ESOTERICISM
OF the
popol vuh

The young Maize god. Limestone sculpture from a temple at Copán, Honduras. The British Museum, London. *(Reproduced by courtesy of the Trustees of the British Museum).*

ESOTERICISM
OF THE
POPOL VUH

RAPHAEL GIRARD

Translated from the Spanish with a Foreword by
BLAIR A. MOFFETT

THEOSOPHICAL UNIVERSITY PRESS
PASADENA, CALIFORNIA

THEOSOPHICAL UNIVERSITY PRESS
POST OFFICE BIN C
PASADENA, CALIFORNIA 91109
1979

First English Edition

Originally published in Spanish in 1948 as *Esoterismo del Popol Vuh*,
by Editorial Stylo, Mexico City, Mexico.

Library of Congress Catalog Card Number 78–74712

Hardcover ISBN 0-911500-13-8
Softcover ISBN 0-911500-14-6

Manufactured in the United States of America

Contents

Foreword

THIS BOOK was first published in the Spanish language in Mexico City in 1948. It has since gone through three editions in French, one Italian, and four Spanish editions. The present translation, from the 1972 Mexico City edition, is the first to appear in English. *Esotericism of the Popol Vuh* is published by Theosophical University Press as a service to all English-speaking students of the ancient wisdom of humanity.

A Swiss-born ethnologist, Raphael Girard came to the New World in 1919 as the director of a six-man French scientific mission to study the native forest peoples of Honduras. He returned in 1924 to live in Guatemala and begin an archaeological and ethnological survey of the country, which resulted in a lifetime of association with and research in Amerindian cultures ranging from Patagonia to Canada. From the eminent anthropologists, Dr. Eugène Pittard of the University of Geneva, and Dr. Paul Rivet, then director of the Musée de l'homme in Paris, Girard learned the interdisciplinary method of analysis — employing mythology, ethnography, archaeology, and linguistics — which has characterized and enriched his many published works.

In his early career the author was active in forming and participating in professional bodies in Switzerland, Honduras, and Guatemala to further the study of native American cultures. Over the years he has represented the Government of Guatemala at a number of international Americanist congresses, on four occasions serving as honorary vice-president of the congress. A distinguished Americanist whose work is well known throughout Europe and the Americas, Professor Girard has received fifteen honors and decorations. The latest of these is the Diploma of Merit awarded him for his more than 50 years of research and publication by the Organization of American States in October, 1978, at a ceremony in Washington, D.C. In 1977 he was nominated for the Nobel prize in Literature for his pioneering methods of study of native American cultures and his monumental writings clarifying their prehistory and history.

With regard to his analysis of the meaning of the *Popol Vuh*, the Mayan "Book of the Community," Professor Girard's comments from a recent letter to me are revealing:

> My first experiences disclosed that the *Popol Vuh* constitutes a key document for understanding the spirituality, culture, and history of the Quiché-Maya. But no exegesis had been made of that celebrated document owing to the disregard of its esoteric meaning, and so it was never employed as a research tool. Much the same held true for Quiché-Maya religion and its symbols which, it was claimed, were completely inaccessible to our mode of thought. . . .
>
> It was vital and necessary to study their sacred way of life. Only this method, in my view, would allow us entry into the mental universe of the Mayas and bring comprehension of their mythology and thus of their culture.

To accomplish this, the author went to the tribal elders of the Chortí and Quiché-Maya tribes, where he quickly encountered the barriers of impenetrable reserve which those spiritual leaders — guardians of their sacred traditions — erect to defend these precious values from the unworthy and the potential despoiler. Only after more than twenty years of direct association with the elders was Girard able to obtain the fundamental aspects of their secret doctrines which he reports upon in this work. *Esotericism of the Popol Vuh* demonstrates beyond question that at the heart of Maya religion and custom there is a sophisticated spiritual philosophy with clear correspondences not only to ancient Mexican as well as Andean cosmogony and creation mythology, but also to the mythoi and cultures of other parts of the world.

The author fully credits the "native gnostics," as he respectfully calls the Mayan elders, with enabling him to distill and elucidate the hidden sense of the *Popol Vuh*. But I believe he would be the last person to claim any ultimate finality for his work. His findings, nevertheless, comprise a genuinely authoritative approach to the solution of many of the so-called enigmas surrounding our knowledge of pre-Columbian Mesoamerican cultures, and are unprecedented in American ethnography. In his exposition, the author takes us behind the elliptical wording of the text into the spiritual heights and depths of conception that form the archetypes on which Amerindian metaphysics is modeled.

We begin to realize that we are looking at a magnificent expression — unchanged in essentials during thousands of years — of that archaic wisdom-religion which in one or another measure can be found at the core of all the world's religions. The *Popol Vuh*, properly understood, sheds light on the whole reach of native American spiritual thought. A true Mystery-document, it has strong and definite links with every other Mystery-tradition, and belongs in the highest class of scriptural literature. At present there are German, French, Spanish, and English language editions of the *Popol Vuh*, all of which are, as Professor Girard notes, acceptable literal translations of the original codex. The best English rendition is perhaps that of Delia Goetz and Sylvanus G. Morley, from the Spanish translation made by Adrián Recinos, published by the University of Oklahoma Press in its series titled *The Civilization of the American Indian.*

For the Maya the universe is a multilevel, multiplane production or emanation of primeval sevenfold creative forces or "gods," which continue to inspirit their production. Thus, there are a number of other "worlds" or "planes" "above" as well as "below" our physical world of the five senses, and closely linked with it. There is always a multiplicity within and behind the unity of our material world, which can be compared to one octave in a complete piano keyboard representing the total manifested universe. To retain this perspective is absolutely necessary for an understanding of the Indian's metaphysics. The various combinations of the creative forces and their worlds are allegorized in the god-Seven, god-Five, god-Thirteen, and god-Nine, etc., described by the author from Mayan sources. Each allegory thus has a range of meanings, standing for the complex workings of these forces and the relations among the "worlds," fully known only to the adept of the tradition who is accustomed to raise each basic idea in the allegory to progressively higher orders of conceptual magnitude.

Employing the same method with the textual contents of the *Popol Vuh*, we can understand that the four "Ages" with their respective humanities which it discusses, refer not alone to the ancestors of the Quiché-Maya but more correctly to the whole of mankind in existence on earth in each of those periods of time. For example, the *Popol Vuh* calls the latest, or Fourth-Age mankind, Quiché Mayas: that is, those who had achieved conscious spiritual linkage with their creative progenitors through the mediation of the man-god Hunahpú. Here we have an Amerindian expression of the better known Promethean allegory of classical Greek myth which explains the origins of man's self-consciousness, distinguishing him from an animal. The Christian biblical statement of this momentous experience is the allegory of the casting out of Adam and Eve from the Garden of Eden as a result of their having tasted of the knowledge of good and evil. In Hindu scriptural record, the same event is hinted at in the descent of the mānasaputras or "sons of mind," spoken of in theosophy as having come from higher worlds to awaken in man his mental potential. Some sort of allusion to this destiny-laden happening in early human history can be found in almost every spiritual tradition.

Readers acquainted with authentic presentations of modern theosophy, as in the writings of H. P. Blavatsky, principal founder of the Theosophical Society in 1875, will recognize much in this book that is familiar, albeit having its own form and language. The *Popol Vuh* clearly teaches, for example, that the simians sprang from an early humanity's racial experience, and not the reverse as asserted by the Darwinism of our day. Moreover, on page 227 Professor Girard explains the esoteric Mayan doctrine that the individual cannot realize the perfected state of True Man, or Hunahpú, except when the whole community shall also have attained that divine perfection. This is an unmistakable reference to the doctrine of compassion, its path, and the hierarchy which sustains it.

The concept of advanced men, or man-gods, beings of the evolutionary grade or rank of what Oriental tradition terms the bodhisattva or buddha of compassion, is not foreign to native American spiritual tradition. As seen, it is present in the *Popol Vuh* in the figure of Hunahpú as the paradigm of the spiritually perfected, illumined human being who sacrifices himself for the community, a word that here stands for the race or for humanity as a whole. We have only to examine the iconography of the magnificent carved stone figure of the young Maize god which once adorned the façade of a temple at Copán, to find it (see the *Frontispiece*). Above the serene countenance of that personage can be seen a pointed crown of maize leaves. This is a form of the protuberance of the Oriental *ushnīsha*, Sanskrit for "crown," a sign of the spiritually perfected one who is *buddha*, "awakened," such as is found in numerous buddha and bodhisattva figures in the Far East. The hands of the Mayan young Maize god are, moreover, extended palms outward, one raised and one lowered, in a classical teaching gesture or *mudrā* characteristic of the bodhisattva and buddha as seen in Oriental iconography. Professor Girard emphasizes the spiritual nature of Mayan ethics and the Indian's recognition of their importance in his aspiration to achieve human perfection. In fact, he regards the Mayan ethical system as one of the most beautiful in the world.

But the author has done more than just elucidate the esotericism that is in the *Popol Vuh*. The illuminating objective vision of the Amerindic cultures that the reader obtains from his presentation is not accessible through the unilateral approach of archaeology. This work takes a great deal of the mystery out of our view of Mayan and, by extension, Amerindian culture in general, correcting some of the false assumptions still prevailing. A gifted ethnologist as well as a man who gained the respect and confidence of the Indian elders, Raphael Girard shows us the vital connections between the millennial mytho-history of the Quiché-Maya epic and the monumental structures, codices, glyphs, symbols, and customs of classical Mayan civilization, and therefore of present-day Mayan life and religion, its descendant.

The translation of *Esoterismo del Popol Vuh* into English has benefited greatly from a painstaking and challenging review and reading of it by my wife, Ida Postma, and by Sarah Belle Dougherty, Elsa-Brita Titchenell, and, last but far from least, by Grace F. Knoche. All of these have helped to give it whatever literary polish it may have, and I thank them and also William T. S. Thackara, who was responsible for the production of this book, for their manifold labors. Eloise Hart devoted many hours to typing and retyping the manuscript, and I. M. Oderberg and Ingrid Van Mater to reading proofs, and I am most grateful to them for their help. A special word of appreciation is due to my friend James H. Bothwell, a native Spanish speaker and professional translator, who reviewed the translation and made valuable suggestions for its improvement. For greater ease in using the book, several lengthy word lists have been moved from the text and placed in Appendices A and B, and a glossary and index have been added.

Miss Dora Marina Luna, secretary to Professor Girard, helped me correct several puzzling references in extracts from the *Popol Vuh*, and was unfailingly helpful in assembling and furnishing Theosophical University Press with reproducible photographs from the author's personal archives. The translation itself has been prepared in the atmosphere of regular contact with the author, who lives in Guatemala City, both by telephone as well as by correspondence over many months. It goes without saying, however, that any errors of fact or interpretation which may be found in the translation are mine and mine alone, and I shall be grateful to have them brought to my attention.

BLAIR A. MOFFETT

January, 1979
Pasadena, California

ESOTERICISM
OF THE
POPOL VUH

Introduction

FOUR hundred years ago, in the manuscript known as
the *Popol Vuh*, a Quiché wise man wrote down the
age-old traditions of his people. He transcribed
them in his own language, but used Roman letters.

It has not been possible until now to penetrate into the
esoteric meaning or even the historical validity of this
document because, to put it simply, it is written in a symbolic language not easily understood by us. Nevertheless
those sacred texts, so obscure for the Western mind, are
not only perfectly intelligible to the Quiché-Maya but
form a fully living reality for them.

At the beginning of the 18th century, Father Francisco
Ximénez discovered the *Popol Vuh* and translated it into
Spanish, saying that

> it was conserved among the Indians in complete secrecy,
> such secrecy that not even a written record of such a thing
> was made by its guardians of old; and, being in the parish
> of Chichicastenango and investigating that point, I found
> that it was the doctrine first imbibed with the mother's
> milk and that everyone knew it almost by heart.[1]

---

[1]Fr. Francisco Ximénez, *Historia de la Provincia de San Vicente de
Chiapa y Guatemala*, Guatemala, 1929–31.

Those words eloquently express what the *Popol Vuh* meant and still means to the aboriginal of Quiché-Maya descent, as I was able to prove to my satisfaction during 32 years of ethnographic research among diverse peoples representative of that culture. It is likely that such a document is the reproduction of a prehispanic codex, "written in antiquity," as the author of the *Popol Vuh* puts it.

To interpret this mythic material, at once very old and always young, one must thoroughly understand and be familiar with the Indian's way of thinking, feeling, and expression, explore the deepest levels of his thought, know his mental processes, his religious ideas — in a word, his spiritual reality.

Until now no investigator has succeeded in entering the hidden recesses of the Maya soul because of the systematic concealment the Indian has employed to protect his sublime cultural values.

In my judgment this explains our ignorance of the spiritual reality of the Indian's present and past which pulsates throughout the *Popol Vuh*. Hence, we have many literal translations of this scripture from the Quiché into Spanish, French, English, and German, but up to now none reveals the true meaning of this most valuable document which sums up the history and the soul of the Quiché-Maya.

The historical value of the *Popol Vuh* is evident not only in the text itself, which describes the story of the Quiché-Maya through the ages, but also in the express words of the native scribe, who by way of introduction says: "This is the origin, the beginning of the old Quiché history; here we will put down the old history, the beginning, the origin of the Quiché people and all that they did [their history]."

The Chortís confirm that historical character of the

Popol Vuh in the very title of their drama called "The History," which in a magnificent synthesis reproduces the essential episodes of the Quiché epic.

Interpreting the Quiché's opinion of the book, Father Ximénez titled his Spanish rendition the *History of the Origin of the Indians of this Province of Guatemala.* In this way the Quiché-Maya define their own conception of history by declaring that the mythic accounts in the book are also historical narrations; that is, they form a mytho-history.

One must not, then, look for a part on mythology and another part on history in the *Popol Vuh.* As this study will show, the same style characterizes the whole work from the first to the final page. There are no divisions into chapters, the text of the manuscript is unbroken, and the narration continuous from beginning to end.

Such an arrangement is typical of the Quiché-Maya mentality and moreover projects itself in their system of measuring time. Actually, all of their calendric series, like those of their history, are connected without a break, so as not to disrupt the cosmic order. Their system of chrono-magic is copied from mythical models, archetypes of all their mental architecture. Hence the Quiché-Maya peoples live in continuity with their past, which for them has no mystery inasmuch as the myths are the foundations of their cultural consciousness. We, in fact, are dealing with a unified history that embraces in continuous succession the whole historical-cultural process: history written in terms of mythological thought, which is historical for these people.

It is of paramount interest to learn the method by which the Quiché-Maya express their conception and systematization of history. That method is revealed in the cyclical doctrine of the Ages that contains all the events of the past and the present in a historic totality.

Those events are brought together in four serial historic periods or Ages, of which three comprise periods already ended, i.e., the past, while the fourth corresponds to the present which began with the latest creation. Existing cultural forms belong to the present or Fourth Age; by the same token, those of the past are nonexistent because they were transformed and incorporated into the present.

For distinguishing actual forms from those belonging to the past, and for expressing at the same time their genetic relation, the Quiché-Maya found a wonderfully simple formula. They made a sharp distinction between the now-dead past and the present, inserting between each Age or period a destructive cataclysm that annihilated the earlier one; that is, it is no longer possible to look directly at the former Age because it has ceased to exist.

Since the past is separated from the present, it belongs to prehistory. In this way, the first three racial cycles, which in their time formed actual periods lived through by the Quiché-Maya during their history, were destroyed. Those periods or Ages are at once separated from, yet united with, the present, as necessary parts of a whole; separated so as to distinguish the phases of the past, united so as to preserve the causal connection that relates the parts to the whole. Although the cultural characteristics of the past were erased (symbolically by a catastrophe), since they were replaced by those of the present, their mention is required to explain the living forms which have their roots in that prehistory.

In reality this past has not disappeared but rather has become transformed so as to incorporate itself into the common cultural property of today. Thus, for example, the giants of the First Age were transformed into cosmic bearers; the gods of the Second Age into the demons of today, and the virtues of the prehistoric period into the vices of the Fourth Age.

To understand the genesis of cultural elements, i.e., what they were before being incorporated into the present, one must understand what they are now in order to explain how, why, and in what circumstances they were transformed. What are the determining phenomena of their actual situation? This is very important, because in those phenomena lie the fundamental teachings of religious and historic doctrine.

The features of the past were seemingly erased, but were reinterpreted, and are found alive and vibrant in the present. In this manner mytho-history is narrated in a causal sense. It expresses the process of accumulation from the past into the present, the transmission of the cultural patrimony that grows from one epoch to the next. It enables one to perceive, in the flow of the historic process, variation in cultural elements; to follow, for example, the evolution of ethics or of institutions in relation to changes that take place on all levels of culture.

In other words, present-day culture is the product of the historic totality; therefore, the greater the portion of the past that affects contemporary culture, the higher in the scale of civilization will it be; that is, the cultural level of an epoch is directly proportional to the duration of its prehistoric past.

From this point of view, the conservation of all phases of the past, arranged in chronological succession, is needed to determine and explain the present. Mytho-history expresses, then, the course of the events in which the present originated, and those events are placed in relations of dependence or of succession in the warp and woof of the account known as history.

Upon this background the *Popol Vuh* projects in successive scenes the life of the Quiché-Maya man and people throughout their history. It describes with color and precision, in a simple, clear, and touching manner, the life of the type-family which characterizes the spiritual and material culture of each racial cycle: the family of Vukup Cakix in the First Age; of the Camé in the Second; of Ixmucané in the Third; of the civilizer-hero and the first four true men in the Fourth Age, showing forth the simple and human side of history and also the whole panorama of the type-culture of each epoch, chiefly the spiritual, social, and economic phenomena which formed it.

In the Quiché-Maya conception, history is man and the human group throughout time, a judgment that is not different from the definition modern scientific historiography gives to history as "the science which studies and explains by means of causal connections the facts of the evolution of man and his works (individual as well as collective and typical), as a social being."[2]

We have, then, an original source, written by Quiché-Mayas about the life of man, that embraces the whole process of human life and culture from the primeval horizon to that of civilization. Its historic fidelity is seen in the description of deeds and ways of expressing spiritual life that do not correspond to contemporary culture and were abandoned thousands of years ago, but which express the living reality of bygone cultures. The Quiché-Maya wrote true history before our own historians did so, a history that concerns itself with men, i.e., the living reality of a people and not of official events of no importance for the future.

The mytho-historic episodes exactly record the archetypal acts performed and gestures made *in illo tempore* by the remote ancestors of the Quiché-Maya. Such things not

---

[2]Bernheim, *Lehrbuch d. hist. Methode.*

only took place then but do so anew, continuously, being repeated in the rites, the calendar,[3] the theater, and the customs of today. They are made real at each moment and always in the same way, so that in the practices of contemporary Indians they reach us as a faithful reproduction of history just as it has in fact evolved.

These facts explode the old prejudice (from the time of Montaigne and Descartes) that the American is the model of the man without history, and at the same time confirm the judgment of modern historians that myths have historiographic value. "The most important step modern critical history has made has been to learn, following in Vico's steps, that the greater part of the divine and heroic myths of old traditions . . . represent other kinds of historical reconstructions and explanations . . . in the form compatible with the a-logical and anthropomorphic mentality of the primitives."[4] The study of mythology was some time ago transferred from the field of literature to that of science.

The *Popol Vuh* contributes material that is extremely valuable for deciphering Quiché-Maya history, subject matter that allows us to follow the unfolding of its ideas, art, sciences — of the whole of its culture. And, for the first time in the annals of Americanist investigations, we

---

[3]The structure of the system of time-reckoning copies the mythological models. Like the type-Ages they represent, each calendric series expresses a period that is living and complete in itself and which terminates in abrupt and complete change. These cycles of time, like the series of history, function within a greater unity, as parts necessary to the whole. Despite the abrupt end of each mytho-historical cycle, the text of the *Popol Vuh* shows that their respective realities are displaced not by a sudden change of scene but through progressive modifications.

[4]Enrico de Michelis, *El problema de las ciencias históricas*, Ed. Nova, Buenos Aires; p. 259.

can come to grips with the problem of history, pursuing the logical sequence of events from the oldest horizon up to the most recent rather than from a reverse direction; that is, beginning with causes rather than effects. With this possibility, the hiatus between paleoanthropology and ethnography or history is erased.

But what interests the specialist, perhaps more than the historic methodology of the Quiché-Mayas, is to know if there is a method that is communicable for establishing the correct interpretation of the *Popol Vuh*. And what is the technique within reach of the scientific method that will allow us to prove that such an interpretation really corresponds with the conceptions of these people and their real history?

The main object of this introduction is to explain the technique used in our exegesis, a technique which at the same time offers methods by which it can be tested.

As said, the conceptual analysis of mythologic themes that express the Quiché-Maya spiritual way of life can be accomplished only through an inner comprehension of indigenous thought, of the native's mental processes which are so different and removed from our own.

Lévy-Bruhl has already said that the interpretation civilized man tends to give to the beliefs, customs, and rites of primitive man never or almost never is the right one. Therefore we must place ourselves on the level of the native's mental perspective if we wish to understand his manner of spiritual expression and, even more, to witness and systematically study the secret and nocturnal ceremonies of his agrarian religion, celebrated by native elders in their own places of worship hidden in the forests.[5] Hav-

---

[5]For further details about this method of investigation see my *Los Chortís ante el problema maya*, and also my reply to the critical review

ing become familiar with native thought and its methods of interpretation, the investigator will be able to recognize its spiritual meanings on whatever level these appear and interpret its ancient sacred texts in the light of today's reality.

The myths can be clearly explained by means of the practices and ideas of the contemporary Indian. All his acts, individual and collective, including the physiological, are ceremonies that continually repeat the mythical models. To live and act in accordance with those mythical patterns is the constant aspiration of the Quiché-Maya.

The correlation between the present and the past, between the real, what exists now, and the mythical, is settled thanks to the fact that the myths prevail in the ceremonies. The whole worth of an investigation of this kind turns upon the native elders, unlettered but trained in the school of oral tradition. When they share with us their inner thought, they introduce us to a world until now unknown.

To verify the truthfulness of the information furnished by native theologians, we have recourse to the comparative method by which we can see whether data provided by various individuals who do not know each other exhibit internal agreement. This same method will bring to light systematic correspondences that exist between information derived from ethnography and that provided by primary sources, the writings of the Quiché-Maya themselves. Such systematic correlations between the myths,

---

of Miss Betty Starr (*American Anthropologist* 53, 1951). In this present book I refer the reader frequently to pages or chapters in *Los Chortís ante el problema maya*, using the simple short-title form of: Girard, *Los Chortís*, in view of the inconvenience of reproducing *in extenso* the comprehensive ethnographic, archaeological, and linguistic material, and extracts from written sources, contained in that 5-volume work.

the written sources, and the facts of ethnography and linguistics, establish the solid basis on which our interpretation of the native texts rests.

There is, in fact, a strict parallelism between the mythic episodes and current ceremonies and customs; not only simple correlations of facts which correspond with and explain each other, but also — and this is the most important thing — regular correspondences of features between the whole mythological structure and the ritual system, the measurement of periods of time and native dramatic art. These are brought together in the same way, follow the same order of succession, express the same thematic development, and are based on the same doctrine, the same cosmo-theo-astronomical principles. The present explanation of the *Popol Vuh* is based, then, on presentation of actual, concrete facts which are available to ethnographic investigation.

But there is even more: since the myths, equally with the ceremonies, express the religious ideal of past, present, and future epochs, which all began in mythic times, it follows that this ideal is to be seen in both the racial culture as well as the archaeology, on whatever historical level these may be found. From this it follows that the prehispanic art of the Quiché-Maya, which was strictly religious in character, translates into the language of forms the same religious ideas that live and breathe in the pages of the *Popol Vuh* and in the religio-metaphysical way of life of the contemporary Indian.

Thus the range of correlation between the myths and the ceremonies extends to the field of archaeology (monuments, paintings, ancient codices). As with all Quiché-Maya cultural expressions, the interpretation of native art through history must begin from within and from there emerge, proceed from the spiritual to the external or objective form. This reveals the emotive impulse which gave expression to the forms and explains the meaning of millennial figures and symbols that, until now, have remained as enigmatic to the outsider as has the spirituality of today's Indian.

One must add to these test elements the documentary proof furnished by the testimony of written sources of the Mayas, Quichés, and Toltecs themselves, as well as Colonial sources reproducing native reports. This book establishes the fundamental soundness of those sources, which are all expressions of one mother-culture whose history is summarized in the *Popol Vuh*.

J. Imbelloni has already shown that these Maya, Quiché, and Mexican sources form a closely-connected unity and that their mythic material is identical.[6] Thus Maya, Quiché, Cakchiquel, and Mexican sources furnish an excellent tool for analyzing the *Popol Vuh*.

From all this it becomes apparent that the study of Quiché-Maya mythology can be tackled by the methodology of modern science and subjected to the kind of rigorous analysis now employed in the anthropological disciplines (ethnography, linguistics, archaeology, written sources, etc.).

The essential truths expressed by the myths concern interrelated concepts. Cosmogony, theogony, ceremonies, calendar, mathematics, astronomy, economy, family, society, government, etc., are derived from the identical patterns or models. We are faced with a reciprocal grafting of all into a cosmic whole at each moment. No cultural element can be extricated from that whole to which it is solidly linked.

---

[6]*El Génesis de los pueblos prehistóricos de América*, Buenos Aires, 1940–41. Imbelloni gave his attention to the doctrine of the Ages and made felicitous interpretations of this part of Quiché-Maya mythology.

For this reason there can be no question of arbitrary personal interpretations of any of the cultural phenomena. This would be almost impossible, since any interpretative error would become evident at once owing to the multiple ways (internal and external proofs) we now have at our disposal for establishing the truth of the matter; and moreover, it would result in an evident disagreement with the marvelous internal unity of the cultural complex.[7]

Such are, in broad outline, the methods employed in this analysis of the *Popol Vuh*, as well as the means for checking the results.

Of course, those who examine the spiritual phenomena of the native culture from the point of view of the Occident will have difficulty comprehending them, to say nothing of accepting that the myths, like the traditions, have suffered no alterations or deformations because of the passage of time.

Quiché-Maya culture, essentially mythological, is a case where science and history have not yet separated from mytho-religion. The Indian still lives in a mythological Age, the fourth of his cyclical history: that is, in a sacred space and time. That fact shows that his culture has been

---

[7]When I was carrying on my investigations among the Chortís, I would at times doubt the exactitude of information given me by the elders, which sometimes seemed to be confused or illogical. But, on noting the agreement between the theological versions, their application in the ceremonies, and their correspondence with the myth paradigms, my skepticism vanished. The native elders were never in error in the routine employment of their old symbols, and they adhered in every smallest detail to the teachings of the *Popol Vuh*. In all the cases where I doubted them, it was I who was in error for believing, as do the majority among ethnographers, that the Indian must unfailingly conform to our manner of thinking. The reader will find specific references in this book to such incidents.

impervious to Western influence, and that the explanation of his cultural features is found in his myths.[8]

Although our exposition focuses on the historiographic aspect of the *Popol Vuh*, the historical facts cannot be separated from the mythic material into which they are integrated. For this reason, study of the *Popol Vuh* as a source of history must include the whole of that mythic material, which has a satisfactory explanation as well as many kinds of proofs in the primary sources mentioned above. Consequently the mytho-history expresses actual and not hypothetical truth.

The salient features of this history, which is many thousands of years old, fill the pages of the *Popol Vuh*. They are summarized in the conclusions and synoptic sketch given at the end of this book. They include all the fundamental problems of the Quiché-Maya humanity, as well as the type-events of man's life and destiny throughout its whole period.

The *Popol Vuh* forms a complete treatise of theogony, cosmogony, and astronomy. It gives us theology: the birth

---

[8]The Amerindian is not an unusual case. Leo Frobenius in his book, *Schicksalskunde* tells us of the "Mythological Age of humanity," showing that our own history knew a phase in which culture was shaped by mythic norms. Sir George Grey, in his *Polynesian Mythology and Ancient Traditional History of the New Zealand Race* (1855), noted that the Polynesian people still lived in complete dependence upon their myths; that is, mythology among that people was a way of life. The primeval Asian people as well as the archaic Hellenes lived according to the same kind of norms (Miguel de Ferdinandy, "En torno al pensar mítico," *Anales de Arqueología y Etnología de la Universidad nacional de Cuyo*, vol. 8, 1947). Max Müller has shown that the texts of the Vedas have been handed down orally for a period of more than two thousand years, with such exactitude that there can hardly be found a doubtful accent anywhere in them (*La ciencia de la religión*, Ed. Albatros, 1945).

and formation of the gods, of men, of species and things; that is, the birth and formation of the words with which they are designated. It explains the creation of the universe, the place of the human being in the world, the relations of Deity with man, the ethical mission of the individual and group, the concatenations of events, the proper organization of society. It reveals the Indian and his world, his means of support, his spiritual aspirations, and the process of development of his institutions; in a word, the historical-cultural evolution of the Quiché-Maya people through their history, a unified history that contains all aspects of life and culture.

It is, then, a document that is unique in the annals of humanity, which explains the first moment of the life of a religion, a society, an art, a language: of a culture coming to birth, as well as the series of later developments composing the formation, growth, and evolution of Quiché-Maya culture.

For these reasons it will always be the source that must be consulted, the indispensable vade mecum of the ethnographer, archaeologist, linguist, historian, sociologist, and mythographer, and all who investigate the fields of Quiché-Maya religion, economy, and other phases of their culture. Until now these investigators have lacked a historical basis for orienting their researches.

The *Popol Vuh* gives identifying and classifying criteria for those cultural elements corresponding to each one of the Ages of Quiché-Maya history. Thanks to this masterwork of anthropology, we can now study phenomena formerly restricted to the area of theory and see that the evolution of Quiché-Maya culture is not always a straight-line progression. During its emergence, brought about through racial fusions, there is great progress, but at the same time notable retrogression, in relation to the primeval horizon. This prodigious work of Amerindian genius, which sums up the soul and history of the Quiché-Maya people, describes the activities, ways of life, and psychology of the men of the caves, as if it all were taking place before our eyes. The beginning of Quiché-Maya history coincides, in fact, with the first traces of man on this continent, which go back thousands of years before the Christian era. It follows, therefore, that the *Popol Vuh* is the oldest document that we know of concerning human history, earlier than the Rig-Veda and the Zend-Avesta, until now held to be the most ancient collections of sacred texts.

The spiritual contribution that the Mayan and Toltecan civilizations now offer us, stripped of the mystery that has enveloped them, is a factor of great value in this critical moment for humanity. The *Popol Vuh* concedes nothing in philosophical value to the great books that have guided the human conscience. Its revelations illumine not only Quiché-Maya history, until now so obscure, but also the history of mankind itself.

2

Esotericism of the Popol Vuh

W E HAVE various sufficiently acceptable literal translations of the *Popol Vuh*, and this is shown by the agreement between the text of the codex and the native customs, rites, beliefs, and theater in which the myths are dramatized so as to bring them within reach of the popular understanding by means of easily comprehended allegories. This makes possible useful comparisons as well as mutual corroborations between the text itself and the data of ethnography.

Learned Americanists such as Ximénez, the discoverer and first translator of the *Popol Vuh*, Brasseur de Bourbourg, Stoll, Brinton, Porohiles, Krickeberg, Douay, Seler, Max Müller, Sherzer, Lewis, Spencer, Beebe, Chavero, Batres, Jáuregui, Raynaud, Villacorta and Rodas, Imbelloni, Schulte-Jena, Recinos, and others, have tried to penetrate the dense veil of mystery that envelops the famous Quiché narrative. But hitherto no mythographer has succeeded in giving us a satisfactory explanation of the esotericism contained in that sacred book.

Even persons such as Flavio Rodas[1] and Antonio Villa-corta, who have been born among and lived with the Indian, believe it is impossible to clarify the abstract and philosophical conceptions buried in the Quiché legend. Most of its interpreters consider the esoteric meaning of the *Popol Vuh* to be lost, or else they formulate their hypotheses contrary to the native manner of thinking. Such is the judgment of the author of the prolog to the latest translation by Raynaud, published by the National University of Mexico in 1939.

J. Imbelloni, who has recently devoted his attention to the critical and comparative study of pre-Columbian sources, avoids analysis of the episodes concerning Hunahpú and Ixbalamqué, which form the most essential and extensive part of Quiché mythology, embracing five of the seven chapters into which Villacorta divides the mythic part of the Chichicastenango Codex.[2]

J. Imbelloni considers those myths to be "an interpolation of episodes much larger than the central discourse, the inclusion of which has made it extremely difficult to follow the connection between successive chapters, leading to misunderstanding even by persons who have worked on this codex for many years." Starting from that view, it is proposed to separate the more contingent portions from the basic framework of the text so as not to confuse such less essential elements with the permanent structure of the narrative, bearing in mind that the *Popol Vuh* has as its object to narrate the formation of the universe; moreover, that the development of this thematic unity includes the whole manuscript, but that the narrative sequence is inter-

---

[1]Flavio Rodas and Ovidio Rodas Corzo are those in Guatemala who best know the Quiché customs.

[2]Imbelloni, *El Génesis.*

rupted by the insertion of a number of episodes in sections 2 to 6, or, in other words, practically the whole of the account.

Some translators have tried to "improve" the style of the Quiché text to make it conform to Western literary taste. Yet in the architecture of the Indian's language, as in that of his monuments, each word or sign has a very precise meaning, so that any modification or poor interpretation of one single word can completely destroy the meaning of a sentence.

From Ximénez, who rated "all these accounts as children's tales,"[3] down to Imbelloni, the most substantial part of Quiché mythology has remained hidden. This shows a failure both to penetrate deeply into the Indian's mentality and to comprehend the essence of his religious conceptions, and therefore of his culture.

The fact is that these "puerile" legends, transmitted orally from time immemorial, contain the whole evolutive process of Quiché-Maya culture, its religion, society, and economy. They are an epitome of religious laws or articles of faith that are still in force and which were given to man by Deity before the Old World had the Hammurabi Code. Hunahpú — the civilizing hero of Quiché-Maya culture — is a redemptor-god, son of the Supreme Being. He is born immaculately like all the great religious founders and sacrifices himself for humanity, many centuries before the towering figure of Jesus the Christ becomes outlined in the panorama of human history. Hunahpú proclaims the tenet of the soul's immortality before Plato taught his doctrines, when the Greek mythology created by Homer and Hesiod did not yet exist. Hunahpú and Ixbalamqué transform

---

[3]Fr. Francisco Ximénez, *Las Historias del Origen de los Indios de esta Provincia de Guatemala*, 1857.

themselves into human beings, have the same substance
and experience the same life that man does, in order to
establish the latter's patterns of conduct.

Before Heraclitus, the Quiché-Maya had the concept
that men are mortal gods and gods immortal men, with
the difference that among the latter, man, on dying, was
transformed into an immortal being provided that he had
complied with the precepts of religious ethics. The corol-
lary to this idea is the conception of a harmonious world
system and a relation between man and Deity and cosmos
so close that perhaps no other religion equals it in this
respect.

With his own example, Hunahpú establishes the rules
for worship and for the cultivation of the fields and lays
down astronomical, ritual, and time-reckoning procedures
inseparable from those rules. He also provides the standards of natural law and ethics contained in religious
morality of a utilitarian character, based on the conservation of the individual, family, and society, and the principle of authority and economic security for the well-being
of humanity. Hunahpú exemplifies the kind of ethical
action which characterizes the ideal human type.

In the *Popol Vuh* are resolved those spiritual anxieties
which have in every age troubled the human soul: the
creation of the universe, the divine functions, the relation
between Deity and man, the problem of the human condition itself, of duty and truth, virtue and sin, the origin of
beings and things, of life, death, and human destiny, the
causative laws of phenomena, etc. The Maya religion,
which is one of salvation, has as its ultimate goal the
development of inner tranquillity of soul within a harmonious social order wherein injustice cannot prevail,
leading man to a happy afterlife, one merited through
virtue, in conformity with the divine teaching exemplified

by Hunahpú in one of those hitherto uncomprehended episodes of the famous Quiché codex.

The authenticity of this masterwork of Mayan thought has long been accepted by authors such as Brinton, Müller, Raynaud, Rodas, Villacorta, Recinos, and others who have shown that even though it was written during the Colonial era it is completely native and foreign to Western thought. But there is even more than that: the *Popol Vuh* is a document of retrospective history, unique among human annals. Its mythology, theogony, and cosmogony are projected on a historic background that faithfully registers the events which took place in different epochs or racial cycles, and describe the particular features of those periods, even where many of them were not known or had undergone modifications by the time the codex was written. We will furnish evidence for that in this study, in which will be described the successive prehistoric and historic epochs with their own customs, beliefs, implements, arms, and mode of life, drawing a picture of times past which differed from conditions that prevailed when the famous book was written. It also gives us a geographical description including the flora and fauna of the place where the original homeland of the Quiché-Maya culture was found. And those traditions, which have not mixed up the characteristics of one historic period with another, state explicitly the difficulties encountered in the beginning, during the primeval horizon, because of differences in language, doubtless referring to groups of distinct ethnic relationships which chance migrations had brought together into one area. Later on they tell us of the language differences found among peoples of the same racial and cultural background, details of considerable value for Americanist studies.

So, then, we have an extensive panorama of historic-cultural conditions firmly located in time, which, by means of the myths entwined in the history, enable us to reconstruct the evolution of Quiché-Maya life from its remotest past.

The veracity of the facts set out in the *Popol Vuh* is susceptible to many kinds of proof, thanks to comparative ethnology and archaeology on the one hand and, on the other, to the traditions and written sources of American peoples who, separated from the same cultural trunk in different epochs, conserve in distinct degree the features corresponding to the successive eras through which Quiché-Maya culture has evolved. Without leaving Maya territory, in Honduras we find a coexistence in the same country and the same moment of time of indigenous tribes belonging to the historic period (Chortís) and to the pre-historic (Sumos), according to the classifications of the *Popol Vuh*, while others (Hicaques and Payas) hold intermediate positions.

This process of cultural differentiation is repeated when the Quiché branch itself divides off from the Maya, evolving from then on in a parallel but independent manner. Starting from the Quiché-Maya separation, the *Popol Vuh* relates episodes that belong exclusively to Quiché history and do not concern the Maya. On the other hand, the sources and traditions of the latter record cultural advances in which the Quichés did not participate, such as the extraordinary and unique development in astronomy and time-reckoning, about which the Books of Chilam Balam and the Chortí tradition of the Dance of the Giants (see chapter 16) inform us.

Those achievements of the Maya are due to the fact that, as demonstrated by a study of the Tzolkín, they were the only people who did not move very far away from the astronomical baseline upon which the Mesoamerican calendar was constructed. When the two peoples separated, the essential features, character, and institutions of both had already acquired definitive form, unchanging and perfected, because patterned on a cosmo-theogonic model that would undergo no future alteration. This explains the basic difference between these two and other peoples who left the common homeland earlier, when the Quiché-Maya culture was still in process of coming to birth, and clarifies a fact that has appeared strange to some Americanists who, like E. Pittard, show that the Quichés have the traditions of the Mayas.

The comparative study of the features that characterize those diverse human groups which in different eras emigrated from the area wherein Maya culture was being formed, and that correspond to those which the *Popol Vuh* assigns to consecutive cycles of Quiché history, are dealt with in the chapter "Ethnography and Comparative Religion."[4] We find that that study gives us a correlation between the information in the Quiché manuscript and what is derived from ethnography. The former — offering us a short vertical history that starts from the most primitive horizon of the hunter-gatherer period and passes on to the matriarchal-horticultural cycle corresponding to plant domestication, and culminates in the patriarchal-agrarian era — exhibits the evolutional process of Maya religion, its socioeconomic system, its art, and its means of subsistence: inseparable elements that shape a culture in constant motion. Thus groups which separated from that development at a given moment in time and, for one or another reason, kept their original features thereafter, exhibit a culture distinct from the one the Mayas succeeded in forging.

---

[4]Girard, *Los Chortís.*

Thus, then, we will be able to follow Quiché-Maya history by means of truthful, written sources; and it is this history that is most essential because it explains the evolution of human thought, the progress of ideas, of the arts and sciences — in a word, of culture. And for the first time in the annals of Americanist science we will be able to address the historic problem, following the logical sequence of facts beginning with the primeval period and not the reverse. That is, we need not proceed from the most recent strata to the most ancient, in accordance with the research technique heretofore employed to try to infer the unknown from the known. That method, which in the past we have had to adopt in attempting to penetrate the mystery that envelops the remote pre-Columbian past, had its necessary limitations. For as we moved away from known facts and continued retreating in time, we found less and less information, problems multiplied, and the historic panorama became ever more complicated until it was reduced to a purely hypothetical exercise. It is, in fact, very difficult to go back step by step toward the commencement of a culture by beginning at its near end. Thanks to the instruction in the *Popol Vuh*, susceptible to proofs by ethnography as well as the other native sources, a decisive and definitive step has been taken toward the solution of the many and great Americanist problems, placing them on a new basis which future studies will go on to consolidate and perfect.

This is the transcendental importance of this work of the Mayan genius, a work that concedes nothing in philosophical value to the known great books which have guided the human conscience such as the Bible, the Vedas, Avesta, I Ching, the books of Brahma, Talmud, Koran, Tantras, or Puranas. Because of its historiographic merits, the *Popol Vuh* outreaches all of those and henceforth will wholly transform the course of Americanist studies.

For our exegesis of the Chichicastenango manuscript, we will use mainly the Villacorta-Rodas rendition because, in spite of its errors, we consider it the most faithful to native thought. For certain passages we will use the translations of other authors such as Raynaud and Recinos. As said, the *Popol Vuh* is divided into two parts. The first contains, besides the myths referring to creation of the universe, the history of the Mayas and Quichés up to their separation. The second part is concerned solely with the Quichés. In human history, as in that of nature, there are no abrupt changes; but as time passes, one notes the different phases that elapse and join during a culture's formative process. Then artificial divisions are established for the identification of those phases, making an abstraction of the transition periods between some and others.

This is the method employed by the authors of the *Popol Vuh* in their synthesis of history, showing that the traditions were faithfully transmitted from generation to generation and formulated after the events referred to. The important thing is that those events of the prehistoric epoch in which the deep roots of Maya and Quiché cultures are to be found, should not have been forgotten and should have come down to us, thanks to the extremely conservative character of the native and his form of government. The anonymous elder-chiefs, representatives and interpreters of divine laws and conservers of tradition, have in fact succeeded one another without a break, transmitting from one to another the cultural legacy just as this still occurs within the Chortí caste of elders. Thus they appear in the course of history as a single personality that perdures in their successors and repeats without alteration those ethical fables that continue to serve as models for conduct among today's Indians.

The classification in the *Popol Vuh* embraces four cultural horizons, three prehistoric and one historic. They correspond to the four Ages or Suns of Toltec mythology, and in both of these cultures — which stem from a common trunk — this historic synopsis is linked with sections of the calendar governed by "Regents," in accordance with the method by which Mayas and Toltecs recorded outstanding facts of their history in the very substance of their chronology and its change of calendric bearers. As we shall learn, the *Popol Vuh* projects the important events of Quiché-Maya history in the primary series of Imix, Cimi, Chuen, and Cib.

3

Cosmogony and Creation of the Universe

THE QUICHÉ codex begins by referring to the creation of the universe. Divinity — preexistent to its works — creates the cosmos, which extends through two superimposed, quadrangular planes — heaven and earth — their angles delimited and their dimensions established. Thereby is established the geometric pattern from which will derive the rules for cosmogony, astronomy, the sequential order in which events occur, and the marking out and use of the land, which for the Maya are all reckoned from that space-time scheme. The cosmic quadrangle the *Popol Vuh* refers to is determined by the four solstitial points and is divided into four equal parts by the astronomical cross whose arms align with the cardinal points. From most remote times the Indian, a great observer of nature, had noted the regular annual oscillation of the points where the sun rose and set. Then he observed that the star "sought the angles of the firmament, measured what was there, and quartered the measurements, establishing the points of what is in heaven and earth," inferring the squaring of the universe, a model that was applied to the quadrangulation of territory, of the village, the field and its labors, the altar, the house, plaza, etc.[1]

The Book of Chilam Balam of Chumayel completes this information from the Quiché manuscript, stating that the four directions were indicated by landmarks (such as flint markers, trees) whose respective colors — red, white, black, and yellow — compose the gamut of ritual hues. There were created the four chiefs or regents of the directions, inasmuch as the existence of that quadriform plane automatically implied that of the four cosmic gods or suns and, therefore, of the light which tears aside the shadows of chaos. And this conception is explicit in the *Popol Vuh* where, some lines before mention of how the cosmic quadrangle is measured, "the birth of light by the mediation of Tzakol, Bitol, Alom, and Cajolom" is narrated.

For the Chortí wise man, solar light always has a double significance: actual light and metaphoric light, since from the sun both material and spiritual light is received, so that in accordance with native thought the preceding paragraph can be interpreted in its double sense.

It should be noted that at the beginning the *Popol Vuh* mentions only two cosmic planes, and says nothing about the underworld, whose integration into the universal system will take place in a time later than that of the creation. The Chilam Balam of Chumayel concurs with this when it places the creation of "Hell" in Nine Cauac, at an interval of eight stages or epochs removed from the formation of heaven and earth. This creation, incomplete to start with, reflects the imperfect and rudimentary state of knowledge

---

[1]Girard, *Los Chortís*, chapter 16, "Cosmogony."

of primitive man, who is able to conceive only the visible divisions of the world: heaven and earth. Later, on forming the idea of a subterrene astral world at the same time as new spiritual doctrines, inseparable from the phenomenon of the germination of plants, the existence of a third dimension to the cosmic structure was conceived.

With such a preamble, the Quiché scribe begins his narration, telling the reader that his intent is to conserve the traditions of his ancestors.

He then goes on to describe the creative process, which takes place through successive stages — along a ladder, says the Book of Chilam Balam of Chumayel — in which heaven is formed first, then earth and its contents: the mineral, vegetable, and animal kingdoms, and finally man — a theory that accords with modern scientific thought.

Both the *Popol Vuh* and the Chilam Balam of Chumayel agree on the progressive order of creation carried out by a creator, which is an uncreated Divinity and the first cause of all that exists. This uncreated god exists before all being and antecedes its works. The Chilam Balam of Chumayel says in this regard: "On One Chuen, [Divinity] took out from itself its divinity and made heaven and earth. On Two Eb, it made the first ladder in order to descend in the middle of heaven and in the middle of the water." That is the ladder of clouds to which we have referred elsewhere.[2] And, further on: "All was created by our Father God, and by his Word, there, where before there was no heaven or earth, was his Divinity, which through itself made itself into a cloud, and created the universe. And its great and divine power and majesty made the heavens tremble."[3]

---

[2]Girard, *Los Chortís.*
[3]*Chilam Balam de Chumayel*, trans. A. Mediz Bolio, Mexico, 1941.

With this the ontological aspect of the Supreme Being becomes defined, in the view of the Quiché-Maya. Heaven existed, says the *Popol Vuh*, even when there was nothing that had any resemblance to it. The tranquil heaven and the sea existed consubstantially[4] in the quiet of the shadows, where shone with cosmic clarity Divinity itself, called Heart of Heaven or Cabahuil, and its hypostases: Tzakol, Bitol, Tepeü, Gucumatz, Alom, and Cajolom, the formative aggregate of the Creator god or god-Seven, whose nature and functions have been defined elsewhere. Before creating the universe, the Supreme Being created the gods which are no more than vital extrusions of It itself.

The Chilam Balam of Chumayel is more explicit about this, declaring that "the one that is the Divinity and the Power, brought into being the Great Stone of Grace, there, where before was no heaven, and from it were born Seven sacred stones, Seven warriors suspended in the spirit of the wind, Seven elected flames, and then seven times were lit the seven measures of the night." Further on the seven gods are spoken of in the singular as "the Descendant of seven Generations," produced by the Eternal, all of which is perfectly in accord with Chortí theological teachings.[5] The former quotation from this Quiché manuscript assimilates Divinity to heaven, an idea that has not varied even among contemporary Indians and has its linguistic correspondence (*ut' e q'in:* heaven, solar eye, God).

Cabahuil, according to the Quiché version, is the name of Divinity, synonymous with Heart of Heaven and Hunrakán. The etymological value of this word has been extensively discussed, but some time ago Gerónimo Román gave the definition of that "name of the supreme deity of

---

[4]As explained in Girard, *Los Chortís*, chapter 16.
[5]Girard, *Los Chortís*, chapters 7 and 17.

the Guatemalan Indians which resides in the central point of the firmament." Francisco de Coto and also Father Varea point out that "*gabuil* means idol, picture, or image of God, or a statue or painting adored by the gentiles." The very same term is still used by the Quichés to designate their small idols as well as the incense containers which, like the small figures, represent the deity. In the Chilam Balam of Maní the central Deity is called Itzamná-kauil, a term equivalent to the Heart of Heaven or Cabahuil of the Quiché tradition.

The Supreme Being, after creating and delegating its powers to god-Seven, which is the creative Deity, assumes an essentially passive role, confining itself to the supervision and management of the universe; while the created gods, its sons, begin an active role, taking charge of "all the work," thereby exemplifying the duties of the sons with relation to the patriarch in the macrofamily. Thus the created gods, sons and hypostases of the Supreme Being, are those who continuously act on the mythopoeic stage. But in order that their acts be perfect, the individuality of Heart of Heaven or god-Seven must be integrated by means of all of its cosmic components. Accordingly, the *Popol Vuh* underlines this when it states that "with the coming of Tepeü and Gucumatz, there arrived the Word."

In earlier paragraphs Tzakol, Bitol, Alom, and Cajolom were identified as the Regent-gods of the four cosmic corners. These, on coming together in heaven in union with Tepeü and Gucumatz, form god-Seven or Heart of Heaven, an entity that is distinct from each one of its components but which embraces them all, agreeable to the Quiché-Maya's monotheist conception. In this view Tepeü and Gucumatz correspond to the sun at its rising and at its setting along the ecliptic, when the star moves through the zenith to form the astronomical cross by crossing the line of parallel with that of the meridian.[6] In this moment god-Seven, or the agrarian or creative god, acts, since only then are present all the hypostases composing it. Thus, "when Tepeü and Gucumatz arrived then was the Word"; that is, the act took place which created the earth. As explained elsewhere, Word and Action are equivalent terms with and are used in the same sense by the Mayas, Quichés, and Mexicans. The divine Word implies instantaneous creation, or the thing done. Accordingly, by this rule it is required only that the Chortí rain-magician say clearly what will be, that it should be. Identical conceptions are expressed in both Mexican and Mayan sources; for example, we read in the Vatican Codex that Tonacatecuhtli created the first human pair with his Word.

It should be noted that the general name Gucumatz, the counterpart of Quetzalcoatl, is applied as much to a particular god — one of the septemvirate — as to the creative gods in general, which radiate light and are called Gucumatz "because they were covered with a green mantle like the quetzal bird." Gucumatz literally means "serpent-quetzal" or "serpent-bird." It can be translated also as "serpent with quetzal plumes," since the voice *guc* or *q'uc* means both quetzal (*Pharomachrus mocino*) as well as the long and beautiful green tail feathers of that bird; and *cumatz* means serpent. There is a synonymy between the solar ray as a symbol and the divine feathers or hairs of the plant-life mantle, whose magical properties are held to be equivalent. But the gods clothe themselves in the green mantle, the color of vegetation, only when they are involved in a creative act. The production of maize is equated with this, and it occurs during the rainy season determined by the passing of the sun through the zenith. At the

[6]Girard, *Los Chortís*, chapter on the Tzolkín.

same time and in imitation of the agrarian deities, the Chortí elder puts on his "dress suit," green in color like the divine raiments, and again we see the extremely close linkage between the myth and the ritual that is practiced by the Chortí. When the elder, called Hor Chan (head of the serpent), puts on his green mantle, he is compared to Gucumatz, the serpent with quetzal feathers; that is, the Agrarian deity of which he is the earthly representative. All this shows that the Chortí rites maintain a practice that has continued with little change since very remote times.

Continuing the account of the *Popol Vuh*, we find that when they come together in the center, the gods deliberate, offer their opinions and views to each other, consult, confer about the future existence of the beings they propose to create, take care to assure that the latter have sustenance, and finally reach an agreement which fills them with satisfaction. And this celestial assembly occurs each time there is to be a creative act, which cannot be accomplished without the complete accord of all the parts. The same proceeding is mentioned in Mexican sources (the Franciscan, Gama, Chimalpopoca, and Mendieta Codices) whose thematic correspondences with those of the Quiché and Maya are clear. Elsewhere we have illustrated the Chortí theological concept by which the agrarian gods come together, deliberate, and cannot take any action that is not of common accord. "They call each other and convene in heaven in order to join together in one headship and decide unanimously what has to be done."

Aside from its theological meaning, this mythological allegory expresses the pattern which determines the parliamentary form of indigenous government wherein the "principals" come together, deliberate and discuss until they reach an absolute accord upon a resolution which thus becomes unappealable. Both this council of chiefs and

the divine assembly are exponents of the social and monotheistic conception whereby the All is the sum of the con-
stituent parts of a collegial body whose destiny must be
decided by a unanimity. This is the precise political principle that governs the administration of the Indian's communal group, at once parliamentary and autocratic. The
executive power is in the hands of a democratic theocracy,
and all decisions taken by an accord among the "principals," representatives of the group, must be respected as a
divine order.

The creative gods or Creative God having pronounced
the proper word for Earth, this is born at once. " 'Earth!'
they say, and then it is formed." The voice of Heart of
Heaven is made objective in the trinomial — Lightning
Bolt: its Brilliant Flash: Thunder. These instruments of the
divine Word are spoken and written in the immensity of
the heaven. There is a perfect concordance on this among
the Quiché, Chortí, and Mayan theologies; and such concepts are illustrated in the Mayan codices which represent
god B — the equivalent of Heart of Heaven — manipu-
lating the lightning bolt, lightning flash, and thunder.

At this point in the account, the name of Hunrakán is
mentioned for the first time — "he of a single foot" — as a
synonym of Cabahuil and Heart of Heaven. Hunrakán as
a variant of Heart of Heaven involves a very precise functional meaning in relation to the creative act. The mythological disappearance of the foot of Hunrakán externalizes
the theogonic concept by which the god of Maize —
which is born in the bowels of the earth from the foot of
Heart of Heaven — is an extruded part or hypostasis of the
Agrarian deity. In this case, and following this reasoning,
the Earth as a cosmic plane is an unfoldment or image of
the celestial plane and, moreover, as a goddess is an extruded part or hypostasis of Hunrakán, the god of Heaven.

It was a miraculous thing, says the *Popol Vuh*, strange and marvelous, how the mountains, the coasts, and the valleys of the earth were formed; how at the same time populated forests appeared on its surface. Then was formed "the roadway of the waters" and these began to flow forth at the foot of and among the mountains. Before the formation of the earth, the waters had vacated the place where it was to appear. Such picturesque description of the earth, "flat like a plate," and of the formation of the coasts and water courses speaks to us of a maritime landscape of broad coasts, limited by mountains and cut by rivers. This quadrangular plane — a paradigm of the altar table, the maize field *(milpa)*, the patio, the floor of the house and of the ball court, perfectly level — was contiguous to the sea. Thus it was not the rivers but, instead, the "road" along which the waters flowed that was formed, a conception that corresponds to an apparently real geological phenomenon based on the water table or water level, the subterranean circulation of water, and its emergence in springs. In the permeable earth of the coasts, the water level appears generally at the level of the sea and resembles an underground extension of the ocean. From this came the belief that the earth is surrounded by water and built upon the sea. Since the waters were before the formation of the earth, it was necessary only to trace out the roads along which they should flow.

The *Popol Vuh* concludes by saying: "Thus was the earth formed, when it was created and populated by the Heart of Heaven, the Heart of Earth."

It should be noted that in the narrative the central deity is now termed Heart of Heaven *and* of Earth, and that this new variant appears as a result of the act which created the earth, to show that the god of Heaven is also the god of Earth. This new functional aspect of the same

deity is a consequence of its earlier form — or name —
which shows the god of Heaven deprived of his foot, which
became the earth. The Book of Chilam Balam of Chumayel offers us the same allegory expressed in terms of the
katún count. This source says that in Seven Caban the first
earth was born, where for us it had not been before. The
association of the glyphs Seven (exponent of the Agrarian
deity) and Caban (Earth), expresses the same idea as the
name "Heart of Heaven and of Earth," and this theogonic
unity is externalized in Indian art by a two-headed entity
or by the positioning of god-Seven upon the umbilicus of
the Earth goddess. All this confirms the native conception
that the variants of the name of a deity express distinct
functions that it has or performs.

4

The First Three Ages of the World

The First Age

FOLLOWING the formation of the earth with its mantle of vegetation, the gods proceed to populate it with animate beings who, in exchange for their having been given life, must worship their Creator. Therefore "they covered woods and mountains with their animals. From then on the guardians of the maize fields and the inhabitants of the thickets were the birds, pumas, and jaguars, and of the creeping plants the rattlesnakes and large snakes." Each species was given its respective habitat: den, nest, or burrow. Immediately Tzakol, Bitol, Alom, and Cajolom, gods of the four sectors of heaven, gave each animal its peculiar means of expression: cries, howls, grunts, separating each group "according to its manner of being understood." (This evinces a notion of zoological classification, applying to the animal kingdom the same rules for differentiating the human kingdom into linguistic groups.)

Only four cosmic gods take part in this. They are the equivalent of the Chac of Maya mythology who are in fact the *owners* of wild plants and animals. The Chortís continue to regard the animals as the *guardians* of the woods, a term that is also applied to the keeper of the temple *(mayordomo)* — *u wink ir e tecpan:* guardian of the temple — in order to show that the woods as much as the temple are divine property. The Indian continues to turn to the Chac when he needs to hunt some animal, a plant, or a tree, having to ask their permission and justify his need to take this or that thing, and *pay for* the concession granted him by them.

The gods concede life not as a free gift, but only on condition that their creatures acknowledge their dependence upon the Creator, invoking it, paying it tribute and homage. For that reason they command the animals to pronounce the name of their Creator, "since we are your mother and father." Speak to us, invoke us, praise us, adore us, the gods tell them. But the animals are unable to comply with this divine order because they lack a fit language; neither can they communicate with each other owing to their differing vocal expression.

Lamenting their failure, the gods resolve to exchange these creatures with others, and to punish them, changing their mode of speech, food, and manner of living and eating, condemning them thenceforth to have their flesh sacrificed and eaten: "and solely for that reason all the animals which live on earth would be killed."

It is a characteristic of Indian thought that it expresses many related concepts in a single allegory. In this case the creation of the animals, whom the gods tried in vain to raise to the category of rational beings, has, aside from its intrinsic meaning (creation of animals), a profoundly ethical, religious, and socioeconomic significance, reflective of the conditions of human life during the primeval cycle of Mayan prehistory.

As shown so often, the native community composes a perfectly homogeneous unity, culturally and linguistically, and identifies itself by the use of the common word its members employ to designate the Divinity. Any change or alteration in pronunciation of the divine name implies a dialect differentiation, therefore political separation, since language is consubstantial with the tribe and spreads with it. This fact is not exclusive to the Quiché-Maya groups since, for example, the same is found among the peoples of Asia Minor who have different names to designate the goddess Ishtar. The first human generation tried repeatedly "to express its adoration [of the gods], but because of the [differing] speech of its members, they failed to understand each other when they were together, nor did they feel affection for one another, and so the Creators did nothing for them." This tells us that then there was no linguistic homogeneity nor the kind of social organization characteristic of Quiché-Maya culture. Because he was ignorant of how to honor his Creator, man was condemned to live in caves and hollows like the animals and Deity did nothing for him, abandoning him to his own fate.

The life of primeval man could not have been sketched more vividly, nor the ethnical features of the country during its first cultural stage, corresponding to the hunter-gatherer cycle. At that time the horde lived in caves and ravines, where it also left its dead. Its means of life were very precarious; man covered himself with leaves or went naked. He had rudimentary religious principles; although he recognized the existence of a supreme Creator, he gave it no worship at all; that is, there was no ceremony, and therefore "the gods did nothing for them." The men of this epoch were likened to animals because of their way of living and thinking. In modern terminology, such a comparison corresponds to the state of savagery, a classification that is evidenced in another way by this Quiché source which equates the Third Age with the period of barbarism, the era of culture being initiated only with the Fourth Age. This way of looking at uncultured man as an animal is not exclusive to the native American mind inasmuch as the first creatures of Phoenician cosmogony were compared to "animals without understanding," according to references from Sanchuniathon and Philo, given by J. Imbelloni.

The veracity of the *Popol Vuh* is confirmed by ethnography, linguistics, archaeology, and the comparative study of native American sources. With respect to the latter, we find a notable description of primeval man — agreeing with the Quiché version — in the account of Guaman Poma.[1] Guaman Poma says that during the First Age, called Pakarimok Runa, the equivalent of the First Age of the Quiché codex, men lived in caves and among the rocks, and fought against the wild beasts. They didn't know how to make anything, especially houses and clothing, covering themselves with leaves from trees and grass matting. Their whole occupation was to worship God: in loud voices they said, "How long will I cry and you not hear me, how long will I speak and you not answer me!" With these words they invoked the Creator, but they had no idols, temples, or sepulchers. They had some sense of the knowledge of the Creator and Maker of heaven, earth, and all that is in it. Their worship consisted solely in the exclamation, *"runa camac, pacha rurac"* (Creator of man,

[1] *El Primer Nueva Corónica y buen Gobierno*, by Felipe Guaman Poma de Ayala, Paris, 1936.

Maker of the world) and, says Guaman Poma, "it is one of
the greatest things, even though they did not know the
other laws and commandments of God." They wandered
like persons lost in unknown terrain. These people, known
as *uariuiracocharuna* (autochthones, first people: *uari* connotes also the idea of native to, primeval, ancient, savage
animal;[2] compare this with the identical conception of the
Quiché) lost their hope and faith in Deity and so they were
lost also, much as in the Quiché story Divinity abandoned
the first people. These peoples were ignorant of their
origins. They worshiped neither the sun, moon, stars, nor
demons, in temples. They lacked rites or ceremonies (they
didn't know how to worship Divinity, says the *Popol Vuh*).
Nevertheless, "they were living without strife or feud and
without evildoing. They had places set aside for calling to
the Deity and those they kept clean. Kneeling, they lifted
high their hands and looked toward the sky, asking for
health and crying out, 'Where is our Father!' They buried
their dead without any idolatry or ceremony."

From the collation of both native sources we can form
a judgment about the way of life and spiritual and moral
condition of the primeval inhabitants of the continent:
those of the First Age in the classifications of the *Popol Vuh*
and the *Nueva Corónica*. Quiché-Maya civilization starts
from this horizon, which contains in seed the institutions
that gradually evolved forth through the succeeding Ages
of their history. According to the testimony of these two
sources (the *Popol Vuh* saying that the first creatures tried
to give expression to their worship of the Creator), monotheism characterized the oldest cultural cycle, since primeval man recognized a "Creator of man and Maker of the

---

[2]Toribio Mejía Xesspe, *Las primeras edades del Perú, por Guaman
Poma*, Empresa Gráfica T. Scheuch, S.A., Lima, 1939.

world" which he worshiped on bended knee, looking toward the sky, a posture and belief that has not varied to this day. This contradicts those such as Lévy-Bruhl who believe that the idea of a single and universal God is at variance with the primitive mentality. But the primeval religion lacked rites and ceremonies; favors were asked of the Deity but there was no knowledge of how to worship or pay homage to it. Neither idols, temples, nor sepulchers existed. On the other hand, a place was expressly set aside for entreating the Creator, and this was always kept clean. Such places in the open air formed the initial phase of the patio or plaza, inseparable from the temple, where the multitudes came together to pray for divine favors. And that custom has not changed to this day, continuing through the epoch of the Old Empire, it being worth noting that a meticulous cleansing of the patio is still a requirement of worship — as during the First Age — inasmuch as the plaza where the people make their petitions must be "clean like the pathway of the sun." The first people also had no ceremony for the death of their relatives, which tells us that they then lacked animist ideas; but they were of a peace-loving and good disposition, basic qualities of the Maya of today.

Survivals of that archaic form of culture still persist on this continent and, as might be expected, are found in areas of refuge where they were preserved by farming peoples. Populations which retain a high degree of "First-Age" characteristics, as described by the native sources, live in Baja California as well as on the islands of Tierra del Fuego at the southernmost extreme. Both populations display notable similarities, and in terms of nature and physique appear to be the oldest and most primitive people of the hemisphere. Baja California is or was peopled by the Yumas, Guaícuris, and Pericu; and the Seri — now

confined to an island in the Sea of Cortez. All of them
belong to the primitive hunter cycle and, excepting the
Yumas, are dolichocephalic. They have a very primitive
type of physique, like the Tierra del Fuego Indians of the
extreme south and the Botocudos of Brazil. Like their
remote ancestors, the Fuego Indians, whom W. Krickeberg regards as direct descendants of the oldest immigrants,[3] preserve a religion based on the purest monotheism and have almost no ritual acts. They have neither tribal
organization nor institution of chiefs, living in nomadic
hordes of two or three families, small consanguinal patrilineal groups. They produce neither pottery nor weaving
and live by hunting and fishing, feeding on mollusks, fish,
birds, and seals. A piece of sealskin covers the shoulders of
the men and serves as an apron for the women.[4] They do
not know the fire drill, employing instead two stones and
tinder, a very primitive method still used by the Chortí,
particularly in connection with the interment of the dead.
In the south of Patagonia in former times caves were used
for habitations as well as for burials, as W. Krickeberg
notes; and the same author indicates that estimates based
on archaeological remains and island middens show that
the Fuegians have lived in that region for at least two
thousand years, their culture undergoing very little modification during that time. These data tend to confirm the
cultural stability as well as the great ethnological age of
those people.

Stratigraphy verifies the presence of this primeval culture as the oldest of which we have knowledge, and shows
its coexistence in different parts of the hemisphere with a

---

[3]W. Krickeberg, *Etnología de América*, Mexico, 1946 (Spanish-
language edition).

[4]A. D'Orbigny, *L'Homme Américain*, Paris, 1839.

rudimentary stone tool kit (excepting the Folsom points). This tool kit is sometimes associated with bones belonging to a human type similar to the contemporary Fuegian, as well as with extinct fauna. Such finds give a picture of the life of the first immigrants that corresponds to the one left us by Guaman Poma, depicting for us man's struggle with the wilderness when he first trod American soil — a description that we find in another form in the *Popol Vuh* and the Mexican sources which tell us of the struggle against the "giants."

Those peoples were ignorant of their origin, says the *Nueva Corónica*, a fact that implies the passage of considerable time between their arrival in the hemisphere and their slow migration toward the south. But while this exodus of predominantly dolichocephalic peoples was taking place, another human wave of distinct racial character but similar cultural conditions made its appearance. Of this we have a record in the present Maya population itself, particularly that which still lives in the area where the native American culture was gestating, and which, according to anthropometric statistics, demonstrates beyond dispute the coexistence of two different physical types. It is logical to think that these two groups, coming from distinct ethnogenetic homelands, spoke different languages and had distinct manners of thinking. The *Popol Vuh* alludes to such a heterogeneity of the primeval population occupying the slopes of the Pacific during the First Age when it tells us of creatures who "because of their speech were unable to understand each other on meeting" and because of their different ways of thinking felt foreign to each other and "felt no kinship."

The course of mixing and of spiritual sharing that would culminate in the formation of a historic race that later would be characterized by great mental homogeneity and stability of language and customs, must have continued for a long time. That process of gestation of Maya culture extends across the three periods of Quiché prehistory preceding the present or historic era.

But we have not yet concluded the exegesis of the First Age because the sequel to the formation of the primeval and imperfect man is his destruction or transformation into an animal, as punishment for his inability to invoke the Creator. In the same way the succeeding creations will be destroyed, their human creatures becoming animals of a superior zoologic type, there being registered in this way a progressive ascent in cultural evolution. The degree of genetic affinity between human being and animal is also established, explaining present beliefs that in former times the beasts could speak. The perfect man, the True Man, will not appear until the human line will have succeeded in so developing itself as to acquire the Maya form of culture. On the other hand, the order by which man is the final product of creation follows the logical sequence the world itself obeys in its formation, with the successive appearance of heaven, earth, its vegetation, animals, and finally man, as found in the Chaldean cosmogony.

Divinity ordains "the flesh of the animals to be sacrificed and eaten, and therefore they were trapped and eaten by the civilized people." This is an express mandate of the Creator by which civilized man is authorized to kill, hunt by trapping, sacrifice, and eat the meat of animals. We find in this divine law the origin of the institution of animal sacrifice, established by Divinity itself. This is borne out in another part of the Quiché codex wherein human sacrifices are regarded as pertaining to a barbaric people and their epoch, and not sanctioned by divine laws promulgated for "civilized" peoples, who can only sacrifice animals. In observance of this command of the Crea-

tor, the Quichés and Mayas sacrificed only animals so long
as they preserved their orthodox ceremonies. The Chortís
who never trespassed this custom continue to sacrifice animals to this day for the benefit of the community itself, as
well as an offering to the gods. The explicit limitation
allowing animal sacrifice only for those ends reveals moreover the principle of a protective law for fauna which the
Chortís continue to observe. Such a law was imposed because of economic necessities, inasmuch as man passed
from nomadism to fixed habitations and had then to take
care not to heedlessly destroy his hunting reserves.

The Second Age

Faced with the failure of the first creation, the gods try
to form new beings capable of paying them homage, "con-
structing them of damp mud," as in the ancient Hebrew
conception. But having done so they realized that their
creatures lacked consistency, falling apart if they became
wet. They had no form and resembled "a pile of mud
having only a neck,[5] no head, a very wide mouth, and eyes
looking only to each side. They could speak but had no
feelings.[6] Then Ajtzak and Ajbit told them: 'You will exist
only until the new beings appear. Struggle to procreate
and multiply yourselves.'" Later they destroyed their
handiwork, and tried to devise a way to construct more
durable creatures who would be able to see, understand,
and invoke their creators.

The Chilam Balam of Chumayel relates the failure of
this creation in similar terms, saying that "on Thirteen
Akbal, it came to pass that God took water and moistened

---

[5] "The neck was their only face" — A. Recinos translation.
[6] They lacked understanding, according to the A. Recinos version.

earth and constructed the body of man. On One Kan he became dispirited because of the poor thing he had created. On Two Chicchan, the poor results became known to the people."

This period shows some slight progress over the former, since now men "knew how to speak, but still lacked understanding"; i.e., they lacked the Maya mentality, and because of that the gods destroyed their second creation. Such an idea is perfectly explainable in terms of Maya thought because, besides the reference that the men of the second creation lacked understanding, they disintegrated when in contact with water, a feature clearly expressing the antithesis between Second Age and Maya culture.

The Chortí is bathed by this divine element with which he is consecrated at both birth and death. The temple for agrarian worship is kept in a state of continuous dampness, and its elders have to sprinkle themselves with water during specific ceremonies designed to magically attract the winter, thereby following the procedures laid down by the gods. Rain is as indispensable for the crops as water is for human life.

This allegory expresses the opposition between the way of life of the hunter-gatherer and that of the agrarian cycle. While tropical rains limit activities of hunting and gathering, they are vital for the work of agriculture. During the first cycles of Maya prehistory, the search for the means of subsistence was carried on during the better conditions of the dry season, while for the Mayas cultivation of the *milpa* is "the proper work," during which the Indian exposes himself to get wet. Therefore he must be "resistant to water," a quality that men of the Second Age lacked.

And those characteristics of the respective cultural cycles are projected in the gods representative of the

Second and Fourth Ages, since rain is beneficial for the god of Maize but troublesome for Kisin, the malignant being of Maya mythology (Tozzer) into which the god of the prehistoric epoch is converted, as will be explained.

Nevertheless, the Second Age marks a stage of cultural progress in regard to linguistics, since people "are able to speak." That is, they can make themselves understood, something they were unable to do in the earlier epoch. On the other hand, they were made of mud, misshapen, and lacking in definite form, this being the salient mark of the second creation.

The specific function of the Creator of the men of mud is found in the proper name of the deity: *Aj bit*, literally "that which makes things of mud," which for the first time appears in the theogonic list.[7] Both Maya and Quiché sources agree upon the production of those unformed creatures modeled of damp earth during the prehistoric epoch. It is interesting to note that during the Second Age of Peruvian mythology, named Wari runa by Guaman Poma, Viracocha, the Creator god, is called *allpa manta rurak*, or "that which works or makes with mud," according to the translation of T. Mejía Xesspe, a name and function equivalent to the Ajbit and Ajtzak of the Quiché codex. This concordance among the sources from the three high American cultures (Maya, Quiché or Toltec, and Andean) speaks to us of their common genesis and brings out, by general agreement, a reality of American ethnology: the beginning of the pottery industry. The artistic poverty of the first ceramics is seen in the description of those grotesque beings who disintegrated in water because lacking in firmness of material substance.

---

[7]Aj bit and Aj tzak correspond to the singular of Bitol and Tzakol, the "builder" gods.

One of the characteristics of native mythology consists in projecting in divine figures certain activities proper to humanity. In this case we have in Ajbit the archetype of the incompetent and uncouth potter who can produce nothing better than counterfeit and impermanent beings. But the gods, like men, perfect their knowledge, and during the Maya era the "Builder" god — the equivalent of San Manuel of Chortí mythology — models in its image and semblance exquisite stone and wooden statues, laying down the standards for Mayan artists, as can be seen on page 45 of the Tro-Cortes Codex.

Nevertheless, the material with which human creatures are made is always that which typifies the salient mark of their cultural cycle: mud during the Second Age, wood in the Third, and maize in the Fourth and latest cycle.

It should be noted that the Fuegians — who by their culture belong to the First Age — do not know the potter's art, a fact that confirms their extreme racial antiquity. Another sign of the progress that is made during the Second Age is seen in the divine decree by which its humanity must struggle in order to procreate and multiply, since that is the Divine will. Thus the Peruvian *Nueva Corónica* tells us that "since the Second Age people multiplied . . . and began to care for and respect their fathers and mothers and lords, and to obey them, . . ." — all this shows a progression in family and social relations. As these appear in company with advances in language and material culture, we can infer that during this period the nomadic peoples reaching the rich areas in which Maya culture was coming to birth felt a continually greater tendency to stabilize, which produced in turn some degree of demographic increase — attested to by our sources — in contrast with what happened in the first cycle. Those conditions imply a slow transformation of the economic regime in which human subsistence depended as much, if not more, upon collection of roots and wild fruits as it did upon hunting and fishing. This paved the way for the arrival of the Third Age, corresponding to the matriarchal-horticultural cycle. Meanwhile the struggle for existence was still difficult. " 'You will struggle to procreate and you will multiply,' said the gods, thereby ensuring that their will would prevail."

Guaman Poma's account completes the description in the *Popol Vuh* by saying that in the Second Age human beings dressed just as they did in the earlier epoch, "had no occupation or craft, no benefits, or war, or houses." Nevertheless, they began to till the virgin soil and construct little shelters called *pukullo,* which looked like large ovens. They had neither idols nor temples, and did not know the art of weaving. The Mexican sources in addition take special pains to tell us of the vegetarian fare of the Second Age, consisting of the "fruits of the earth" according to the anonymous manuscript commented upon by Paso and Troncoso; of wild fruits, says the Vatican A Codex.[8] The Franciscan Codex names pine nuts and an herb called *centencupi,* according to the Thévet-de Jonge manuscript.[9] This grass is described as "a seed like maize, which they call *cintrococopi,*" a reference of capital importance since it refers to wild maize discovered during the second cycle of Quiché-Maya prehistory, an event that later was to be the principal support of their civilization.

---

[8] This source mentions "a certain kind of wild maize, which was called *atzitziutli,* known from the First Age."

[9] "Hystoire du Mechique," *Journal de la Soc. des Américanistes,* Paris, Vol. 2, 1905.

The Third Age

Immediately following the destruction of the second creation, the divine quorum came together anew to consult and discuss how to form beings superior to those of the second, beings "who should see, understand, and invoke us." The celestial council resolved that the four cosmic deities should be responsible for setting "a new day of manifestation and creation," because events of such transcendence should be put into effect at the moment of a new Dawn, Day, or Sun, terms equivalent to a new Era or Age. This meaning of a New Day as a period of time is confirmed in the terminology used in Mexican and Mayan traditions to mark those historical epochs, regarded as Suns in the former and determined by dates of the katún count in the latter.

From within the cosmic tetrarchy — which now includes a Coyote- and an Opossum-god — is selected one "who is the grandmother of the sun, the grandmother of light," the choice going to Ixpiyacoc and Ixmucané. So for the first time on the theogonic stage there appears a feminine deity (Ixmucané), the personification of the old Lunar-earth goddess, who will thenceforth become the center of attention inasmuch as Ixpiyacoc — a masculine deity — plays an essentially passive role. Under the regency of Ixmucané is begun the matriarchal-horticultural stage, whose unmistakable characteristics are described in the traditions of the Third Age as well as in the account of the life of Hunahpú and Ixbalamqué, grandchildren of Ixmucané. This cycle corresponds to the Sun of Water of Mexican mythology, the epoch governed by Chalchiuhtlicue, goddess of the Moon and of Water, which ends in a watery catastrophe. Ixcanleos, the mother of the gods, is in Mayan mythology the functional replica of the Quichés'

Ixmucané, and the etymological affinity between the two names should be noted.

For the first time the *Popol Vuh* mentions the election of a Regent, which despite the tardiness in naming her, explains the position of Ixmucané in the series of regents. This event accompanied the creation of cosmic bearers, also during the Third Age, as will be explained further on.

After selecting the Regent, the central deity — integrated by the three suns of the line of the parallel — "says to those of the sun, to those who make the sun appear and disappear [an allusion to the gods of the cosmic points or the four heliacal gateways], that they should come together again and determine what kind of beings would be created and formed and which they would sustain so that these beings should adore them as being their superiors." The constant preoccupation of the gods was to form beings who would know how to venerate them, recognize them as superior, feed them and give them the necessary offerings. The recurrent failures of the previous creations show how difficult and time-consuming was the introduction of correct ritual into religious practice, and at the same time explains the origin of the agrarian religion, based upon the principle that man is an eternal debtor of the gods and should sustain them if he wishes to enjoy divine protection. As in all ancient religions, before the appearance of the doctrines of humanism, man is counseled to recognize his dependence on the Creator; in exchange for this he has the right to demand the Creator's protection, since the obligations are reciprocal.

Then the Quiché manuscript enumerates a series of twelve divine names, specifying that "thus they were named by our Creator." Here is outlined for the first time the individuality of the god-Thirteen, formed of the solar deity in its zenithal position and its twelve stellar compan-

ions which, in the conception of the Chortí elder as of the
Popol Vuh, were "named" (created) by the great Agrarian
god. For that reason he too must "name" them during the
rites established for the Tzolkín. Those twelve gods are
mere hypostases of the great god of Heaven[10] and so par-
take of its qualities; and this is clear in the listing in the
Quiché epic since all the names given correspond to distinct functions of the Creator, such as: the wild Boar (this
is how it also appears in the Mayan codices), the Lord of
the emerald, the resplendent Lord, Lord of the penetrat-
ing rays, of the extension of the firmament, of the luminous face, the Maker, etc. This union of the thirteen gods
in one could not be more eloquently expressed than it is in
the paragraph of the Book of Chilam Balam of Chumayel
wherein is mentioned Oxlahun-oc, "Lord of the thirteen
feet," measured by Deity the Verbum at the request of the
Mistress of the World (the Lunar goddess).

In both these sources the lunar deity appears in close
connection with the stellar gods, and this association —
which accords with astronomical reality — is confirmed
in Chortí theology, which regards the moon as the "Captain of Heaven" and the stars as its subordinates. The
moon, functioning as the Water goddess, and the latter as
rain gods, "work" in unison and in most perfect harmony,
pouring down the celestial waters for the benefit of mankind. But such religious conceptions can only evolve parallel with the evolution of horticulture, when the rains
become indispensable to the success of the plantings. From
this it follows that the first astronomical observations
among the Mayas grew out of economic necessities, during
the matriarchal-horticultural cycle. The superior importance of the goddess of the Moon and of Water, projects

---

[10]Girard, *Los Chortís*, "The Tzolkín" and "Theogony."

on the theogonic plane the privileged social position of woman, linked with the apogee of horticulture. On the other hand, the importance attributed to the worship of the Lunar goddess reflects the existence of a system of time computation based on the revolutions of the moon, a fact confirmed by the Chilam Balam of Chumayel in the following terms:

> When anciently the world had not awakened [allusion to the precultural epoch, according to the Maya concept] the Month [moon] was born *and began to walk alone.* . . . After the Month [Deity] was born, it created the one called Day [young sun] . . . and this one walked with the mother of his father and with his aunt and with the mother of his mother and with his sister-in-law.[11]

This is authentic testimony to the existence of the lunar before the solar calendar, explained in terms of family succession, since a mother precedes her son. The relationship according to the female line, mentioned above, also points to the existence of a matrilineal state contemporaneous with the computation of time by lunations.

And with the first astronomical observations were born magic and the astrological sciences, facts that are stated in the *Popol Vuh* which tell of gods practicing divination with grains of corn and red *tz'ité* seeds for the first time during the preparations being made for the Third Creation. Ixpiyacoc and Ixmucané are the progenitors of "divination with the seeds," and correspond to Oxomoco and Cipactonal of Mexican mythology who appear as the inventors of the calendar. The etymological relation between Ixmucané and Oxomoco should be noted. As said, the feminine deity assumes the principal role, since Ixpiya-

---

[11]Mediz Bolio, *Chilam Balam.*

coc does not act during the Third Age and is only mentioned as the companion of Ixmucané who takes the full
initiative. On the other hand, the role of the young god
(Hunahpú), grandchild of Ixmucané, becomes more pronounced and foreshadows his apotheosis at the end of the
Third Age. This agrees with the order of succession set out
by the Book of Chilam Balam of Chumayel. The *tz'ité* or
fruit of the *palo de pito* (*Erythrina corallodendron L.*,
native in Guatemala) has a form similar to a bean seed,
but its color is red.

Following the tradition established by the gods of the
Third Age, the Quichés still use grains of maize and seeds
of the *palo de pito* in their divination practices, calling
these seeds beans (*frijoles*) or *tz'ité*. This intimate association of beans and corn stands out better in Chortí theogony, where both plants, deified, form an inseparable pair
in the native pantheon and *milpa* (planting field), corn in
the role of masculine and bean in that of feminine companion deity. Such functions demonstrate the relation of
each plant to the respective age it characterizes. Thus,
while the Maize god is the theogonic exponent of the
Fourth Age, i.e., of the patriarchal-agrarian age which
begins with the formation of human beings from maize,
the Bean goddess represents the Third Age or the matriarchal-horticultural cycle which commenced with human
creation based on the *palo de pito* or bean. Despite the
immense antiquity of wild maize, which was already
known during the Second Age, the bean was apparently
more easily domesticated and had reached its full development before maize, so that it can be seen as the basic food
of the Third Age. According to the Book of Chilam Balam
of Chumayel, people then fed upon three classes of beans
and ate tender branches of *yaxum*, ground tubers and
white beans, calabash seeds, and small and large beans, all

well crushed. It is most important to show that during the matriarchal-horticultural period, when according to the Chilam Balam of Chumayel "sons had no fathers and mothers no husbands," beans and tuberous roots formed the basic food of the Maya-Quiché. The great antiquity of the bean is seen by the fact that the ordinary type (*Phaseolus vulgaris*), native to Guatemala, offers features showing that it was domesticated since the most remote times. That class of bean was diffused from Guatemala to South America, and its area of distribution, embracing a considerable geographic extension, is another proof of its great antiquity as a domesticated plant. Such diffusion implies concurrent migratory dispersions, a fact confirmed by the series of cultural features associated with bean cultivation in the southern Americas, which in the Quiché classification took place during the Third Age.

A phenomenon of linguistics reinforces the above postulate. Elsewhere we have drawn attention to the fact that in languages emanated from the same linguistic subsoil the word for bean (*frijol*) either passed from a particular to a general meaning or suffered a displacement in meaning by becoming the word for another plant or food.[12] Such changes lead us from the ethnologically oldest languages to those representing a more advanced state of culture. The word meaning bean in the former becomes in the latter the designation of the *milpa* or of maize. We have singled out some cases, such as the Pacific Maya language group, which most fully preserves the archaic word forms, wherein the word signifying bean has in the Chortí language come to mean *milpa*. Likewise the root *at*, *et*, which in Talamanca means bean, is the name for the tortilla in Zapotec, Lenca, and Otomí, and synonymous

---

[12]Girard, *Los Chortís*, chapter 4.

with the number one (*et*, *at*) as indicating the principal food. So we see that when maize became the most important food, displacing the bean, it also took over the name and number that formerly identified the bean. When maize gained the principal importance as food, its name became identified with the "one," because it was the food of the chief, the "number one" in the household and the person who ate first.

There is even more to this, because if we extend the comparison to the South American language groups, we find that the words *frijol*, *mandioca*, *maíz*, *chile*, *patata*, or the names of products made from these food plants, usually proceed from equivalent roots in one or another of them. In order to avoid citing too many examples, we simply observe that the root *im* < *am* or *ma*, the metathesis of *am*, which is found in the word *maíz* in Central American languages, changes in meaning in languages to the south, where it chiefly designates *mandioca* (manioc or cassava). See Appendix A for an extensive comparative listing of such words.

Many pages would be required to present an exhaustive comparison of words designating food plants among the languages stemming from this common linguistic subsoil, and this is not our intention. We wish only to cite from among them all some examples of displacement in meaning undergone by the same root. This development can be explained by imagining that there was one original word that came to indicate the food plant and that it was applied by each people to their own particular varieties, in some cases maize, in others the bean or manioc, as they came to know these plants and adopt them as the basis of their alimentation.

As said in the *Popol Vuh*, there arose the new humanity formed like "puppets of wood resembling human beings, human beings who spoke," and modeled by Ajtzak and Ajbit similarly to the earlier Second Age humanity, with the difference that this time wood of the *pito* (*tz'ité*, or bean) was employed instead of wet mud. This change in material implies an evolution in creative technique and at the same time notes the progress made in the epoch. In the theogonic order the Third Age, which because of that essential feature can well be called the age of wood and beans, reflects a real advance in human technology in the matriarchal-horticultural period. And this is once more confirmed by comparative ethnology because the cultural horizon corresponding to the Third Age shows us peoples who are principally wood-using, such as the Taoajkas of the Mosquito Coast whose society is purely matriarchal and whose economy is based on horticulture, hunting, and fishing. Their work implements are mainly of wood, an industry in which the Taoajkas excel.

Mayan culture has its roots deeply submerged in a prehistoric past, and it preserves features that derive from the most primeval levels of its development. As that culture evolved, the elements which went to make it up continuously increased in number. The first notions of agriculture, of the calendar, of magic, of worship, and of wood carving — which culminated in the sophisticated artistic lintels of Tikal — stem from the oldest phase of its prehistory.

The creatures of the Third Age mated among themselves and produced offspring, but they had no hearts or feelings, and were unaware that they were sons of the Creator. They wandered about like strangers and without purpose, according to the *Popol Vuh*. Since they were unable to know and understand the Heart of Heaven, they fell into misfortune. They could speak, but their faces were stiff and only had a mouth for eating. They had no feet or hands and so could not defend themselves, no blood, and no extremities. Thus they only resembled but were not true human beings. This picturesque description vividly portrays the condition of things in that age, in which the population of the earth increased as a result of the stable and growing sources of subsistence, human language was evolved, and certain aspects of human culture were developed. That an abundance of food was a characteristic of this Third Age is also noted by Felipe Guaman Poma de Ayala in his Andean account: in those times people "multiplied like the sands of the sea and overran the land." This explains the migrations which took place in that age as well as the extensive geographical diffusion of human cultural features that occurred. Social evolution continued at the same rate as material and intellectual development. The "mating, cohabiting, and producing offspring" tells us of a change in the social and family regime as well as of the appearance of exogamic clans. Every demographic increment brings with it a complication of the structure of society, a fact recorded in Quiché tradition. But despite this progress, the beings of the Third Age still lacked the mental and religious character typical of Maya culture. "They had neither hearts nor feelings." This indicates how long and difficult was the process of the formation of the Indian's psychological nature, developed through three racial periods, and at the same time explains the profound stability of the Maya mentality. It also sets forth the fact that it was not racial but cultural factors that shaped the native mentality.

As in the previous age, the description of the anatomy of the beings of wood reflects the art of the time. The fact is emphasized that the wooden puppets lacked members, had neither feet nor hands, and their fingers did not protrude from their bodies. We find these very features in the archaic statuary; the carving of the extremities was the most difficult part for the artisan of the protohistoric era.[13] Of course sculpture in stone followed that in wood, but the statuary found in the most ancient archaeological horizon reproduces those features described in the *Popol Vuh*, which suggests that the process of artistic development took place over a considerable period of time. When the Mayas first began to cut statues in stone, they had already had a long artistic tradition of working in wood, continued in the statuary of the archaic period. The lack of human extremities also speaks to us metaphorically of the lack of moral as well as of physical strength, such as humanity has today, and which would be obtained only in the great age to follow. It was in that later age that appeared Hunahpú, the civilizing hero of "strong arms," according to the Chortí Drama of the Giants. And this weakness of the men of the Third Age was natural, since they "had no blood"; that is, they had not been formed of maize, which is the blood, the divine substance. This allegory also expresses the essentially inferior legal position of men to women in the Third Age.

The gods resolved to destroy the beings of the third creation because of their imperfections, "condemning them to disappear by dying." For the first time the word *death* appears in the Quiché codex, and the same thing is seen in the Book of Chilam Balam of Chumayel, which mentions the "invention" of death on a date later than that of the second creation, since "On Three Cimi, there occurred the invention of death. It happened that Deity Our Father invented the first death."[14]

Such a tardy reference to death doubtless indicates a

---

[13] Girard, *Los Chortís*, chapter on archaeology.
[14] Girard, *Los Chortís*.

religious innovation involving veneration of the dead, a thing unknown during previous ages and in consequence an evolution of thought in the direction of beliefs of an animistic type.

An inundation, a great flood, came to wipe out the beings of the third creation. There fell torrents of resin from the heavens (a probable allusion to a volcanic cataclysm, a frequent occurrence in the original territory of Maya culture). Finally strong winds from the sea concluded the destruction of the wooden beings, whose eyes were torn out, heads lopped off, their flesh and bowels devoured and nerves and bones eaten by the agents of the god of Death, who is also now on the stage as a result of the creation of death. All this the *Popol Vuh* offers to us in an apocalyptic picture, which also explains the existence in that era of a funeral ritual whose purpose was to liberate the dead from such terrible adversaries. Even the animals and household implements are shown in the *Popol Vuh* as helping to destroy the "men of wood," contributing to the heavenly punishment. The earthen jars, and pans, bowls, pots, dogs, and chickens reproach their masters for the mistreatment they gave them or the misuse made of them. Besides showing us the existence of domesticated animals in that age, this episode contains a profound moral meaning and recounts the beginning of the custom whereby the Indian uses domestic implements with moderation, and treats his animals with respect.

It is interesting to note that the account of the revolt of household implements that is given in the *Popol Vuh*, also forms part of the traditions of the Chiriguanos of the Tupi-Guaraní family (located in the Gran Chaco region of South America), according to information sent the author by Dr. Alfred Métraux. An account of this nature, which can be explained neither by transcultural influences from the Quiché or the Maya nor by spontaneous invention in two distinct cultural areas, seems to indicate that at one moment in their history the Chiriguanos and the Quiché-Maya shared a common culture.

In this manner the people were destroyed, thus was their end, and according to tradition there was left as a sign of their existence only the monkeys which live now in the woods and fields. In them persists the appearance of those who were made of wood. For that reason the simians are the beings most like man.

With this epitaph concludes the account in the *Popol Vuh* of the Third Creation, with a curious doctrine that reverses the order of the ancestry of man and of simian from the one found in Darwin and Haeckel.

But that is not all, since the events taking place during the prehistoric ages are again spoken of in a different manner and with greater detail in the part of the *Popol Vuh* that describes the life and miracles of the hero-gods, Hunahpú and Ixbalamqué, the part that constitutes the center of interest of the Quiché codex. This repetition of the same theme in a different form recalls to mind the system of double reconciliation or adjustment found in Maya-Quiché chronology, which, projected in the literary structure of the manuscript, contributes an informative supplement of the highest importance, as we shall see in the following section.

5

The Marvelous Story of Hunahpú and Ixbalamqué

HUNAHPÚ AND IXBALAMQUÉ CONQUER THE GIANTS

AS SAID, the history of Hunahpú and Ixbalamqué gives a synthesis of the whole prehistoric period of Quiché-Maya culture and culminates in the arrival of the cultural era. These facts are dramatized in the Dance of the Giants, which with good reason the Chortí call "The History." In this theatrical work, the two actors who represent the sun and the moon appear with faces covered by a veil, something that agrees with the following prolog from the *Popol Vuh:* "At that time only very little light was found on the earth because the sun did not exist. The faces of the sun and of the moon were still covered." At the end of the Chortí drama the two actors remove their veils, symbolically illuminating the scene of the fourth creation following the triumph of Gavite, who embodies the role of Hunahpú. These allegories — as will be shown in the course of what follows   rcfcr to the era of ignorance or spiritual darkness that marked the prehistoric epochs, in contrast with the spiritual illumination of the era of true culture when the gods uncover their faces.

In those times, says the *Popol Vuh*, there lived an extremely vain being called Vukup Cakix — Seven-Macaw, or Seven Feathers of Fire, a title usurped from the solar god which in Maya mythology is named Kinich Kakmó (*kak:* fire, *mó:* bird) — who aspired to be the sun and moon but lacked the qualities of those gods. While the world was still enveloped in semiobscurity, i.e., before the dawn of civilization, Vukup Cakix boasted that he was the sun which would illuminate and civilize humanity, proclaiming in a loud voice: "I will be their Sun, I will be their splendor, I will also be the moon because my eyes are like emeralds, my teeth glisten like precious stones, my nostrils dazzle from afar, like the moon; my house also shines."

In this paragraph are made known qualities proper to the starry gods, who have a house in which they enclose themselves and from which they come forth to move through the firmament to light up the universe. By mentioning that the "elements of splendor" are found in the teeth, eyes, and nose of the god, the *Popol Vuh* expresses a typically Mayan concept which we find objectified in iconography and statuary. Think, for example, of the faces of Ahau at Copán, in which the nose is represented by the glyph for the solar ray, the teeth and eyes by pearls or *kin* signs or even by a half-moon when the feminine goddess is being depicted. The gods, likened to precious stones broken off from the "Great Stone of Grace," radiate light from all of their being, but especially from those parts which, according to observations made by human beings, shine brighter or reflect better the solar rays. Because of this, it is natural that the eyes, teeth, and nose should have particular importance, to such a degree that in the majority of faces of Ahau, which we find on monuments and in codices, the only facial features shown are the mouth or teeth, the nose, and eyes, which are also chronographic elements. Later on the fingernails play the same role and, like the eyes and teeth, are likened to pearls or precious stones.

In reality, says the Quiché codex, Vukup Cakix was not the sun or the moon, and his vision did not embrace everything that was under the sky. The sun was still not to be seen, nor had true daylight appeared, and thus Vukup Cakix boasted of being something that illumined like the sun because the light of day had not commenced to spread itself. Following this we are told how Vukup Cakix became hopeless and discouraged when the new humanity was formed by Ajtzak and Ajbit, and died at the hands of Hunahpú.

Besides giving us an eloquent description of Venus, the brightest planet in the sky after the sun and moon, but whose light vanishes when the daystar appears — as the shadows of barbarism are dissipated by the rise of civilization — this account illustrates some fundamental principles of Maya ethics, based on theological virtues. The failure and death of the false god exemplify the punishment that awaits the proud and vain as well as those who usurp attributes that do not rightfully belong to them.

There can be only one Deity, and this monotheistic principle is proclaimed aloud by Hunahpú and Ixbalamqué:

> Cabahuil only is the Creator; and they saw that what Vukup Cakix, full of pride, was thinking, what he wanted to do in the presence of the Heart of Heaven, was bad. The birth of people like that on the face of the earth in that manner was not good.

This anathema is also a sentence, since the young hero-gods will punish arrogance with death. To that end they went to the place where Vukup Cakix customarily ate fruits, so they could shoot him with their blowguns, causing the sickness that was to bring on his death.

The drama between the young gods and Vukup Cakix unfolds in two parts. The giant was accustomed to climb a berry tree (*Byrsonima*) whose yellow fruit, fragrant and delicious, was his sustenance. Lying in wait for him at the foot of the tree, Hunahpú fired his blowgun and hit Vukup Cakix in the mouth. The giant fell on his back upon the earth. This position prevented him from dying (for reasons that we will explain). Hunahpú ran to seize him and a struggle began in which Vukup Cakix grabbed Hunahpú by the shoulder, threw him to the ground, and brutally tore off one of his arms, which he carried to his house.

Vukup Cakix had two sons, Zipacná and Caprakán; his wife was named Chimalmat. Zipacná had made the mountains and volcanoes whose names are given in the text, and which correspond with Guatemalan geography. Caprakán busied himself moving the large and small hills and volcanoes. "I am the sun," Vukup Cakix said. "I made the earth," said Zipacná. "I am the one who troubles the sky, moving and stirring the earth," said Caprakán.

These are, then, four giants, the Atlas or Hercules of Maya legend, which in the Chortí drama are represented by the Black Giant who "with one kick of his foot makes the earth tremble." And, like Gilgamesh of the old Mesopotamian traditions, who in the time before Judea had to fight with giants in order to win immortality, Hunahpú confronts the giants of Quiché mythology, which he has to vanquish before the reign of the true gods and civilization can be established. This struggle also expresses the antagonism prevailing during the precultural cycle between the forces of heaven — and of culture, represented by Hunahpú and Ixbalamqué — and those of earth — personified by the giants — when cosmic harmony did not yet rule.

Later on, the four giants, having been defeated by Hunahpú, would become the four heavenly bearers, placed in the
corners of the cosmos.

The first episode of the struggle between Vukup Cakix
and Hunahpú represents among other things an astronomical theme made evident in the return of the giant to "his
house," carrying with him a part of the celestial body, and
this cut-off portion must appear in the firmament. The
constellations whose configurations reproduce the personage who lacks one of its extremities are those of Orion and
the Great Bear. Both offer to the unaided vision a group of
seven brilliant stars of which four are located in the corners
of a square, but in Orion the other three are within the
square (these are the Three Marías of Chortí theogony),
while in the Great Bear the three form an arc of a circle
that begins in one of the corners of the same square. In the
group of seven stars is projected the ideogram of god-
Seven, i.e., the name of Hunrakán, Heart of Heaven,
whose etymology (the one having only a single leg:
Sherzer) corresponds to the figure of the Great Bear. This
is confirmed by another source, for in Mexican mythology
Tezcatlipoca — the one-footed god, a counterpart of
Hunrakán — also sallies forth to slay giants as did Hunahpú (the alter ego of Hunrakán). "And this appears in the
sky, because they say that Ursa Major descends to the
water because it is Tezcatlipoca and commemorates him,"
says the *Historia* of the Mexicans in its pictures.

Nevertheless, there is a discrepancy between the version of the *Popol Vuh* and the etymology of Hunrakán
itself, which tells us of a one-footed and not a one-handed
god. But this difference is more apparent than real,
because at bottom this allegory, aside from the astronomical theme we describe, deals with a basic principle of
monotheist theogony whereby the gods are only hypostases

of one single deity, an idea that is expressed by the tearing off of a member of the divine body to signify that one god is a part divided off from another god. Elsewhere we have expanded upon this principle and have demonstrated that

FIGURE 1. Xochipilli (after Hugo Moedano Koer). Note the seven points which adorn the throne and suggest the numeral god-Seven.

the foot which Tezcatlipoca lacks appears in the earth, converted into the Maize god. But this idea is not always rendered through the lack of a foot, since in Mayan art it is usually symbolized by a head lacking the lower jaw, while in Mexican codices one-handed gods appear. The figure shown here, depicting Xochipilli without one hand, is an example.[1] The equivalence of Xochipilli and Hunahpú with respect to Hunrakán is seen in the very name of

[1] On page 3 of the Borgia Codex.

Xochipilli, which W. Lehmann translates as "son of the foot." On page 18 of the Borgia Codex one sees descending from the sky a bird which has in its beak a human arm, whose symbolic value is identical to that of the foot wrenched from Tezcatlipoca, since both allegories equally represent the descent of the Maize god into the underworld. There is a correspondence in the field of linguistics, where the words foot, hand, leg, and arm, regularly proceed from equivalent roots in the various languages derived from the proto-Mayan trunk. For example, in Maya, Chontal, Tzental, Tzotzil, Chañabal, Chol, Quekchi, Poconchi, and Chortí, *ok* signifies foot, while in Huastec *ok* is hand or arm. Quekchi, one of the most archaic of the tongues belonging to the Mayan family, uses the same word to designate arm and leg, a phenomenon leading one to think that in its primitive state Maya language had only one root for the words foot and hand, or leg and arm. In a more advanced period, when an effort was made to differentiate the terms hand and foot, recourse is generally had to a transposition or metathesis, whereby some languages designate the hand by the same term that in others means foot, all of which indicates that later differentiations stem from a common primitive term. Such a situation is seen in the oldest manifestations of aboriginal art, when the sculptor did not even know how to figurate the extremities of the human body, imitating thus the rude creatures of mud of the second creation.

All this leads to some interesting deductions that serve to enlighten us about the life of the primeval hunter-gatherers, whose family — exemplified by that of Vukup Cakix with his two sons — was quite small compared with the ideal type of family of the Mayas which should have at least six sons. The common weapon for the hunt was then the blowgun — nowhere is the arrow mentioned — and the blowgun was also the emblem of the solar ray, as was the arrow in more recent epochs. Thus the gods of the primeval epoch were blowgunners. Like the solar ray and the invisible dart of the witch, both these weapons "prick," and this is the method employed by Hunahpú to cast upon Vukup Cakix the spell that will make him fall sick and die.

Here is illustrated the procedure used by the sorcerer to bring harm to a person, the foundation of the belief still existing among the natives that there is no natural disease or death: these they regard as produced by conjurations. And this contrast between the methods of battle used by Hunahpú and Vukup Cakix, the former having recourse to magic and the latter to brute force, shows the superiority of intelligence over force, of science over ignorance. Here the actors of Quiché mythology play a part similar to that of Minerva against Mars in Roman mythology.

Following the tragic encounter, Hunahpú and Ixbalamqué go to speak with two old white-haired people (the white hair symbolizes the color of the First Age, corresponding to the First Regent, an idea that the Chortís objectify in the white handkerchief with which the elder covers his head when he assumes the function of the First Regent. Also, in the Vatican Codex the "white head" characterizes the First Age and its cosmic Regent). These old ones are the protectors of the young pair, who ask their help in recovering Hunahpú's arm and in completing the punishment of Vukup Cakix. For that, the two youths disguise themselves as poor orphan children, while the old ones play their grandparents who are also healers (elsewhere the grandparents are identified by the names of Ixpiyacoc and Ixmucané), as a way of visiting Vukup Cakix without arousing his suspicions. Under pretext of healing the giant, wounded in the jaw by the blowgun, the two old people tell him they will take out his broken teeth and damaged eyes, and replace them with new teeth and eyes.

But Vukup Cakix protests that "this is not well because, being a Lord (Ahau), my teeth and my eyes are my riches" (attributes of rank and power; see what was said above about the symbolic value of those elements in the face of Ahau). The old ones insist upon the necessity of the operation, offering to replace the teeth with others that look like bone, intending to replace them with grains of white maize which resemble bone in appearance. Note the symbolic relation between bone, teeth, and maize grain, a relation that is also found on the level of linguistics. Finally the operation is performed; then the giant no longer feels pain, his presence as a great Lord rapidly fades, and he suddenly dies, having lost his attributes. Then Chimalmat also dies, and Hunahpú recovers his arm. The simultaneous death of the giant and his wife illustrates the concept of duality by which every divine pair forms an indivisible whole, the female aspect being an unfolding or alter ego of her "husband." The same idea prevails in contemporary beliefs concerning nahualism, i.e., when a person dies, his nahual or double also dies instantly.

The action wherein the supposed healer "takes away the emeralds which glittered in the beginning here on earth" reflects the triumph of the true gods over the false, of heaven over earth, and explains why the macaw has no teeth. This allegory also reveals the mythical origin of the servitude imposed upon Venus by Hunahpú in his role as god of the Dawn, as will be shown later on. For that reason *Iko Kij nima chumil*, the great star, carries the sun on its shoulders, and it is so represented in the Tellerianus Codex. Although Tlahuiscalpantecutli has been correctly translated as "god of First Light" or "of Dawn," (*dieu de l'Aube du jour:* Thévet), or "the Lord of the rosiness of morning" (Beuchat), and not as Venus, the two have frequently been confused, as the cosmic bearers are wont to be confused with the Regents of the angles of the cosmos. The relation of Venus with the god of Dawn is the same as that of the bearers to the Regents, and this is projected in the sequence of time where Venus has the value of "introducer of the sun" (tables of eclipses). In Mexican iconography Tlahuiscalpantecutli is presented at times as a hypostasis of Tezcatlipoca, who in Aztec mythology plays the same role as Hunahpú in the Quiché. Hunahpú is the equivalent of Ahau in the calendric series as the final day of the month, and that title he takes in a spectacular manner from Vukup Cakix, despoiling the latter of his "elements of splendor" which from then on will be Hunahpú's. Perhaps this scene also symbolizes the demise of the ancient worship of Venus, which could have existed during the hunter-gatherer period and which we still encounter among certain American tribes of lesser culture.

THE FOUR HUNDRED BOYS

After defeating Vukup Cakix, the hero-gods using magical arts destroy Zipacná and then Caprakán. These episodes in the *Popol Vuh* are introduced by the legend of the 400 boys who drag an enormous beam with which to build their house. To cut that beam, they begin by burning the trunk, the accepted method of that time for felling trees.

This group of 400 individuals uniting their forces to transport the unusually large piece of wood affords a beautiful show of cooperation, highlighting the principle governing the communal type of society as well as the origin of a custom preserved to this day by the Indians: when anyone proposes to construct a dwelling, the whole group voluntarily offers to help him so that the labor is quickly done. The scene of the Flying Pole (*Palo Volador*), in which a large number of Quiché Indians (the equivalent to the number 400 of the *Popol Vuh*) transport an enormous beam from the woods into the plaza where it will be erected on end as a mast, reminds one of this passage in the *Popol Vuh* that the ceremony perpetuates. The same scene is reproduced in those places in Mexico where this curious custom still survives. Patricia Fent Ross says that in Panhuatlán, Hidalgo State, 200 Otomí youths carry a pole of 130 to 160 feet in length (see Figure 10).

On their way the 400 boys encounter the giant Zipacná, who offers to help them, and carries the heavy beam himself after asking the boys, "What do you intend to do with that pole?" "It is going to be the centerpost of our house," the boys reply. This question and answer give in a few words the contrast between the habitation used in the hunter-gatherer period and that used in the civilized epoch. In the First Age — that of the giants — men didn't know how to make houses and this ignorance is reflected in Zipacná's curiosity and his innocent question: "What will you do with that pole?" Then, picking it up, he throws it on his shoulder and alone carries it to the boys' camp. This spectacle expresses in vivid image the antagonism between two social concepts: communal cooperation, personified by the 400 boys who work in unison, and the individualism embodied in Zipacná who "works alone," and in this picturesque way expresses the opposition between the two cycles. The idea is accentuated in the sentence which follows, voiced by the group of boys: "What Zipacná did, in taking up and carrying a beam *by himself*, is not properly done." Then the boys "think together about the matter and reach an agreement" (the identical procedure employed in the divine assemblies, exemplifying the model for human communities) as to how they can slay the giant, using astuteness instead of force for that purpose, and always proceeding in unison.

Employing a stratagem, they will lure the giant into the bottom of the hole they dig for setting up the mast and, once he is there, will crush him with the heavy wooden pole.

But Zipacná, who was the Earth god, had the ability to hear at any distance, a thing the Chortís explain by saying that all natural apertures in the earth — caves, precipices, grottoes — are the "ears of the earth" and allow this deity to hear all that is said in the world; a curious belief whose origin goes back to the myth of Zipacná.[2] Having learned of the plot, but without letting on, the giant went down to the bottom of the hole and there dug a lateral tunnel to save himself when his adversaries would let fall the heavy beam intended to kill him. Believing Zipacná dead, the 400 boys, now happy, prepared "their drink of three days" to celebrate their triumph, which had spared them taking Zipacná into their community. In the community's social structure there is no room for strangers, and that rule, which even now governs native custom, is here exemplified.

The three-day drink is today called *chicha*, the Indian's native beer, a fermented, alcoholic fluid whose preparation requires three days. As with all indigenous customs, this too is exemplified in the mythical part of the *Popol Vuh*. When there are reasons for rejoicing, the Indians still drink the *chicha* together, as did the 400 boys celebrating

---

[2]Compare the name Zipacná, Earth god, with Cipactli and Cipactonal of Mexican mythology.

the supposed death of Zipacná. On the third day when the *chicha* was ready, the boys proposed to drink it on the very spot where they thought they had killed the giant, hoping then to see the ants attracted by the cadaver. But Zipacná, who heard everything they said — as explained above — had cut hair from his head and chewed off his nails to give them to the ants and so deceived the boys. Seeing these remains of Zipacná being taken by the ants, the boys became drunk on the *chicha* and fell into a stupor. The giant then tumbled the house down upon them and killed them all, so that "not even one or two of the 400 boys saved himself." This legend, dramatizing the fatal consequences of drunkenness, illustrates another rule of native morality which prohibits excess in drinking liquor, limiting its use to a number of cups determined by ritual figures (four or five). As a notable example of the temperance of Quiché-Maya Indians, we can cite the case of the community of Nahuala (Guatemala) where there is no tavern because the indigenous community prohibits it, paying the government an annual tax to cover the estimated revenue that would ordinarily accrue from sales of *aguardiente* there. Thus the Indians are freeing themselves from the "benefits" of civilization.

The native belief that the foundation of the four "world pillars" (*horcones*) or cosmic bearers are set in the underworld where they nourish the spirits of the dead is illustrated in the legend of the 400 boys. But that story dealt with a malign spirit located in the bottom of the hole, and explains the Quiché custom of burning incense in the hole where the mast will be placed for the Flying Pole ceremony in order to expel bad spirits which, like that of the giant, could harm the actors.

Hunahpú and Ixbalamqué felt "dismay in their hearts when they learned of the death of the 400 boys." Some

lines before this in the Quiché epic, the destiny of those
boys is mentioned, which was that they became incorporated in the stars which thereafter, to commemorate the
events recounted, were called Motz (those reunited in a
group), that is, the Pleiades. But it is not until the final
victory of Hunahpú and Ixbalamqué, when they are transformed into sun and moon, that the 400 boys come back to
life through the intervention of these divine twins and are
converted into the Pleiades, like the Atlantides (Hyades
and Pleiades) of Greek mythology. Besides illustrating the
religious doctrines of the immortality of the soul and the
native belief which places life after death in the stars —
and that explains why, in the Mexican glyphs, a seated
dead person replaces a star in the figure of the sign for the
day of the dead — this myth contains a profound astronomical meaning. As the Chortís say, the Pleiades "are
angels that lift up the Lord" on the day of the sun's first
passage through the zenith. Then "they shine in the
Glory," repeating the act whereby Hunahpú revives the
400 boys. According to Chortí observations, the position of
the Pleiades determines that of the sun at the zenith, an
event which marks the beginning of the rainy season and
the base line of the calendar. This precise linkage between
the star and the constellation is seen in the Quiché codex by
the intimate relation between Hunahpú and the 400 boys,
a relation that, on the other hand, evinces the social soli-
darity between related elements. The fact that the
Pleiades come forth at the end of the Third Age indicates
that from then on there was a perfect knowledge of the
positions and movements of that constellation, so important in the Quiché-Maya astronomical system, and similarly the calendar of 400 days was used, a number that was
in the beginning the highest mathematical and chronological expression known and, therefore, embraced the

notion of innumerable. We will return to this point later when the apotheosis of the hero-gods is discussed.

The importance of the myth of the 400 boys and its great antiquity is evident in the versions of this legend preserved by peoples whose separation from the Quiché-Maya trunk goes back to very remote epochs such as, for example, the Lenca, who have among their traditions the following, as recounted by Fray Alonso Ponce in his *Relacion Verdadera.* One day as 400 boys were dancing about the spring at Uluapan, and with them an old one who accompanied their steps by drumming, they tired so much and were so sick of dancing that, despairing of life, they all decided to leap into the spring and drown themselves. So that none of them could escape, they brought up a long, strong rope and tied themselves together and, throwing themselves into the water, they were transformed into fish. Despite its variation, one sees in this the same social concept and the same relation between the boys converted into fish and Hunahpú who also, as we see later, is transformed into a fish, his nahual. The boys' invention of the intoxicating drink compares with a Mexican mythological account of 400 rabbits, gods of *pulque,* the Mexican alcoholic drink. In the *Historia de los Reinos de Colhuacán y México* (1563–1579), the starry gods are called the "400 cloud-serpents." But in Aztec mythology the 400 Huitznahua, copied from the Quiché tradition, are defeated by Huitzilopochtli who, being a copy of Hunahpú, nevertheless plays the role of Zipacná, for reasons of history.[3]

The mythological connections between the Pleiades, the sun, and the moon are reflected in the field of linguistics. In the various languages emanating from the trunk-language, the expression of a common ancient cultural

---

[3]Girard, *Los Chortís,* "Ethnography and Religion."

subsoil, the words sun, moon, and Pleiades are related
genetically and substituted for each other through displacement of meaning. For example, in Xinca the term
áhua is used for moon (R. Shuller); and in Chuj, moon is
pronounced *ahau*. On the other hand, *ahual* is used to
designate the name of the Sun god which follows the last
day of the month in the Tzental calendar. The unusual
term *po*, designating moon in Quekchi, Mixe, Pocomam,
and Tapachultec (*poya en zoque*), is related to the root *pu*
which in South American languages enters into the composition of names meaning moon and the Pleiades (Shuller)
and in the words *pu pu* (Pleiades) in Miskito, *pu pu* (east)
in Xinca and *bul* (star) in Hicaque. This goes to show once
again that the origin of the word goes back to the age of
myth and that, like cultures, languages emanated from the
same trunk separated from each other in different historical moments and dispersed over a considerable area to the
north and south of the country that was the cradleland of
those cultures.

In order to avenge the death of the 400 boys, Hunahpú
and Ixbalamqué go in search of Zipacná, whose preoccupation was the search for fish and crabs by the rivers,
wandering through the woods to get his daily sustenance.
At night he busied himself by moving mountains about.
This descriptive picture of human life during the hunter-
gatherer period is noteworthy; previously the *Popol Vuh*
told us that the favorite meal of Vukup Cakix was the
yellow fruit, and has this personage saying, "If they had
killed me, I would be hanging over a fire and roasting
there," illustrating the First Age method of preparing
foods. Both Mayan and Mexican sources refer to the time
when primitive man depended on a parasitical economic
regime. In the memorial of the Cakchiquels there is described the epoch of "misery, when people nourished

themselves on wood, leaves, wanted nothing but earth, and couldn't speak."[4] Similarly, the Mexican codices specify that during the First Age man nourished himself with acorns (compare the yellow fruit of which the *Popol Vuh* speaks), pine nuts, pine resin, and mesquite fruit, etc. That not only confirms the thematic unity of Mayan and Mexican sources; it also gives a true description of primitive man's *modus vivendi*. And this, as with all that the *Popol Vuh* has to say about the life and customs of people during prehistoric cycles, is confirmed by comparative ethnography.

Having learned Zipacná's habits, the young pair of hero-gods work out a subterfuge for overcoming the giant, and construct an enormous crab, perfectly reproducing the form of the crustacean, making its eyes of *ek* (a Guatemalan parasite called *pie de gallo*) and then placing it in a cave at the foot of the mountain named Meaguan (a Guatemalan mountain). Then they go and find the giant wandering by the banks of a river, hungry because he hasn't eaten in two days (a notable description of the precarious state of life of the hunter and of his uncertain food supply). The youths approach and tell him where the beautiful crab is located, which "filled the giant with pleasure because of the hunger that constantly tormented him." When they reached the cave, the youths persuaded the giant to enter it lying on his back, so as to trap the crustacean. But when Zipacná's body disappeared inside the cave, Hunahpú and Ixbalamqué "let fall on him the mountain that they had bored into through the middle, crushing the giant who became transformed into stone."

This episode, like all the others in the Quiché epic, has many meanings. In the first place, it illustrates the native

[4]*Memorial de Tecpán-Atitlán*, A. Villacorta, Guatemala, 1936.

belief in the immanence of living beings in stones, inasmuch as Zipacná was transformed into rock, becoming the soul of the hill, therefore embodying the image of the cosmic bearer. Since he had positioned himself with his mouth up when he was crushed, his spirit could not escape and he remained imprisoned within the hill. In fact, according to native beliefs, exemplified in this account in the *Popol Vuh*, witches and the defunct must position themselves on their backs so that their spirits can leave and return to the body. As we saw, that position prevented the death of Vukup Cakix when he fell on his back. To prevent the repetition of this with Zipacná, the youths, having learned from experience, sealed up the giant's mouth by letting the mountain fall upon him and so imprisoned his spirit within it. In their word *p'a kma* (bad, depraved, boaster), the Chortís preserve the characteristics attributed to the giants by the Quiché source, linked by analogy to the name Zipacná, showing once again that the origin of the word is tied to the origin of the myth.

Moreover, the Maya traditions cited by A. Tozzer say that the sun had scarcely appeared when the first men were transformed into stone.[5] And the Book of Chilam Balam of Chumayel explains the magical act whereby Hunahpú bored through the center of a mountain to cause the death of Zipacná, as an effect of the divine Word: "The Word of the Deity sounded and separated from the stone, and fell in the second time . . . and its Word . . . pierced and sundered the shoulder of the mountains."

We have already mentioned that Word and Action are magical equivalents, and we have an eloquent demonstration of this idea in the text of the Dance of the Giants (the

---

[5] A. Tozzer, *A Comparative Study of the Maya and the Lacandons*, New York, 1907.

Chortí dramatization of the *Popol Vuh*) in the scene specifically related to the death of Zipacná (personified in the Dance by the Black Giant). "Let death be spoken to this boastful giant," says the Chortí version, preserving in its Castilian diction the original semantics. This demonstrates once again the native authenticity of the Chortí drama.

That divine Word *tells* the twins that they should now do away with Caprakán, the last of the giants, since " 'this is our will, because what he does on earth is not good, pretending to equal the sun and the moon in grandeur. Therefore, tactfully see to it that he goes toward the place where the sun comes up,' Hunrakán told the two youths." And these, replying that what they have seen is not good, reaffirm the doctrine of divine unity as follows: "Aren't you the only one that should exist and live as the Heart of Heaven which you are?"

The youths leave to search for Caprakán (the theogonic antithesis of Hunrakán, expressed in their very names: "he of two feet" versus "he of one foot") and find him busy moving the mountains as expected, because being the god of Earthquakes that is his profession — a malign being to whom the Chortís give the name of "he of the earthquakes."

Seeing the two youths, Caprakán, curious, asks, "Why are you here? I don't know your faces. What are your names?" (in the primitive mentality, the name is the person). But never in their adventures do Hunahpú and Ixbalamqué reveal their identity, since "he who knows the name is master of the person," and magically dominates that person, according to the Indian manner of thinking. Carrying out Hunrakán's order, the youths maneuver the giant toward the place "where the sun comes forth" which, in Mayan cosmogony, is the "good" side of the cosmos wherein the beneficent gods reside, whose influence will help the twins gain victory.

During the trip Hunahpú and Ixbalamqué aim their blowguns and, simply by breathing into the tube without using any darts, capture some birds, which exceedingly amazes Caprakán. This incident explains the esoteric value of the blowgun as symbol of the solar ray, which operates magically. All mythologies are in the habit of identifying the instrument that symbolizes the power of their solar deity with the chief weapon of the epoch in which the myths were formed: dagger, sword, hatchet, or arrow. In a recent epoch of their history, the Quichés adopted the bow and arrow, weapons that, as in Mexican mythology, replaced the blowgun as the emblem of the Solar god. Mention of the blowgun as the divine attribute at a time when it had been displaced by another weapon confirms the historical validity of the *Popol Vuh*.

The twins prepare a fire to roast the birds over the coals (showing the technique for preparing food), but they smear one bird with white earth, a procedure that by means of imitative magic should bring about the death and interment of Caprakán, since "just as the earth would cover the body of the bird, so it would enclose the giant within earth and in earth would he be buried."[6]

Since Caprakán "thought only of eating, his heart desired only that," said the twins to each other as they cooked the birds. The roast gave off an appetizing smell which aroused Caprakán's wish to eat: "His mouth watered, it gaped, and saliva fell from it." Note the contrast between this primitive behavior and the ethical values of Maya culture. Caprakán's reaction to the vivid picture of the steaming bird is no different from that of a dog anxious for its food. The giant implored the twins for at least a mouth-

---

[6]This section has been translated perfectly in the version of A. Recinos, which we have reproduced here.

ful of the savory meal, and they gave him the bewitched bird, which caused his downfall, for going eastward, he could no longer move the mountains, and fell unconscious "because of the earth on the bird." Instantly the youths tied him up "with hands behind, the collar tied to the feet, and then they buried him in the earth. Thus ended Caprakán, because of all the evil that he had done here on the earth."

Caprakán is tied up like an animal that is transported home by successful hunters. Then he is placed on the ground where he is buried according to the rules of primeval interment (horizontal position). And with his burial ends the era of the giants, the close of the first ethnical cycle of American prehistory. A painting in the Vatican A Codex illustrates the destruction of the First Age by a giant interred in a horizontal position under the surface of the earth.

The mythical giants, compared to animals by the *Popol Vuh*, are in popular belief associated with the remains of bones of now extinct beasts. Through such beliefs, wrapped in the mantle of legend, we see a background of fact, since man of the First Age had really to fight against animals which were gigantic in comparison with those of later times. Primeval man's coexistence at the end of the Pleistocene Epoch with species of a now extinct fauna, such as the mammoth, giant bison, and camel, etc., has been scientifically confirmed.

Guaman Poma draws a vivid picture of the "first Indians who trod on American soil, who wandered as though lost in an unknown land, and had to fight against wild beasts. They killed these, conquered and ruled over the land, having entered it by order of God."

Thanks to the discovery at Tepexpan, that description corresponds to events which have been reconstructed. Tepexpan offers us the picture of a hunt for the imperial mammoth, cornered by its pursuers in a bog. Those very hunting techniques are still employed by the primitive Gés

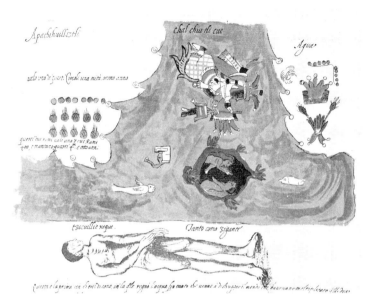

FIGURE 2. End of the First Age, as pictured in the Vatican A Codex.

— contemporary representatives of the oldest ethnical horizon — who, employing lances to hunt the tapir, surround this pachyderm by burning great extensions of the *sertao* (W. Krickeberg). The great merit of these native sources is the information they afford concerning the way of life of primitive man about which we previously knew nothing.

6

The Biography and Genealogical Tree of Hunahpú and Ixbalamqué

THE INFORMATION in the *Popol Vuh* about Quiché theogony does not differ from what we learn from Mayan sources of Yucatán or the present-day practices of the Chortís. The Quiché codex states that the parents of Hunahpú and Ixbalamqué are the seven Ahpú, i.e., god-Seven, which is Heart of Heaven itself. But here for the first time is given the number of the divine hypostases, with numbers instead of names, thereby comparing the seven Ahpú with Uuc-cheknal, the god-Seven of Maya mythology, which according to the Book of Chilam Balam of Chumayel came from the seventh plane or stratum of heaven and descended to the earth. In the same way, the seven Ahpú descend to earth, where they become human beings and, after undergoing a number of trials, die at the hands of the Camé.

This variant of the divine name expresses a specific function of the god of the Firmament, who descends to earth to fecundate it with his blood and later, in the underworld, is transformed into the young Maize deity, thereafter assuming another aspect and another name, as we shall see.

The seven Ahpú were produced by Ixpiyacoc and Ix-mucané, the name the *Popol Vuh* gives here to the supreme pair, the great Father and great Mother of Quiché-Maya humanity. As the Supreme Being, Ixpiyacoc has no life history: the Ahpú, who become human, are its hypostases; and it is the life and miracles of the Ahpú that are narrated, for they exemplify Mayan cultural standards. Ixpiyacoc is the equivalent of Hunab ku, the Supreme Being of Mayan traditions, of which Fray Diego López de Cogolludo said that "it had no form and could not be configurated because incorporeal, and from it proceeded all things." Hunab ku had a son who was known as Hun Ytzamná or Yaxco Cah Mut (other appellations of god-Seven).[1]

A kind of foggy cloud enwrapped the seven Ahpú, says the Quiché text, making allusion to the epoch of barbarism or of semi-obscurity, which the Chortís represent by the veils that cover the faces of the actors playing the roles of the sun and moon. The same idea is repeated when it is said that the seven Ahpú "were born during the night," i.e., when neither the sun nor moon nor Maya culture had yet been produced. The Book of Chilam Balam of Chumayel also tells us that when Uuc-cheknal descended, "the earth had not become lit, there being no sun or moon."[2]

Although the seven Ahpú are the parents (or parent) of the civilizing heroes Hunahpú and Ixbalamqué, one only of the seven has two sons, Hun Bátz and Hun Chouén, cousins or brothers of the former. The native word-list makes no distinction between those terms of kinship,

---

[1] *Historia de Yucatán*, Madrid, 1688.
[2] Girard, *Los Chortís*.

whose origin, as well as the origin of the macrofamily that those terms imply, goes back to this remote epoch. This is confirmed later on in the story when the cousins treat each other as brothers.

Because of their divine nature, Hun Bátz and Hun Chouén were great sages: all the arts were passed on to them as an inheritance by one of the seven Ahpú; they were singers, orators, jewelers, writers, engravers, and sculptors of stone. Here are mentioned for the first time those cultural features that appeared only very late in Maya prehistory, such as the invention of the ball game, a favorite pastime of the Ahpú "who every day dressed up to play ball, competing two against two and even four against four when they came together on the ball field."

Origin and Significance of the Ball Game

The *Popol Vuh* is the only American source to speak of the origin of the ball game and place it in time. Not only does it tell us of the game's ethnological antiquity, it also explains its symbolism. It in fact establishes a parallel between the ball players and the solar gods, which from the angles of the universe — to employ the phraseology of the Chumayel manuscript — meet in the center, in this case in the ball court, where they can convert themselves into two and even four persons with no loss of their theogonic individuality, at once a unity and a multiplicity. During the ball game they wear their resplendent ceremonial gear — that is, they exhibit their insignia as solar deities. Two by two they come from the eastern and western sectors of the cosmos and, meeting in the center, forge themselves into the individuality of Heart of Heaven. This fusion of a number of forms under "one single head," as the Chortís say, is expressed in the principal rule of the game which is that the players can touch the ball only with their body but never with their heads, feet, or arms; each time this happens a point is given the other team. The continual contact of two or four bodies with a single ball makes clear the monotheistic principle whereby the deity integrates itself through the union of its hypostases. This idea is objectified in the group of ball players unable to use their heads or extremities since the ball — the symbol of the Star or Sun god — is alternatively the head of each. This figure of a single-headed god having many bodies is characteristic of Maya thought. We need only to remember Oxlahun-oc ("it of the thirteen feet"), who is mentioned in the Chilam Balam of Chumayel. The motion of the ball imitates the trajectory of the sun, a figure that the Chortí actors also reproduce in their dramatization of this part of the *Popol Vuh*. Besides this, the Quiché codex represents the descent of god-Seven from the Center of Heaven to the center of the earth by the solar bird which, coming down from on high, "came to see them play." As said, in Chortí religious allegory the bird of prey, which is the mask, nahual, or messenger of the deity of Heaven, descends vertically to the center of the earth — like the sun's rays — when the daystar goes through the zenith, symbolizing the descent of divine grace.

The seven Ahpú were taking the road to Xibalbá (the underworld)[3] when their coming was felt by Hun Camé and Vukup Camé, Lords of the subterrene regions, who, disturbed by the noise the Ahpú made, challenged them to play a ball game on the Camés' court in their kingdom. We have here a contest between opposing forces, since those of Xibalbá cannot tolerate that " 'anyone greater than they, or any having greater power, should exist,'

---

[3] An allusion to the setting of the sun.

they all said unanimously." From this passage it is seen
that the organization of the false gods is similar to that of
the true since, like the latter, the false gods compose a
sevenfold entity whose components must get together and
reach decisions by a unanimity. This shows an evolution of
the idea of Divinity that parallels the social evolution expressed in a collective religion as a projection of the divine
corporation. We are now far distant from the kind of individualism or egoity personified by the giants, as well as the
pure monotheism of the First Age. But there still is no
harmonious, universal order, since the celestial and terrestrial forces were antagonistic.

The *Popol Vuh* then lists the names of the malignant
beings which inhabit the Quiché Avernus, giving their
respective functions as the originators of specific diseases or
as those responsible for the misfortunes that afflict humankind. Here we have the origin of native ideas whereby
sicknesses are conceived as psychological and not as patho-
logical conditions. In the Indian concept, Deity takes
away its protection from those who infringe against the
laws of religious morality and who from then on are subject to the influence of malign beings, whose earthly representative is the black magician (*brujo*). The latter busy
themselves in casting spells and, like the messengers from
Xibalbá, can transform themselves into owls, a bird which
for the native continues to be the messenger of death. The
popular saying based on this belief is well known: "When
the owl sings, the Indian dies."

The owl-messengers from Xibalbá were four: Chavi
Tukur, Hunrakán Tukur, Cakix Tukur, and Jolom Tukur.
These come to the ball court to give the Ahpú the following
message: "The Lords say you are to come, that you will
play ball with them, each one to make himself known by
his face, and that you should bring your playing gear,

lances, gloves, and also the rubber ball." The intention of the Xibalbans was to take away from the Ahpú their accoutrements of splendor, i.e., their divine attributes.

In order to dominate them by magic, the Camé had to know the face of each of their adversaries; for the person is the name, and knowing it one gains dominance over the person. Elsewhere we have referred to this peculiarity of native thought, which explains the absence of the two verbs for *to be* (Spanish: *ser* and *estar*) in languages of the Maya family, since those grammatical categories are implicit in the personal pronouns.

The Ahpú hurry their preparations for the trip to the regions of the underworld; but first they go to say goodbye to their mother, "because only she was there." During this period and throughout subsequent episodes, the role of the woman is emphasized and that of the man diminished as the head of family. The personages who successively come on the scene, such as the Ahpú, Hun Bátz, Hun Chouén, Hunahpú, and Ixbalamqué, have only a mother or grandmother. Before leaving, the seven Ahpú ask Hun Bátz and Hun Chouén to continue cultivating the arts, their singing, and oratory, and to keep the fire in the house going as well as "the warmth in the heart of your grandmother."

With these simple words there is established the family veneration of the grandmother, instituting at the same time a new theogonic category, the god of the Hearth, the nahual or representative of the Ahpú. The flames of the hearth fire remain as substitute for the seven Ahpú, in the same circumstances as, later on, the shoots of maize are to remain in place of Hunahpú and Ixbalamqué when these descend into Xibalbá. This is an interesting datum regarding divine nahualism, and at the same time explains the reason why the god of Fire (Ahpú) is father of the god of Maize (Hunahpú), and precedes Hunahpú on the journey to the underworld. The same order of succession governs in the series of the Nine Lords of the Night, headed by the god of Fire.

The custom of keeping the hearth fire continuously lit, as well as the social forms that it implies, go back to this mythical episode. Such a custom continues to be scrupulously observed by the Indians.

It is interesting to note that in the theogonic order the god of Fire preexists the agrarian deities and that its worship, deriving from such an immense antiquity, has been preserved in Maya culture, which regards the god of Fire as an ancient god, the oldest in the pantheon.

Disregarding the injunction of the Lords of Xibalbá, the Ahpú took off their splendid gear, "tying them together to store them with the rubber ball in a space in the roof of their house." Thus they frustrated the Camé, who now would be unable to take their attributes of rank, even though they should sacrifice the Ahpú's bodies. This is a beautiful allegory of the triumph of ideas over matter. Following their touching farewell to their mother, which caused her to weep, the seven Ahpú, guided by the Tukur, undertook the journey to Xibalbá.

Descending through a rough way, they saw by a river the openings of two ravines. They had arrived at the entrance to the underworld, where the earth's surface divided from the subterranean floor. The Chortís still locate that place in the defiles of their real world, known by the name of "the hills which come together there," equivalent to the Greek Sympleiades. After having crossed the four infernal rivers without incident, the Ahpú reached an intersection of four roads, where they decided they were lost because they did not know which was the correct road. One was red, another black, the other two respectively white and yellow (the first mention of the underworld's

FIGURE 3. Stele standing at the foot of the western stair-
case of a temple of the ball court, Copán. Note the solar
ray glyph on the wristbands, the ear ornaments, and the
headdress: the "elements of splendor" referred to in the
Popol Vuh and the Chortí drama.

geometry, identical with that of the other cosmic planes,
as well as the first reference to the ritual colors). The glyph
of Mictlantecutli, god of Death in Mexican mythology,
which is as follows, ⊕, exhibits the arrangement of the
roads of Xibalbá with their respective colors.

The black road then spoke: "I am the road of the
Lord." It was there that the Ahpú became lost (a word
used here in a double sense, both actual and figurative),
for by that road they went directly to the mat-covered

residence of the great Chief of Xibalbá, where they were vanquished.

In these few lines is explained the origin of the native belief identifying the cosmic routes with animate beings that feel and speak, the Chortís not sleeping in sacred paths used ceremonially so as not to injure their spirit; the ignorance of the times about the configuration of the lower world — an idea corresponding to the preamble wherein only two cosmic planes are mentioned; and, finally, the Regency of Hun Camé. The latter, signaling a new epoch, is confirmed by the double circumstance that Camé is the Ahau (Lord) who enjoys absolute dominion during the period when the struggle for control in the world takes place between the Lords of Xibalbá and the Ahpú. The former win and preserve the title of Ahau, or the gods of the Age, eclipsing all the rest, taking over the regency from Ixmucané. Another indication of this is seen in the principal feature of the "house" of Camé, which is covered with mats (*popobal*), a symbol of power and the distinctive mark of the Regent (Ahau, Pop, or Katún). In the Book of Chilam Balam of Chumayel this allegory is expressed in the following statement: "The Black Regent was carried upon his mat and seated on his throne." Camé is the equivalent of Cimi, second of the Regents in the primary series, a series that will complete itself in later episodes, as we shall see.[4]

Coming to the end of their journey the Ahpú see wooden figures disguised as human beings and, believing themselves in the presence of the Camé, greet them. But the

---

[4]The color black symbolizes both barbarity as well as its authentic exponent, Hun Camé, god of Death and of the Underworld, represented in the Chortí drama by the Black Giant. This characteristic color of the underworld is employed later on in the Mayan codices to indicate the Lords of the Night.

wooden dummies do not reply, and this provokes uncontainable laughter on the part of the Lords of Xibalbá, who are watching.

Here we have a new confirmation that these events occurred during the Age of wood, when wooden idols were constructed. Moreover, the artifice used by the Xibalbans to deceive the Ahpú points to a tactic of war employed in that epoch, consisting of dummies disguised as soldiers and placed on the field of battle to deceive the enemy. The same trick was used in Honduras only a few years ago by the Indian Ferrara.

Hun Camé and Vukup Camé immediately invite their guests to be seated (in agreement with the native protocol), but the seats are hot stones which burn the backsides of the Ahpú, causing them to jump up, which again causes much hilarity among the Camé. "They were dying of laughter like people with heart palpitations. Even the bones of the Lords of Xibalbá moved because of such laughter." This vivid description of those whose pleasure is found in causing pain, depicting a vice of the barbaric age, allows us to follow the progressive evolution of ethical conceptions in Maya culture.

On the other hand, the sketch given of the Xibalbans "moving their bones" in merriment evokes the figures of the god of Death represented as a skeleton in the Mayan codices.

Here use of stone benches as an important part of the furniture is mentioned for the first time; also the custom of offering guests a seat; and this cultural element, going back to the Second Age, is inseparable from the figure of the god of Death depicted in the Maya codices. As can be seen in the following illustration, that deity is shown seated on a rough stone, a primitive form of the stone benches or thrones that later Mayan art would perfect.

This seemingly insignificant detail is really of considerable importance if we take into account the concepts inherent in the figure of the seat, which in Maya culture is a symbol of authority.

This symbolism of the stone seat is so deeply rooted among the Chortís that although they have forgotten the

art of stone cutting and use only wooden seats, they preserve in their vocabulary the words *ah pah caa* and *ká*, with which they respectively designate a carpenter, calling him a worker in stone, and the wood bench, which they call stone. There is even more to it: the use of stone during the Second Age seems not to have involved seats alone but was extended to the first grinding stones, judging by the etymological relation between that instrument and the word Camé. Such relation becomes more noticeable in light of the covariation of the roots employed to designate respectively the grinding stone and the god of Death. For example, in Quiché the *metate* is translated by *caá, kaá*, the radical of Camé, while the Chortís call the grinding stone *cha* and the god of Death *cha mai*. In the Villacorta edition of the *Popol Vuh*, Camé is translated by *caá*, grinding stone, and *me*, to break into pieces; words that perfectly render the Chortí, Hicaque, and Lenca beliefs in the existence of a gigantic grinding stone or millstone by which those condemned to hell will be ground over by the "bad enemy." This idea, contained in the name Camé, eloquently ex-

FIGURE 4. The god of Death on his stone seat (Dresden Codex).

presses the technique of crushing food grains by the *metate* as is done even in our day by housewives when preparing tortillas.

The distant origin of the word as well as the use of the grinding stone becomes evident in all this. It also shows that all the peoples who employ a common word root to designate the *metate* in connection with the word for death, from the area of the Tarascos to that of the Chibchas and Caribs, at one point in their history shared in a common culture.[5]

Following the episode of the hot stones, the Xibalbans force their victims into a black cave, while they think out the way they may slowly kill the Ahpú (the characteristic of cruelty proper to a barbaric people, but foreign to Mayan ethics). The torture of the black cave is to remain in that hellish cavern that is filled with smoke from torch pine and cigars, which by order of the Camé the victims themselves must keep lit: a refinement in cruelty that converts the cave into a hot, stinking, and suffocating oven. The *Popol Vuh* describes the torch pines (*chaj*) of Xibalbá as a stick of pinewood covered with turpentine; the chips of the burning pine fell off like pieces of bone — a description that corresponds in every detail to the pieces of resinous pine that from those remote times until today the Indian has used as a torch. Besides instructing us in the lighting method of that epoch, the smoke-filled cave reminds one of the vapor bath even now so popular among the Quichés. The repeated reference to cigars (four times

---

[5]See what was said in chapter 1, Girard, *Los Chortís*, about the root *caá*, *chá*, and its variations in both geographical areas as well as in time. That list is incomplete and could be amplified by the addition of many more words such as *uka*, stone in Coroado, *aka* in Tunebo, *kági* in Changuena; *ak* in Guetar and Bribri, *kaya* in Jívaro, *kaka* in Quechua, *taka* in Rama, etc.

in several lines), to the smoke they produce and the method of lighting them with the pine torch — just as do today's Indians — leads one to think that these references explain the invention of the cigar following discovery of tobacco and its properties. The relative antiquity of that invention is apparent in the widespread distribution of cigar smoking in prehispanic America, paralleling diffusion of the word *zic* (cigar) used in the *Popol Vuh*. The word cigar in fact originated from *cigale*, the name long ago given in the Antilles to the rolled-up tobacco leaf, and is connected with the root *zic* of Mayan languages, as for example the Jacalteca, which better preserved its primitive forms. The god of Tobacco is called Zic-Ahau among the Quichés, according to references in Sapper and Termer. On the other hand, the root *zic* and *sic* (tobacco) enters the composition of place names in the Pacific zone of Guatemala (Sicalla, for example), and this can happen only in a country where that plant was intensively cultivated.

Following the agony of the black cave, there followed that of the freezing cave, where "it was cold and an icy wind blew." Then the victims passed on to the cave of jaguars, "which roared and killed each other with their claws, both male and female." The fourth place of torment was the cave of vampire bats where "there were only bats, and these screamed, screeched, and fluttered about within the cave from which they could not escape." The fifth hell was the cave of flint knives where "there were only pointed flints over which the tortured victims were made to run rapidly."

But the Ahpú had no chance to learn about all those places of torment described by the Camé because, on emerging from the black cave, the return of the cigars and pine pitch torches intact was demanded of them. Since they had earlier been required to burn these, they could not satisfy the demand, and so were sentenced to death by the Lords of Xibalbá.

The Ahpú were then beheaded and cut into pieces. Their remains were buried in the place called Pucbal-chaj, and their heads hung on the branches of a tree. Such practices, typical of the epoch, continued among those peoples who remained fixed on that primitive cultural level.

After the heads of the seven Ahpú were hung up in the tree branches, they were transformed into gourds (fruit of the calabash tree). This amazed the Xibalbans beyond measure, and they thereupon decreed that no one should go near or touch the miraculous tree, which continued to produce gourds.

Here the *Popol Vuh* gives us a new discovery of Quiché-Maya culture, the gourd, whose importance can be appreciated from its still indispensable religious and domestic use. The immense importance of this utensil, at a time when pottery-making was in its infancy, is not difficult to imagine. Later, potters imitated the forms of this fruit, which because of its mystical significance and practical utility was the archetype of ceramics through all later periods of Maya history. The relation between the gourd and the skull is expressed in the common term by which they are designated (*ruč* in Chortí), and once more we see that the origin of the word and its etymological explanation go back to the age of myth.

The genetic connection between the words for gourd and skull proceeds, moreover, from the interchangeable use of those objects as receptacles. It is probable that before the invention of ceramics and the discovery of gourds, the skullcap was employed as a drinking cup. That hypothesis is based on the practices of peoples such as the Caribs, who preserve the cultural features characteristic of the age of predominance of the Xibalbans. Miguel Acosta Saignes mentions that among Carib customs is the drinking from skullcaps of persons sacrificed as well as the quartering of living prisoners, as the Xibalbans were accustomed to do. Use of the skullcap as a cup by the principal wife of the dead man has been noted among the Caribs of Chaimas, Cumaná, Chiribichi, and Caracas, while in Palenque the chief used the cranium of quartered prisoners as a cup.[6]

The gloomy infernal regions so clearly described in the *Popol Vuh* imply the development of animist beliefs that did not exist before, and this image of the underworld which appears for the first time in the panorama of prehistory is the same as that on which Quiché-Maya conceptions of life after death are based. The Chortís dramatize the captivity of the Ahpú in the scene in which the White Giant falls prisoner to the Black Giant, and the latter brags of having "conquered seven kings" (the seven Ahpú) embodied in his adversary — an eloquent demonstration of the conception of plurality within divine unity. The same is seen in the *Popol Vuh* where the seven Ahpú are the father of Hunahpú, just as the White Giant of the Chortí drama is the father of Gavite who personifies Hunahpú (see concluding chapter).

The Book of Chilam Balam of Chumayel recounts the same episodes in similar terms when it gives in serial order in "Book of the Ancient Gods" the descent of the god-Seven — the equivalent of the Ahpú — to earth, during a time of darkness; the reign of the second and of the third period, corresponding to the Second and Third Age of Quiché classification.[7] The heavenly gods weep before Chac, as

[6]M. Acosta Saignes, *Los Caribes de la Costa Venezolana*, Mexico, 1946.

[7]Mediz Bolio, *Chilam Balam*.

Ixmucané does before the Ahpú. The immensity of the earth reddens (because of the shedding of divine blood). There were then living great spiritual sinners (the people of that period). The era of power (of the true gods) had not yet arrived. The people then believed themselves to be gods but were not, because they did not sow seeds or produce rainfall. They said they were united piece to piece,[8] but they did not say what they loved (the false gods lack power to fructify the grainfields and, although their theogonic organization is similar to that of the true gods, they were not exemplifying the Mayan virtues as were the latter). Thus their countenance was hard and under their rule great misery befell everyone. When they did seat themselves on high, the fire of the sun came to life and drew near them, burning the earth and the clothing of the kings (a cataclysm by fire as depicted in the *Popol Vuh* destroys that human generation, which still lacked the ritual rules of the Maya culture; moreover the earth-heaven opposition bespeaks cosmic disharmony).

Despite their elliptical and metaphorical style, the traditions set out in the Chumayel manuscript do not differ from those of the Quiché text.

Aside from the information on the forms of social and family life, economic and religious development, and new ideas about the division of labor which the *Popol Vuh* gives us, it is important at this point to underline two features of great historic interest.

The invention of the ball game, resulting from the discovery and use of rubber, took place in prehistoric times and in the area of incubation of Maya culture. We have

---

[8][I.e., the opposite of a fully integrated entity in which the part is inseparable from the whole. A stage of imperfection from the standpoint of complete integration of all parts. — TRANS.]

authentic testimony to this in the *Popol Vuh*, the only native source that tells when, where, and in what circumstances this cultural element appeared, explaining its symbolism at the same time. Moreover, the word *hule* (rubber) belongs to the Maya language. *Ule*, the Chortí name for the tree and the gum from which the rubber ball was made, connotes the idea of roundness. In Maya and Tzotzil, it means play; in Tzotzil and Tzental, *bol* is roundness, and in Mayan it is *uol*. According to Pío Pérez the expression *hun vol* is used to count round things. The word *bo* and *po* are etymologically related to those for play, rubber, and roundness: in Tapachultec *po* means the moon and *poo, po*, which in Mixe and Quekchi mean the same, produce an association of ideas which the Chortí elders explain by saying that the moon is "the great circler of the earth." This genetic connection between the words for play, ball, rubber, and round expresses the association of ideas that went into the formation of the word when the ball game was invented.

Nowhere is the symbolism of the seven Ahpú so well represented as in the monumental ball court at Copán, where fixed into the side walls above the sloping platforms we find six stone carvings of the macaw, aligned three on the east and three on the west side of the court, in accordance with the astronomical positions of the respective hypostases of god-Seven. The line of the parallel, i.e., of the passage of the daystar through the zenith, crosses the center of the court from east to west, symbolizing the "road of the sun," according to Chortí expression. The ball, together with the six macaws, completes the symbol of the god-Seven. As said, the macaw was for the Maya the disguise or nahual of the Solar deity, whose attributes were for a time usurped by Vukup Cakix. Those elements of splendor, associated with the figure of the solar macaw, are seen in the Copán sculptures where, as the focus of interest, the sacred birds' eyes, feathers, and beaks are finished in exquisite workmanship.[9] Kayab, depicted by the head of the macaw, is the sign of the next to last uinal of the tun, and falls on the summer solstice, one of the positions of the Solar god, marked by a macaw at the ballcourt. The relation between the seven Ahpú and Hunahpú is expressed in the monumental group at Copán by the association of the statue of the young god, a representation of Hunahpú, with the figures of the macaws symbolizing the Ahpú. The statue is found in the northern end of the ball court, exactly at the place where Mayan mythology locates the underworld, so as to symbolize Hunahpú's triumph over the forces of Xibalbá. Both the Copán monuments and the Chortí Drama of the Giants are faithful reproductions of the Quiché account.

In times before the artistic development of Maya culture, the ball game must have taken place on a simple level area on which was drawn a line to divide the playing field into two equal parts. We have recourse to comparative ethnology for its reconstruction. The widespread diffusion of the ball game toward both the north and south of the continent, as well as into the Antilles, corroborates its great antiquity, and this accords with the relative position in time assigned to it in the *Popol Vuh*. The ball game in its primeval form is preserved in peripheral areas, and therefore it cannot be attributed to Maya or Quiché cultural influences. So that the ball game was spread during prehistoric periods by migrations of peoples who, departing from Central America, dispersed over the rest of the hemisphere. While Quiché-Maya culture itself continued evolving and differentiating more and more from

---

[9]See figures 5 and 6.

FIGURE 5. The ball court, Copán, expressing the symbolism of the seven Ahpú, the inventors of the game.

FIGURE 6. One of the macaws of the ball game. The ball court, Copán.

that of the peoples who had left their common ancient homeland, these latter either stopped progressing or did so more slowly than the Quiché-Maya. Thanks to these circumstances we are able to reconstruct the various stages of Quiché-Maya culture and verify the historical veracity of the *Popol Vuh.*

In the episode about the messengers sent to the Ahpú by the Xibalban Lords, we have another striking proof of the diffusion of cultural features of Maya prehistory to the north and south of the Americas as well as into the Antilles, carried abroad by the migratory currents of peoples. As said, among the Maya the black magician (*brujo*) is personified by the Tukur, and can transform himself into an owl. His work is the casting of evil spells and he represents the forces that are inimical to man, whereas the elder or white magician (*sacerdote*), his opponent, defends the community and represents the true gods beneficent to humanity. In the Chortí conception, the black magicians are ineluctably destined to return to Xibalbá inasmuch as the portals of heaven are closed to that class of being. But the black magicians of Maya culture were the elders of the earlier cycle, which they represent, and they were incorporated into the cultural complex by virtue of the principle of duality or the antagonism between good and evil, personified in the figures of the elder and the black magician. On the other hand, among the southerly peoples of Central America's Atlantic watershed, and in those of similar cultures in South America and the Antilles, the pontiff is still the elder of the Third Age of the *Popol Vuh* and preserves the name of Tukur, from Xibalbá, which among the Maya is a name applied to the black magician or to acts of black magic (*chucu* among the Chortí). Thus we see that the elders along the Atlantic coast of Honduras, Nicaragua, Costa Rica, and Panama are called *tzugur, tzucur, tzugru*

(Shuller) while the Chibchas say *chyquy* (Uricoechea).
Both the Sumos of the Moskito Coast and the Talamancas
(R. Fernández Guardia) as well as the Chibchas are governed or govern themselves socially by the matriarchal
principle, the characteristic feature of the Third Age.
The word in question has undergone little alteration
through the centuries and the cultures. The Tarascos, for
example, continue to call the owl *tukur*, as in the *Popol
Vuh*. The Zoques call the black magician *tzocu*, the
Otomís say *tu kuru* for owl, the Tzentals call the black
magicians *pukuh*, and the Xincas, *tzoka*. The Talamancas
term the owl *tukur* as do the Quichés and Tarascos. *Chu
ku* in Chortí means to fight, thus connoting one of the
functions of the black magician. Etymologically this relates to the root *chu* (to suck). The relation between the
words for black magician and to suck has already been
observed by R. Shuller, and is explained by the former's
function of sucking the sick area to extract the material
cause of the pain.[10] The relation between this function, the
name for black magician, and the malign beings is expressed linguistically by a common root in the Zapotecan
language. For black magician the Zapotec says *benibixio*
or *benibicháa;* for one who sucks, *benigogóba;* and for
malignant, *benigotiaha*. Such a genetic relation is explained by the Chortí belief that the malign beings suck
the blood (or the life) of their victims who slowly waste
away and die. This belief is founded on the functions of
Xiquiripat and Cuchumaquic, beings of Xibalbá mentioned in the *Popol Vuh*, who suck the life from people.

---

[10] [There appears to be some error of interpretation by R. Shuller
here, for healing or the removal of pain is the function of the white and
not the black magician. See several lines below, where the Chortí belief
is that it is the blood (or life) that the black magician "sucks" from his
victim. This appears to be more accurate, and is logical. — TRANS.]

The *suquia* — a corruption of *tzugur* — for treatment of the sick must have as the indispensable requisite a pipe of tobacco which is lit and which, at the right moment, he inhales and exhales, alternating this with sucking the painful area. This is the ceremonial and sacramental use the Talamanca Indians make of tobacco smoking, which also serves to produce in the *suquia* a hypnotic state during which he is said to be in direct contact with the gods (J. A. Lines).

The relation of tobacco with healing among the southerly peoples is seen in the fact that the word meaning tobacco in some Mayan tongues comes to mean healing in others of the south. We have as examples:

sik — tobacco in Mame   *si ka* — healing in Miskito
sik — tobacco in Quiché   *hiska* — healing in Chibcha

This close association of tobacco with the *suquia* is very significant, since it records not only the practices of the Lords of Xibalbá but also discloses a historical fact: tobacco, discovered before copal, was the cure-all of the Mayan elders before the practice of fumigation by incense began in part to replace it. But tobacco preserves its primeval importance among those peoples whose culture corresponds to that of Maya prehistory. All this shows once more that features of the cycle of Maya prehistory were carried to the south by peoples who left the ancestral homeland and its culture in very remote times.

Nevertheless, despite the shift in the meaning of the word for elder in Maya culture to that of black magician, the root *ku* continued to enter the composition of words connoting the idea of sacredness, and in these cases it preserved its primeval signification. We find it in the names of the sacred bird: in Chortí *kut kut;* in Maya, *kuch.* Also in the name for the temples, *ku,* a derivation of its original meaning of house during the protohistoric epoch: a house is still called *ku* in the language of the Guatusos according to Sherzer, *maku* in Xinca, *gü e* in Chibcha, etc. It is found in the name for Deity itself, *Hunab ku*, and for prayer (*Camakú*, the prayer left by Balam Quiché, according to the *Popol Vuh*). *Ku* means the sun in Chuj, and the same root is found in the word for tobacco, a sacred plant called *ku'tz* by the Chortís, *ku* by the Xincas, *kua* by the Lencas, *tanku* by the Jívaros and *chu* by the Guaimis. On the other hand, the Totonacs and Cuicatecs call maize *ku*, the divine plant par excellence (R. Weitlaner), while the Tlapanecs give their god of Earth and of Maize the name of *ku* (Schulte-Jena). In Subtiaba *u ku* means star, and the Talamancas give the name *ku* to the lizard or alligator, their sacred animal. In the Antilles, *savaku* is the name of the messenger bird of Hunrakán, while in Tlapanec *y-ukuu* is the generic name for bird and *sáa* means bird in Mixtec (L. Ecker). In Subtiaba *ku ku* is the turkey, and in Chibcha *kuao* means buzzard; *ku* is the distinctive root for bird in Araua; *kus ma* means buzzard in Sumo-Ulúa, and *kukui* in Uru is falcon; *kute* in Lenca, *kúti* in Xinca, and *kúts* in Quiché and Pocomam mean buzzard. On the other hand, in Miskito and Cuna *kua* is the louse which infects hawks; *kun* in Rama means that louse, and is a metathesis of *uk*, the louse in Maya. The word *tsuku* in Tapachultec does not mean owl but ant, while in Boruca *chúuc* is the frog, and the Hicaque call the owl *sots*, a word that in Mayan languages is applied generally to the bat.

This displacement of the meaning of words for animals is a current phenomenon in language, but it can occur only in languages that are genetically related; and this is another corroboration of the linguistic and cultural kinship of the peoples mentioned above, all of whom are found in territorial continuity.

In regard to the words and symbolisms consigned by the *Popol Vuh* to the early tradition and which therefore enjoy the same relative antiquity, we must still mention the term *wok, guok,* or *guoc,* which designates the mythical bird that descended from the sky to see the Ahpú play ball. This root is found in the word *guacamaya* (macaw), which from the vocabulary of the Arawak of Haiti passed into the Spanish language, as did *cigarro, hunrakán* and *maíz.* The equivalence of the *guacamaya* with the bird of prey about which the Quiché codex tells us, appears in the sound *mo* which in Maya is applied indiscriminately to the sparrow hawk or the macaw, and enters into the composition of the Solar god Kinich Kakmó.

The Chortís of Olopa preserve the name *wak* or *guak* for their mythical bird. *Wara* or *guara* signifies *guacamayo* (male macaw) in Lenca; and *wawá* means macaw or parrot in Araua, in Paya *kawá,* Miskito *raua,* Paya *waro,* Sumo *kaya,* while in Quiché *watas* means crow and *maiwa* goose.

Parallel with the transformation of the elder into the black magician or sorcerer, the gods of the cycle of barbarism become the demons of the Quiché-Maya cultural era. On the other hand, those "demons" preserve their character of true gods, as the sorcerer his function as elder, in cultures corresponding to the prehistoric horizon. And the Quiché-Maya gods are the demons of that cultural cycle.

This transformation of the gods of one epoch into the demons of another is a recurring phenomenon in the history of religions. We know, for example, that before Christianity the root *dev,* in the word now in use in the English language to denote the devil, meant God (*deva,* designation of the ancient gods of India). Percum, the name of the ancient Lithuanian Oak god, was the name used to denote the devil among Christians; and Jesus, their divine savior, was regarded as a devil by the Mandaeans. The Yazida, a neighboring sect of Islam, honored Iblis, the terrible fallen angel of Muhammedanism, whom they believed to be repentant.[11]

Hunrakán, the one-footed god of Quiché culture, was the devil of the earlier cycle, a conception held to this day by the Caribs, Arawaks, and other peoples whose culture corresponds to what the *Popol Vuh* terms the prehistoric cycle. The Galibi call the devil *yurakán*, the Garibisi *yerucan*, the Roucouyenne *yolocan*, the Chayma *yorocan*, the Ipurucoto *iurecá* and the Cariñacu *iroca*, while the Bacairi term the malign spirit *orioca*.[12] The Cahmas Indians call the devil *yorocia'n*, the Tamanacs *yolokiamos*, the Cumanagotas *yoglamo*, the Caribs *yoyoko*, and the Arrúa, *yolok* and *yurakon*.[13] In Talamancan dialects the devil is equated with "white people" (Shuller), the characteristic color of the true god of Quiché-Maya culture, which conversely identifies the malign beings as well as their feelings by the color black.

In spite of being a demon for the southerly peoples and those of the Antilles, and a god for Quiché culture, the semantic value of Hunrakán does not vary, since in both cultural cycles he is the "demon" or "god" of the tempest, rain, lightning bolt, thunder, and the illumination produced by sheet lightning. And good or bad meaning depends exclusively upon the cultural criterion. From the point of view of nonagricultural peoples, storms are injurious and viewed as punishment sent by *maboyas* or evil

---

[11]J. Wach, *Sociología de la Religión*, Mexico, 1946.

[12]R. Shuller, *Las Lenguas Indígenas de Centroamérica*, San José, Costa Rica, 1928.

[13]Lucien Adams, *Matériaux pour servir à l'établissement d'une grammaire comparée des dialectes de la famille Caribe*, Paris, 1893.

spirits of the dead. Du Tertre, who gives us this information about beliefs of the Indians of the French Antilles, tells us of the fear those Indians have of tempests.[14] Of the contemporary Caribs, one learns that "they fear nothing so much as the hurricane and thunder. When dark clouds begin to build up they hurry to their huts, making loud cries, covering their faces with their hands, and crying until the storm passes. This fear of tempests follows them even to the world beyond, since the spirits also fear the thunders and try to hide themselves."[15] Conversely, we have seen that for the Quiché-Maya the subsistence of humankind and the preservation of the cosmic order depends upon the Agrarian god (god of Rain, Tempests, Thunder and Lightning). Because of this, these peoples look with scorn upon the gods of the earlier cycle, who "believed they were gods but were not, because they neither produced rain nor planted seeds."

The great geographical distribution of the myth of the one-footed god, which we found from the Tarasca area (Thares Upeme, the Lame god, according to J. Coronado Nuñez) to that of the Caribs, tells us of the great ethnological antiquity of Hunrakán who pertains to the same mythological horizon from which emanated the Quiché-Maya and Mexican cultures as well as the southerly peoples and those of the Antilles to whom we have referred.

But this is not all: if Hunrakán, the Quiché god, is the demon of the Caribs, on the other hand, Camé, the demon of Quiché traditions, is the god and civilizing hero of Carib myths (Bacairis). In Carib mythology, as in that of the Quiché, the hero-gods are the twins who represent the sun

---

[14]P. du Tertre, *Histoire générale des Antilles habitées par les Français*, Paris, 1667.

[15]Müller, cited by Fernando Ortiz, *El Hunrakán*, Mexico, 1947.

and the moon; but among the Bacairis they are respectively named Camé and Kéri. The same names designate the sun (*camé*) and the moon (*kéri*) among the Arawak-speaking peoples, according to Karl von den Steinen.[16]

It is surprising to discover that the name of Camé has undergone no alteration in languages separated since a period centuries before the beginning of our era.

Of course the zoological nahuals fare the same as the gods they represent. This explains why the jaguar, a god in Quiché-Maya culture, is the malign spirit among certain South American peoples of middling culture.

---

[16]Karl von den Steinen, *Unter den Naturvölkern Zentral-Brasiliens*, Berlin, 1894.

7

The Parthenogenetic Conception of Hunahpú and Ixbalamqué

FOLLOWING the *Popol Vuh's* biographical and gene-alogical summary of the parents of Hunahpú and Ixbalamqué, which expresses the successive stages of cultural development, we have the account of the twins' miraculous birth. For like the redeemer gods of the other great religions, those of the Maya religion also have a divine and a human birth.

Ixquic, daughter of Cuchumaquic, a prominent figure in Xibalbá, felt an irresistible curiosity to see from close up the famous, forbidden tree where hung the heads of the seven Ahpú transformed into gourds. She tried to get her father to accompany her, but in face of his refusal she decided to visit the tree alone. Gazing at the mysterious fruits, the young maiden asked herself: What kind of fruits are these? Do they have a good flavor? Could I reach one? Would anything happen to me if I did? These are questions that must in fact have preoccupied the first people each time they came upon some new botanical species whose properties they did not know.

Then one of the heads spoke, saying: "What is it that

you want? There are only bones hung in these branches. Do you want us?" This response resolves the dilemma: the fruit of the calabash tree is not really edible and only the bonelike rind is useful. Here we have the origin and explanation of the etymological relation between the words for bone, shell, the corncob, and similar hard objects likened to the skulls of the Ahpú or the rind of the gourd, and which are regarded as necessary elements of all bodies (human, animal, and vegetable).

"I want you," replies Ixquic. "Very well, extend your hand," said the heads, their request being obeyed immediately by the maiden. Then the heads let some drops of saliva fall on the palm of her hand; but when she looked at her palm they had disappeared.

"In this saliva that we have cast into you, we have given you our progeny. Our heads no longer have anything over them; they are only bones and worthless. When we lived we were handsome, but now there remain only our heads from that time when we were great lords. Thus when we died we frightened everyone because we became only a skeleton [the source of the fear the natives have of the dead]. In the saliva is passed on to the children the knowledge that one has, whether they are children of lords, wise men, or orators. This knowledge is not lost when the parent dies, but is inherited, because it is the saliva deposited by lords, wise men, or orators, and only thus do the children of those ancestors endure after they begin their existence. This very thing have we done with you.

"Go up, then, to the earth's surface; you will not die. Remember our Word when you arrive there," the heads of the Ahpú told Ixquic, carrying out the will of the Word of Hunrakán.

The maiden returned at once to her house, having conceived the twins solely by virtue of the saliva that penetrated into her being. Thus were conceived Hunahpú and Ixbalamqué.

This is one of the most important passages of the *Popol Vuh*, inasmuch as it expresses a rule of Mayan biology: the law of heredity whereby parents transmit to their offspring their intellectual and moral as well as physical characteristics. Moreover, the divine origin of the caste of elders is also emphasized; its members receive their wisdom from Deity itself, and therefore they have to transmit it within their own lineage, and in this we have the remote origin of the hereditary institution of elders. It also explains the reasons why Chortís and Mayas are so jealous of their lineage. Of this the Chilam Balam of Chumayel says that the noble descendants of princes who ought to know their own lineage, and the kings who were properly governing them, will see that it was the kings' wisdom that gave them authority over their vassals.

The miraculous fertilization of Ixquic through the descent of the spiritual into the carnal exemplifies the mystery both of human conception and of the germination of maize (assimilated with Hunahpú, as will be seen), associating on this occasion for the first time the concepts of human fecundation and fertility of the earth, inseparable in the native mind. This theme will compose the leitmotif of Mesoamerican art, which will reproduce it in the most varied forms, from the sash hanging from the divine member in Maya statuary — like the saliva that falls from the heads of the Ahpú — to the figures in Mexican iconography of gods falling from heaven.

With their sacrifice the Ahpú fertilize the earth, irrigating it with their own blood, thus bequeathing the ritual practices founded on the belief that "the earth needs blood for its sustenance," that divine fluid being correlated with rain, semen, and human blood itself as divine exudations, the essence of maize or of "grace."[1] This association of ideas is exhibited in the figure of the calabashes dropping saliva from high up in the tree, a paradigm of the belief

that calabashes are instruments of the gods of rain, who pour down from the sky the waters which fertilize the earth.

Because of its classification of the god-Seven and its positioning in the top of the tree, the picture the *Popol Vuh* gives us does not differ from one that

FIGURE 7.

we have reproduced from the Chumayel manuscript, showing the god of Heaven at the pinnacle of the cosmic tree, its "grace" falling upon the earth from on high. This resemblance is completed when later the calabash tree is seen to be the equivalent of the ceiba, the cosmic tree, which from then on becomes, like the Christian cross, the sacred emblem of the divine martyrdom. It is through the branches of the ceiba that human generations descend, as the divine twins, Hunahpú and Ixbalamqué, fell into the womb of their mother. Richtofen has said that the tree engenders the first feelings of property and of native land, ideas that could have no better application than in this case, because the cosmic and generative tree of the human species is the primary symbol of Maya nationality, linked with the concept of territory and of population increase. Such is the significance of the ceiba tree that was planted in the center of the public plaza, the center of the communal territory.

---

[1]See the definition of this word in "Theogony," Girard, *Los Chortís.*

Veneration of the ceiba, as that of human skulls and ancestors, begins here. By their martyrdom the seven Ahpú achieve the posthumous honor of being the chiefs of the Quiché people, and this will be reinterpreted centuries later by the Nahua peoples as the legendary Chicomoztoc. The role of savior of peoples that is attributed to the flesh-less heads of the seven Ahpú illustrates another linguistic peculiarity whereby the words for chief, caudillo, leader, and head are expressed by a common word in languages stemming from the proto-Maya trunk.

All this implies a progressive advance in the process of cultural formation that is projected in the ascent of Ixquic from the inferior cosmic plane to the earth's surface, where she will gain the immortality decreed by the Ahpú. Conceived in the underworld, Hunahpú will live upon the earth in order to exemplify the standards of conduct proper for the human race, as well as the development of the maize plant which comes to birth in the underworld like a fetus in the maternal womb, but which evolves on the terrestrial plane.

Just as the Nahuas took from the Quiché traditions the myth of the seven leaders of the people, they also took that of the virgin birth of Hunahpú, projecting this in the Aztec hero-god who, like Hunahpú, Buddha, Confucius, Jesus, or Minerva, had a supernatural parentage. Huitzilopochtli is born on the Coatepeque hill, the equivalent of the Pucbal-chaj (see the explanation below). The Mexican Coatlicue, a functional replica of Ixquic, or of Isis, Devaki, Mylitta, and Ishtar, is the Virgin Mary of ancient world myths.

Six months after the miraculous conception, Cuchuma-quic notes the pregnancy of his daughter and judges it a dishonorable thing — a reflection of the views of the period — and informs the Great Council of Xibalbá of the matter. The Council unanimously resolves to compel the maiden to reveal the name of her lover, but Ixquic can do no more than tell the truth about what had happened, stating that "never had she known the face of any man." This illustrates another Mayan custom which prohibits women, so long as they are single, from looking into the faces of young men, a fact confirmed by Landa who says, "the women were accustomed to turn their backs to the men when they happened to meet anywhere, and also when they served men something to drink. . . ."[2]

Faced with Ixquic's improbable explanations in justification of her sinful act, her own father orders the Tukur, servants of the Ahpop achij (dignitary of the mat, a name that confirms Hun Camé's post as Regent or Ahau) to sacrifice the girl in the fork of a tree far away, and after the execution to bring her heart in a cup, where it would be preserved. Immediately the four servants of Xibalbá went to get the cup and the stone knife employed for sacrifices, and took the girl toward the tree.

In these paragraphs of the Quiché epic we find good ethnological information regarding the manner in which human sacrifices were performed in that age, as also the utensils employed: the cup for preserving the victim's heart (identical with the *cauhxicalli* of the Aztecs), the knife of white stone, and the team of four executioners.

We were told that the heads of the seven Ahpú were placed in the branches of a tree. Now we are told that the body of Ixquic is to be placed in the fork of a tree. These references bring to mind the secondary method of burial characteristic of the matriarchal epoch, practiced by peoples belonging to that cultural cycle. We know, for example, that the Talamancas do not recognize relation-

---

[2]Landa, D. de, *Relación de las cosas de Yucatán*, Mexico, 1938.

ship by the paternal line but by the maternal; and although such relations among two people may be very distant, they never marry. These people do not inter their dead, but wrap them up and hang them in the air *between two tree-forks.* A year having passed, and the judgment having been made that the flesh of the deceased has now become earth, the Talamancas celebrate the funeral with great solemnity. A new wrapping and green leaves of the *bijao* plant (*Musaceae* family) are brought into the house of the deceased, whose bones are placed in order upon them and rewrapped just as done the year before. Then the *suquia* or healer calls to the soul of the defunct to come and witness the celebration. In the afternoon of the third day the *suquias*, adorned with many feathers, pick up the remains and carry them to the *aypuc*, the sepulcher belonging to the family of the deceased. These sepulchers are usually located on slopes or hills about a half-league distant from the houses. If the defunct was a brave or prominent individual, a macaw is carried, killed, and buried with the remains. If the dead person had a slave, he too is killed and buried, and the remains of his master placed above his own. Thus the slave can serve the latter in the afterlife and the macaw will provide feathers. If the defunct is a boy, his blowgun and dart bag are placed with the body; if a girl, her spindle and cotton are put there.[3]

We also know that the Crow Indians of the Sioux peoples practice secondary burial, placing the body *in the fork of a tree.* When only the skeleton remains, the bones are removed and deposited in a cave (Murdock). The Sioux belong to the same cultural horizon as the Talamancas and other North and South American peoples of middling culture.

---

[3]Ricardo Fernández Guardia, *Reseña Histórica de Talamanca*, San José de Costa Rica, 1927.

We might extend these comparisons to many other
peoples, but it is enough for our purpose to bring together
the information given in the Quiché text with that offered
us in ethnography, to show the historical authenticity of
the *Popol Vuh.* We have in contemporary customs (as well
as those of the 16th century) not only amplification and
confirmation of the data provided in the famous manuscript, but also directives for their better translation and
understanding. For example, the name Pucbal-chaj has
not yet been correctly interpreted by the mythographers,
because contemporary Quiché does not take into account
certain archaisms found in the *Popol Vuh.* This obliges us
to have recourse to comparative linguistics. We have a
definition of the root *puk* or *puc* that determines the meaning of the name given above, in the Maya language of
Yucatán (in which *puúc* means hill) as well as in the
account of the Talamancas which calls the site where their
dead are interred, *aypuc*, stating that this site is the sepulcher "made upon slopes and hills at a distance from
their houses." Today that very custom can be observed
among the Hicaques, who still build their cemeteries on
the tops of hills at some distance from their communities,
according to the author's personal investigation. All this
shows the relative antiquity of the root *puc*, found so frequently in Honduras where elevated summits are named
Erapuca, Puca, etc., and whose translation from the languages spoken there during the Colonial era is difficult.

The final *a* means stone, lacking the *k* because of
aphaeresis due to reasons of euphony. The literal translation would be "hill of stone," which in fact describes a
toponymic reality in Honduras where rock summits are
meant. The same word having a similar meaning is again
encountered in the word *pukara* (fortified hill) from the
Quechua, in *quipuca* (hill, or place) in Chibcha, *chuk ka*

(hill) in Paya, *yúku* (hill) in Otomí, etc., all of which shows this word's great age and also the prehistoric custom of burying the dead in hills distant from the population center.

Ixquic protested her innocence when confronted with the wicked decision of the Lords of Xibalbá, remonstrating that she had not transgressed the laws of honor and therefore did not deserve punishment (reasoning that conforms with Maya ethics and justice). She proclaimed that the life she bore within her body was conceived only because she went to express "her feelings to the heads of the Ahpú."

Faced with the dilemma of carrying out their masters' orders and possibly sacrificing an innocent person, the four Xibalban messengers vacillated, and they wondered how they would be able to present physical proof that they had indeed executed the girl. "Very well," said Ixquic to them, "but my heart does not belong to them. You shouldn't obey them or remain in their house, because it is only dishonor to kill persons without any cause whatever. Because they do that, I will overcome the Camé, who do not fear the presence of blood or of decapitated heads."

This is an eloquent profession of faith in the Quiché-Maya religious principles, which repudiate human sacrifice. By her proclamation Ixquic separates herself both spiritually and materially from her kind, and thus her heart does not belong now to them (an allegory having a double meaning). At the same time, the young woman tries to convert the Xibalban messengers to the new belief, inciting them to repudiate the false gods and warning that the prevailing religious ideas will be supplanted by the doctrines of the Ahpú, which contain the worship, articles of faith, and ethical force of the Maya religion.

Ixquic then suggests to her four attendants "that they place the sacrificial cup before the tree." Then a red liquid drops from the tree into the cup, where it coagulates like blood and takes the shape of a human heart. Thus it was that the tree's sap substituted for her blood, and the tree also became the color of blood.

When the Tukur came before the Lords of Xibalbá, they delivered the substitute heart of Ixquic, which was in the bottom of the cup, to Hun Camé. It was then placed in a sack, and when the cup was empty it shone as if covered with living blood.

"Now build up the fire and put the heart on it," Hun Camé told them. His order was instantly obeyed, and when the flames had consumed it and the Lords of Xibalbá came near, they smelled the burning sap and saw the smoke produced by the blood, and realized that it was fragrant. This greatly disturbed them, and the four Tukur went up to the surface of the earth and became the servants of Ixquic.

This is how, says the *Popol Vuh*, the Lords of Xibalbá fared at the hands of the young maiden who made fools of them all.

The episode has many meanings. In the first place, it tells us of a new cultural element in the description of incense and its properties, an invention later than that of tobacco and the manufacture of cigars and which, as with all the important developments in the native American economy, was the discovery of woman and accomplished during the matriarchal-horticultural cycle. Ixquic shows the way to use copal, a tree native to Guatemala, which abounds in the southeast portion of the Pacific region in the same area as the calabash tree (*jícaro*). That country still provides the incense which the Indians of the interior use so abundantly.

In the *Popol Vuh* are spelled out both the essential and mystical properties of this gum resin, which coagulates like blood, gives off an aromatic scent when burned, and in addition has the ability to destroy evil spirits. Reference is also made to the sack used for storing the copal. From that time until today the Indians employ this incense in all their religious ceremonies with the object of warding off the bad spirits and thus purifying the air in both a figurative and literal sense, as well as perfuming the area with an aroma pleasing to the gods because of its divine nature. The Chilam Balam of Chumayel explains that the incense is "the heavenly resin," and that "its aroma is attracted to the central point of the sky." In the same way the peel of the copal is equated to "the waistband; to the vestment of God."

Because of their etymological relation, the liquid exudations of Deity are correlated with those of men, animals and plants; the Zend-Avesta makes the same kind of comparison. Thus the sap of the copal, blood, and rain — that is, the divine substance — are consubstantial, the smoke of incense also representing the clouds, while the rain gods can be figured on Chortí altars by either a solid ball of copal or a receptacle full of "virgin water."[4]

On the theogonic level, the ascent of Ixquic and the four converts from Xibalbá to the earth's surface denotes the appearance of the four cosmic bearers after the destruction of humanity by a cataclysm. This interpretation is based on Ixquic's role as Earth goddess, and as such she is inseparable from the four bearers which the Chumayel document calls the "Wills of the Earth" (*Voluntades de la Tierra*). The will of Ixquic, obeyed by the four acolytes of Hun Camé, is a figure expressive of the same concept. Further on, the Chumayel codex says that the Bacab "went rising up, calling to their Lord," an image

---

[4]See Girard, *Los Chortís*, chapter 12.

which the *Popol Vuh* portrays in the ascent of the four
Xibalban converts to the earth's surface. From other
sources we know that the four bearers of the heaven
"escaped when the world was destroyed by the deluge."[5]

Nevertheless, it seems contradictory that the celestial
bearers whom Mayan and Chortí theologians depict for us
as giants should have their origin in the four messengers of
Xibalbá, and this discrepancy is accentuated if we recall
that the giants of the First Age were also converted into
Atlantes. But such incongruities do not exist from the
Maya point of view which equates the giants with the
Camé, regarding them by the same token as "animals"
because they lacked genuine human culture — that is,
Maya culture — and therefore were made the vassals of
the true gods. In no other source do we find such a clear
explanation of this concept as in the Chortí drama, where
the same actor — the Black Giant — personifies both the
giants of the primeval epoch and also the Camé, in the
beginning playing the role of the earlier giants and later
that of the Lords of Xibalbá, in accord with the sequence
given in the *Popol Vuh*.

Finally, in Mayan calendrics, Ixquic's triumph over the
Xibalban lords marks the end of the period of the Camé
regency and its replacement by another Ahau, of which we
shall speak next.

---

[5]Landa, *Relación*.

8

Infancy of Hunahpú and Ixbalamqué

The Third Regent

THE *POPOL VUH* now offers us a family scene of the times, showing us Hun Bátz and Hun Chouén with their grandmother — whom they call mother — invested with the power of the paterfamilias or head of their family.

Ixquic, coming from Xibalbá, presents herself to them and says, "I am come to you, my mother, I am your adoptive daughter, since I am your daughter-in-law, my mother." But the old woman rejects her, saying, "Who knows where you come from? My sons have died in Xibalbá, their only descendants are Hun Bátz and Hun Chouén. Get out of here," she tells Ixquic, having shown her that she recognizes only those two as her legitimate heirs, the recipients of the wisdom of the Ahpú. Because the latter were their fathers, the two were "singers, writers, orators, and sculptors in bas-relief; these things only did they do as their daily occupation, and because of it they filled the heart of the old woman with pride."

Those paragraphs make us understand that Maya society was then based on the matriarchal principle and its economy on horticulture, i.e., on the work of women. Such a situation permitted the men to devote their free time to cultivating the arts that we see coming into being in this period, as well as the professional activities mirrored in the skills attributed to Hun Bátz and Hun Chouén. These brothers are the heroes of the time; they excel in every line and, following the eclipse of the Camé, occupy without contest the world regency.

This is fully in accord with the Quiché-Maya method of projecting in the change of Regent the successive stages of history, and it moreover agrees with the order of succession of the primary series in which Chuen (Chouén) follows Cimi (Camé). Hun Bátz and Hun Chouén close the period of their regency by becoming transformed into monkeys, and this explains the etymology of their names.

The Third Age, inaugurated under the auspices of the Third Regent, has its equivalence in the Third Katún of Maya prehistory, which in the Book of Chilam Balam of Chumayel is described as

a time of disorder and fury in which he of the false mat, the false throne, reigned: the Monkey of the gods [compare with Hun Bátz], the cunning rascal. And so in the Three Ahau Katún, full of arrogance and with faithless hearts, there walked the descendants of the nobles, the men of royal blood, until it occurred to them to say that they should regain the leadership of the peoples, and they proceeded to do so ["Book of Tests"].

These expressions, until now an enigma, agree wholly with the Quiché account of the Third Age, an epoch in which Hunahpú and Ixbalamqué, descendants of the seven Ahpú, suffer every kind of trial and tribulation, constantly warred upon by their cousins Hun Bátz and Hun Chouén, until at last they castigate the latter, transforming them into monkeys and replacing them as Regents of the Fourth Age which inaugurates the era of Maya culture.

In accord with this, Mayan iconography symbolizes in the figure of god C — having the face of a monkey — the Third Regent of the primary period; and we find it associated with the sign *chuén* as its prefix, on page 43 of the Tro-Cortes Codex. The texts of Mayan and Quiché sources mutually confirm and complete each other. They agree that during the Third Age or Third Katún, humanity was imperfect from the point of view of Mayan ethics, and the vices of that epoch, stereotyped in the character of Hun Bátz and Hun Chouén, caused its ruin. Among those characteristics stand out cruelty, envy, and indolence in the men as seen in the invention of the hammock, which is regarded even now as a symbol of idleness. References to that period also speak of the use of nets, a technical advance in human industry.

The hammock began to lose its importance in the era of Maya culture from the time of the change in the social arrangement (passing from the matriarchal to the patriarchal) that reflected new concepts about work and condemned the vice of slothfulness.

We saw that by way of greeting, the grandmother received Ixquic with marked hostility, saying "I don't want you as my daughter-in-law; you carry only dishonor in your womb. You deceived me, because my sons to whom you refer are already dead." Such repudiation expresses the moral judgment of the time against the woman who bears children the identity of whose father is unacknowledged, as well as the social principle by which ingress into the clan is impossible for anyone who cannot prove his or

her right of admission by consanguinity. Thus Ixquic
insists upon her right by virtue of the offspring she bears
within her and which according to the laws of the time
belongs to its grandmother's clan, equally with Hun Bátz
and Hun Chouén, because it is the child of the seven Ahpú,
which will be proven "by the beauty of countenance of her
child."

Once again we have here a proclamation of the law of
atavism by which the physical characteristics as well as the
moral and intellectual qualities of forebears are inherited,
from which it follows that for Ixquic the physiognomy of
her offspring will be the decisive proof of the truth of her
claims. In native thought — as in Aristotle's — the concept of beauty is inseparable from that of the good. Therefore Hunahpú will be as perfect in body as in character.
This standard is seen in Mayan statuary, since that people
always applied the best of their artistic talents to images of
the young god (equivalent to Hunahpú), and in the period
of their cultural apogee brought its figure to perfect ana-
tomical proportions.

Finally, the grandmother decides to test the truth of
Ixquic's claims by giving her an impossible task: to fill "a
large net to the full with maize," from only one plant of
the precious cereal. "If you are my daughter-in-law, then
help me," said the old woman. "Go and get me something
to eat; we will wait for you here, and come back so you can
keep on helping me." "All right," replied Ixquic. She left
to go to the maize field along the path cleared by Hun Bátz
and Hun Chouén. This paragraph describes the division of
labor in effect during the matriarchal period, it being the
woman's responsibility to work and harvest the *milpa*, providing the family its subsistence, while the man had to
clear the ground.

Turning again to the comparative analysis of peoples,

like the Talamanca, for example, who represent the Third-Age cultural type, we find an identity of custom between what these still employ and those described to us in the *Popol Vuh.* Says R. Fernández Guardia of the Talamanca:

> The Talamanca men cut down and clear the ground for sowing, but only the women sow the maize and collect the harvest. As only women give birth, they say, only they can sow seed that will grow and collect what has grown. . . . Those Indians who are respected because wealthier, with more authority or of greater vigor than the rest, have more than one wife, who ordinarily are their sisters-in-law, and add to their prestige. . . . The menstruating woman, or the one close to giving birth, is considered impure and is not permitted while in such condition to come into the houses or the sowing fields. . . . When women are with child and feel themselves near to giving birth, they go to the woods to do so where they will not be seen.[1]

The same customs can be observed even now among the Taoajka (Sumo) who live in the Mosquitia forests, a people of matriarchal-horticultural culture closest to the area of the classical Mayas, and of considerable ethnological interest. The author made several expeditions among the Sumo, Payas, Miskitos, and Hicaques to investigate their interrelations, finding that the Sumo group is the only one to have a social system based on pure matriarchy. Among these the grandmother holds the predominant place within the family hierarchy. The women cultivate small vegetable gardens and bring the produce to their houses. The men occupy themselves with clearing the woods, hunting, fishing, and making canoes, but enjoy resting in hammocks which they make from vegetable fibers, and their life is less active than that of the women.

---

[1]*Reseña Histórica de Talamanca*, San José de Costa Rica, 1917.

FIGURE 8. A Taoajka grandmother, the family head, together with her daughter who will succeed her. Hamlet of Dimikian in the Honduran Mosquitia.

Manuel Fleury reports the same observation. He says:

> The women are much given to work, and although the men are not totally idle, they are not as industrious as the women. The men are much given to liquor, and when they take it are continually inebriated; but when they can't get it, they get drunk with *chicha*.[2]

---

[2]Cited by R. Heliodoro Valle, in *Semblanza de Honduras*, Tegucigalpa, 1947.

This was, we recall, a vice proper to the matriarchal period. For the rest, the customs of the Sumo are similar to those of the Talamanca, and the same cultural features characterize the peoples who from Honduras (Mosquitia) southward live along the shores of the Caribbean Sea.

Among the surviving elements of that ethnic period preserved by the Chortís, the following are worthy of mention: the linguistic peculiarity that the word *hijo* (son) is different if spoken by the father or if by the mother, because the pronunciation indicates the respective parental role, for, as the Chortís say, it is the mother and not the father who brings the son to birth; the systematic marriage between brothers and sisters of two families; the tabu that prevents the pregnant or menstruating woman from entering the seed field; the custom whereby the woman works in the maize field, but only during the tilling done with the hoe, an implement from the matriarchal period; the special word for maize field worker (*ah čor war išik*) given to the woman; the collection of wild edible fruits, roots, and plants in baskets, at fixed times, exclusively by women, who remain at some kilometers from their houses during the collecting season, following a custom that has not varied since the prehistoric epoch; medicinal and magical use of tobacco; the use by women of cloth bands to carry their children; the bridegroom giving service to the father or father-in-law, depending upon the case, before establishing his own household within the family group; regulation of hunting and fishing, and community hunts and fishing enterprises; use of pits with stakes for hunting animals; the community importance of the old people.

During the horticultural cycle, maize was not yet exactly *the* food or the object of the systematic and extensive cultivation that it became in the era of agriculture.

The maize field of Ixmucané, which had only a single maize plant, appears to bring out this contrast between the economies of the two periods.

Faced with that single plant, from which she had to get enough maize to fill a large net, Ixquic became disheartened at the thought of not being able to accomplish the task imposed upon her by Ixmucané, and so being refused acceptance into her family. Ixquic therefore turns to her supernatural protectors, exclaiming, "I am under obligation because of many faults. When will I be able to take away a netful from that maize field!" She began to implore the being (Chajal) responsible for making the seeds come to fruition, that the food grains should appear. "Ixtoj, Ixcanil, Ixcacau, you who prepare the maize! You, Chajal, guardian of the food of Hun Bátz and Hun Chouén!" cried out the maiden.

In this episode Ixquic inaugurates the rite of confession, acknowledging her indebtedness resulting from many sins, a rite that the Chortís continue by voicing their unworthiness in the same way in front of the feminine deity — the originator of this custom — to obtain the help of the agrarian deities in assuring an abundance of food. This rite is carried out before the ground is sown with seed. There also appears here for the first time the goddess of Cacao (Ixcacau) as one of the agrarian deities, and the name will occur again later on. We can therefore infer the discovery of this American tree during the matriarchal-horticultural period, completing the group of plants on which Maya subsistence was based. As said, cacao is a Mayan word, confirming once again the historical validity of the *Popol Vuh*. The god of Cacao is based on the individuality of the Agrarian god, as explained regarding Chortí theogony, and therefore they are seen as a union in the pleas of Ixquic. But the gods invoked by her are feminine (the *ix* prefix), while in Quiché-Maya theogony they are masculine. This shows the existence of these goddesses — as well as of cacao itself — in the period preceding that of agriculture, and their conversion into masculine deities when Maya society passes from the matriarchal to the patriarchal regime. In Ixquic's invocation of the agrarian deities we have also a paradigm of the entreaties the present-day Indian continues to make to his gods to obtain a good harvest. When the pleas are made with the necessary religious fervor and the person making them has purified himself through confession — as did Ixquic — and in addition has fulfilled the requirements demanded by religious ethics, then the gods listen to the entreaties — as they did to Ixquic's supplications — made in perfect conformity with the ritual that she exemplifies. As a result, the gods invoked "brought the flowering of the maize field," which miraculously produced such a quantity of ears that "when she gathered them and filled the net with them, her protectors had to help her carry the burden."

Here is illustrated the principle of divine-human cooperation, vital for the harmonious functioning of the cosmos and fundamental to the Maya religious system. In fact, man must invoke the gods, pay them homage, feed them, and abide by the rules of religious ethics if he would have them nourish and sustain him. The Indian regards himself as the eternal debtor of the gods, a conception implicit in Ixquic's words "I am under obligation. . . ." But this knowledge is gained only when humanity as a whole shall have achieved a high degree of ethical perfection. Only then will humankind be able to survive because, thanks to the inner communion between Divinity and humankind, that harmony which guarantees the stability of the world will have been established in a manner to impede its destruction by cataclysms such as took place in preceding epochs.

Deity amply rewards those who observe its commandments, and this is represented objectively in the miraculous
harvest achieved by Ixquic. The yield from the single
maize plant in Ixmucané's seed field was such that it filled
"a portable cupboard that was in the house" (showing the
means of storing the maize ears which were placed in this
crate in a corner of the hut).

Having witnessed the miracle, the grandmother told
the maiden, " 'This alone is enough of a sign that you are
certainly my daughter-in-law. I will look after you and
care for the children you will have, who are wise ones.' "

"When their day arrived, Ixquic gave birth to twins,
Hunahpú and Ixbalamqué, born at dawn; but the grandmother did not see them born, because they saw the light
of day in the woods."

What a wealth of teaching in so few words! First, the
custom of that time by which the woman must "give birth
by herself alone" in the woods where she would not be
seen, as still practiced by the Talamanca; then, the principle of predetermination, typical of Maya mentality, is
emphasized. The Chortís signify this in the aphorism: "All
things have their day and their hour," determined by
Providence. But, even more, the explicit statement that
Hunahpú was born at dawn is not arbitrary but shows the
advent of the solar hero who comes forth with the Dawn.

The story of Hunahpú, moreover, reproduces on the
plane of astronomy the course of the sun not only on its
diurnal path but also on its annual sweep, which symbolizes the cycle of human life. Thus Hunahpú is born
with the dawn and dies on descending into the underworld
(Xibalbá), only to resurge again in the east, triumphant.
His birth takes place during the winter solstice, and from
then on he grows according as the day lengthens in duration, reaching his plenitude when the daystar passes

through the zenith and then returns, "flagging in pace" like an old person, during the apparent return movement of the star. The eternal universal renewal is illustrated in the constant repetition of these movements. Weak and helpless like an infant, he has come forth into life during the shortest days and longest nights, and thus is surrounded with dangers during his infancy, since the dominion of the shadows (barbarism, in the historic sense, and rulership by malefic spirits in the spiritual sense) is longer than his reign ("day" identified with "sun"). But Hunahpú surmounts all the dangers and in the end rises triumphant to heaven.

Hunahpú becomes human in order to raise the status of man to that of the divine, by exemplifying in himself the model of the grand True Man (in Maya, Halach winik; in Quiché, Achi). But the ideal of human and social perfection, whether of a culture or of a single man, can be gained only through sacrifices and life-experience. The tribulations suffered by humankind during the course of the three racial cycles that preceded the era of Maya culture, like those that the individual must suffer to make of himself a man, or the man has to undergo to merit eternal felicity, are projected in the troubled infancy of Hunahpú. This parallelism between the stages of history and those of human life reflects the essence of the Indian's mental sense of the flow of time and history, and has its equivalent in the comparison of Ages with Suns. As said, a Sun represents a unit of time that can mean one day as well as a calendric cycle.

In accordance with that conception, the infancy of the twins is lived out in an atmosphere full of dangers and uneasinesses. Scarcely are they brought under the family roof by their mother than the grandmother, vexed at their crying, orders them to be thrown outside, "and immediately they were put on an anthill" by Hun Bátz and Hun Chouén. But there the twins slept very nicely, so they were taken from the anthill and placed upon a spiny plant. Hun Bátz and Hun Chouén really wanted them to die on the anthill or the spines because of their hatred and envy of their younger kin.

But neither caused any harm to the twins, who were invested with divine power. As we shall see, the ants are Hunahpú's faithful servants, as they are of Quetzalcoatl in Mexican myth.

We have in the Quiché account of the torture by ants another testimony regarding customs that were operative in the Third Age and which are still to be seen among groups like the Tupi-Guaraní and the Caribs who belong to that cultural cycle. Alfred Métraux comments that the Mauhé of the Tupi-Guaraní family subject their youths to the ant torture.[3] M. Acosta Saignes notes the trial by savage ants as a Carib cultural feature; young girls are subject to this test at the time of their first menstruation.[4] Such customs were gradually transformed through cultural evolution, losing their character as forms of cruelty or punishment and becoming part of the initiation rite of apprentices to magicians.[5]

Hun Bátz and Hun Chouén prevent the twins from remaining in the family house, so that the latter would not know them, and thus the twins grew up in the forest. This once more highlights the principle of magic by which knowledge of the person implies magical dominion over him. On the other hand, Hunahpú is in his element, exem-

[3]"La Civilisation guyanc-amazonienne et ses provinces culturelles," in *Acta americana*, 1945.

[4]"Los Caribes de la Costa Venezolana," in *Acta Antropológica*, Mexico, 1946.

[5]Girard, *Los Chortís*, chapter 21.

plifying one of his functions as god of the Woods. Hunahpú and Ixbalamqué grow up amidst many labors, sufferings, and sadnesses, finally acquiring — like their older brothers — great wisdom. Consequently they were also singers, writers, sculptors in bas-relief, and knew how to do everything well. Similarly they learned the origin of their line and that

> they were beings with feelings who came to replace the seven Ahpú. From the latter also came Hun Bátz' and Hun Chouén's great learning, although the latter two thought it was only because they were older than the twins. So they never displayed their feelings because of the envy they had for their younger brothers and the ill will toward them which sprang up in their hearts. This was the cause of the hostility they displayed toward Hunahpú and Ixbalamqué.

This paragraph in the Quiché text promulgates the Maya principle whereby within the order of elders the hereditary right is not by itself sufficient for exercise of the post. Besides his birth within the order, the candidate must win the post through personal merit and exemplary conduct. The same, therefore, is true for the individual: his divine descent is not enough in itself for achievement of eternal felicity, and he must prove that he deserves such a destiny through his good conduct — a beautiful inculcation of and incitement to seek personal worthiness of reward. In addition we are presented with an ethical lesson in the picture of discord among brothers, which will have fatal consequences for the older ones. By contrast, a perfect fraternal harmony characterizes the Maya family that adheres to the standards set by Hunahpú and Ixbalamqué. Thus, we steadily learn more in the Quiché-Maya epic about the norms of religious morality whose finality is the development of an ethically and esthetically prepared human being.

But we have not finished with the difficulties undergone by the twins, detested by their grandmother and elder brothers. These give the two nothing to eat and, when meals are prepared, Hun Bátz and Hun Chouén serve themselves first "and only afterwards do the twins come in." When the latter bring in birds for the table, the older two eat them and leave nothing for Hunahpú and Ixbalamqué. This exemplifies the dominion of the older son in the household, a hierarchical order that has not varied down to our own time.

Despite such great oppression by their older brothers, Hunahpú and Ixbalamqué become neither angry nor irritated. They endure it all in silence because they know its origin and purpose, and so give a notable example of self-control, a basic quality of the Maya character.

Hun Bátz and Hun Chouén do not work (confirming the man's status in the matriarchal regime), but only "recite and sing." On the other hand, the twins, by profession hunters with the blowgun, every day bring into the family house the results of their hunting.

The situation cannot last forever, since every evil has its limits and if Deity allows such, it is for the purpose of testing its creatures. When the test has been judged sufficient, it says, "so far and no farther" (a Chortí aphorism). Conversely, in accordance with the rule that "everything has its day and its assigned hour," the time is drawing near when Hunahpú must manifest his power.

One day when the twins have returned to the house without bringing their accustomed provision of birds for the table, the grandmother reproaches them, but they excuse themselves by saying that the prey remained fast, high in a tree which they could not climb. So the twins ask for help from their older brothers to get the birds, and the latter agree to go with them on the morrow at daybreak.

By the very fact that they allow themselves to be taken
to a place selected by the twins, the older brothers have already been defeated. (Compare the same procedure employed for vanquishing Caprakán by leading him toward
the east.) Hunahpú and Ixbalamqué have now changed in
attitude toward their older brothers, since the day of the
end of their regency had arrived. "They wanted to kill us
and cause us to disappear, we who are their kindred. They
have believed that we came to be their servants. So we shall
punish them as a demonstration of our power." Thus the
twins reasoned as the four came together at the foot of the
tree named Canté (yellow wood; called *madre de cacao* in
Spanish, because it is used to give shade to the cacao plants).

Here, thought has the same magical potency as word:
what is thought or what is spoken is a thing done or about
to be accomplished. But, because we are dealing with gods
who, like the twins, embody the theogonic duality and
exemplify the social patterns of the Maya community,
their thoughts or words must come into being in unison.
They will apply the rule of "an eye for an eye" to their
older brothers: these regarded the twins as their servants
and therefore they will be transformed into servants of
Hunahpú and Ixbalamqué in a manner similar to that
applied to the giants earlier.

Hun Bátz and Hun Chouén climbed the tree, but the
tree grew and thickened as if it were inflated; when they
later wanted to come down they were unable. "What has
happened, brothers? Alas! This tree frightens us just to
look at it." The twins answer: "Untie your sashes [*maxtli*,
clothing of the time], fix them below the waist letting the
ends hang down behind like tails, and then you can come
down." "Very well," the older ones replied. They threw
the ends of their sashes out behind, and these immediately
became tails and the brothers assumed the appearance of

monkeys. Then they went about along the branches of the tree through large and small woodlands and hid themselves in the forest, grinning and swinging in the branches. Thus Hun Bátz and Hun Chouén were defeated by the divine twins, thanks to the supernatural power of their nahual (Hunrakán).

We find here the mythical origin of the symbolic equivalence of the sash, lariat, or cord with the tail or the serpent. But the interest of the account is centered in the transformation of the older brothers into monkeys and their position in the top of the *yellow tree*, which is the cosmic tree that is the bearer of the Third Regent. Both in the *Popol Vuh* and the Chilam Balam of Chumayel, the succession of the Regents and of their respective colors follows in the same order: the yellow pole follows the black and the white poles. The Quiché codex gives this equivalence as follows:

First Regent is identified by the white color of its hair, as in the Vatican Codex in which it is called *Tzon Iztak* (white head or hair).

Second Regent, the Camé, with black, the color of its quality of consciousness or of the epoch of barbarism that it represents.

Third Regent, recognized by the yellow color of its bearer, the tree named Canté. In no other native American source do we find so clearly expressed the mythical origin of the ritual colors. The Canté is also the tree that gives shade to the cacao plantations, and so is called *madre de cacao*. Here we have an ethnographic reference to the system of planting of that time, an objectification of the sentence whereby Hunahpú subjects the Third Regent and its bearer to his servitude, just as the Canté serves the cacao. As noted, the god of Cacao is none other than one of the aspects of the Agrarian deity, the alter ego of Hunahpú and Ixbalamqué.

Following this the twins return home to tell their grandmother what has happened. On recounting to her the misfortune that means her separation from her older sons, they tell her: "Don't be sad, grandmother, you will see our brothers again. They will come here, but take care not to laugh when you see them."

Immediately they begin to play on their musical instruments, the flute and drum (note the origin of those instruments in the remote past), the song of Hunahpú-coy to attract their older brothers, now become monkeys. Hunahpú-coy literally means "the monkey of Hunahpú," and signifies the dependency of Hun Bátz and Hun Chouén upon the twins who henceforth are their masters. Regarding the antiquity of the drum and the flute, we also have the evidence of the Chortí drama in which the Black Giant orders *his drum* to be played. The wooden drum is an artifact proper to the matriarchal horizon, typical of those peoples such as the Caribs, Tupi-Guaraní, Arawak, etc., who represent it. Among the monuments at Copán can be seen a gigantic stone *tuncul* on which is sculpted the tongue of a jaguar (the nahual of the feminine deity), expressive of the relation between the instrument, invented during the matriarchal cycle, and the feminine deity which characterizes that cycle.

On hearing the sound of Hunahpú's musical instruments — organs of the divine Word (compare the symbolic value of Tezcatlipoca's flute which is the voice of the Mexican deity) — the older sons draw near dancing. When the grandmother catches sight of their ugly visages, she laughs and is unable to contain her smile, and they run away instantly and hide their faces from her.

Hunahpú reminds the old woman that she must not laugh, saying he will call only four times to his simian brothers. The twins again play the same song and the

monkeys return immediately, dancing; but "their movements were so pleasing, throwing themselves upon the
grandmother in their frolics, making faces, displaying
their bottoms, puffing their muzzles, hiding between her
legs, and making such funny grins that the grandmother
couldn't contain her smile. . . ."

Hunahpú and Ixbalamqué tried to call the simians
back a fourth time but they would no longer come, and so
the twins gave it up. Their calls express the position of
Hunahpú relative to Hun Bátz, the first being the Fourth
Regent and the latter the Third, figures projected in the
number of calls made: Hun Bátz could return only three
times. And so was established the custom of asking no
more than three times, as is done, for example, in requests
to marry, in which the third time is the final one.

Recapitulating these events, the Quiché codex tells us
that in former times Hun Bátz and Hun Chouén were
invoked as artists, "when they lived with their grandmother and mother" (in the matriarchal residence). But
they were transformed into monkeys because they became
filled with pride and mistreated their siblings. The twins
console their grandmother, telling her not to torment herself, that they will stay with and provide for her, because
now they know that she is their mother and their grandmother. In these expressions can be seen the prelude to a
change in the family and social regime, in which from then
on men will labor to maintain the family, taking this
responsibility over from women.

The end of Hun Bátz and Hun Chouén corresponds to
the account of the Third Age that we have already analyzed, and the Third Katún of Maya tradition, an epoch
during which the humanity of the time changed into monkeys. That experience is represented masterfully in the
picture in the Vatican A Codex, reproduced in Figure 9,

showing a field adorned with spirals — serpentlike symbols assimilated with the tails of Hun Bátz and Hun Chouén — monkeys whose genesis the *Popol Vuh* has explained to us. Moreover one sees in this picture the color

FIGURE 9.

yellow, corresponding to that age, whose meaning accords with what is said in Maya and Quiché sources.

Hun Bátz and Hun Chouén are converted into patrons of dance, music, smiles, merriment, pleasure, and lasciviousness inasmuch as they danced naked to the music played by the twins, provoking the irresistible laugh of their grandmother who saw their strange penes. The memory of this episode survives in the song of Hunapú-coy which the Quiché Indians continue to play. But it is in the picture on page 13 of the Borgia Codex that we have the most vivid illustration of the "monkey of Hunahpú." There we see a simian dancing before Xochipilli, who is seated on a throne (in Mexican mythology Xochipilli is the equivalent of Hunahpú). This association of the monkey with the young Solar deity is also expressed in the Tonalpohuali, where Xochipilli is represented by Ozomatli (monkey), the name of the eleventh day in the Aztec calendar. Likewise in Copán, on the altar located in front of Stela D, appears the monkey with attributes of the Solar god. Just as the giants were brought into subjection and converted into secondary gods so, after being vanquished, Hun Bátz and Hun Chouén join the Quiché-Maya theogonic complex, like the sacred ape (*Papio hamadryas*, African monkey) in the mythology of ancient Egypt. In this way the worship of the older gods did not disappear but was transformed, as the older brothers were changed into monkeys through the twins' action.

Nevertheless, veneration of the monkey acquired greater importance on the Mexican altiplano than it did in Maya culture, to judge by the frequency of its reproduction as found in archaeological remains. This becomes more remarkable inasmuch as the monkey is not known in that highland, a fact showing that this element of Mexican mythology is merely traditional and originated elsewhere. To this there must be added that the Quichés preserve in their calendar the name *ba'tz* (big monkey), an animal that is unknown in both the highlands and the Mexican altiplano. On the other hand, simians abound in the original homeland of Mesoamerican culture, a fact that attracted the attention of the Spanish conquistadores coming from Mexico under Alvarado's command. The chronicles of that time tell us of "the monkeys with prehensile tails" encountered on the Pacific coast of Guatemala, a region where there exist all of the animal and vegetable species as well as the mountains described in the *Popol Vuh*. Examples of the latter are the group of great volcanic peaks bordering Guatemala's broad coastal band: Tacaná, Tajamulco, Gagxanul, Atitlán, Pekul, Chikac, and Cajol-Juyub, known to the Indians as the Vukup Camé (seven Camé) according to P. Zamora Castellanos.[6]

ORIGIN AND SIGNIFICANCE OF THE PALO VOLADOR

It remains for us to say that the most spectacular representation of the drama of Hun Bátz and Hun Chouén can be seen in the public performance at Chichicastenango of the Flying Pole (*Palo Volador*), i.e., in the same area and by the same people who produced the *Popol Vuh*.

As in the Chortí Drama of the Giants, the *Palo Volador* reproduces scenes from the *Popol Vuh* that develop in the same serial order as they appear in the famous Quiché manuscript. We have already referred to the symbolism of the bringing of the mast and its relation to the tragedy of the 400 boys, as well as the purpose of fumigating the mast's base with incense to banish evil spirits such as Zipacná — a procedure identical with the one Ixquic used to overcome the Xibalbans.

Between the transport of the mast and the scene that dramatizes the conversion of the elder brothers into monkeys, there fall twenty days or one uinal, it being made known in this way that the two events correspond to distinct historical periods. In the moment of raising the mast two actors dressed as monkeys, representing Hun Bátz and Hun Chouén, attract the public's full attention by their

[6]"Itinerarios . . . ," *Rev. Soc. Geog. e Hist.*, Guatemala, June 1945.

clowning near the mast's tip. Then one of them remains on
the ground while the other rises up into the air as he climbs
up the enormous mast, mimicking the posture of Hun Bátz
in the top of the Canté tree, which grew and grew. Meanwhile, the other actor on the ground diverts the audience
by his grimaces, and dances to the song of Hunahpú-coy.
These actions represent the first born, both in the tree and
responding to Hunahpú's musical summons. In its details
this presentation exhibits variations from one place to
another; for example, in Joyabaj (a Quiché area) the two
monkey-men climb to the tip of the mast where they
remain throughout the performance, while in Chichicastenango the two cling for a moment together on the end of
the great pole and then separate.

The grimaces and contortions of the monkey-men
bring torrents of laughter from the audience, which
unconsciously repeats the role of the grandmother whose
laugh was uncontainable. (In the drama of the Dance of
the Giants, the audience also participates in this way.)
Even the small gestures mentioned by the *Popol Vuh* are
reproduced by the Quiché actors, who stretch their heads
down between their legs and gesticulate as though they
would touch their privates, "that fleshy thing which was
seen below their belly," and which so struck Ixmucané.
That gesture expresses one of the characteristics of the
Simian god, the model of lasciviousness, and gives to this
part of the performance a frankly erotic note that is not
found in any of the Chortí celebrations.

A detail of significance is that the actors do not put on
the monkey mask and tail until the exact moment they
begin climbing up the pole. This faithfully renders the
idea that their transformation did not occur until they
were up in the Canté tree. The masks are of wood painted
black — like that of the Black Giant in the Chortí drama

FIGURE 10. The Quichés carry the Flying Pole, as the 400 boys do in the *Popol Vuh. (Courtesy of Ovidio Rodas Corzo.)*

FIGURE 11. The base of the pole is rendered immune to evil spirits by the application of incense. (*Courtesy of Ovidio Rodas Corzo.*)

FIGURE 12. Raising the Flying Pole in Chichicastenango. The "monkey" climbs higher as the pole is raised. (*Photo: Ovidio Rodas Corzo.*)

FIGURE 13. Top portion of the Flying Pole in Chichicastenango. (*Photo: Ovidio Rodas Corzo.*)

FIGURE 14. The marimba sounds the Hunahpú-coy song, while one of the "monkeys" dances and gesticulates.

— the color symbolic of the bad consciousness the first-born had, as well as of the age of barbarism which they exemplified. This esoteric meaning of the color black had been noted long ago by Father Avendaño who, in referring to the warpaint that covered the faces of the Itzá, compared the blackness of the face with the perversity of the heart. The use of wooden masks goes back to the matriarchal-horticultural era, as we shall demonstrate.

The principal monkey-actor clings to the wooden frame placed over the tip of the mast, and makes as though he would catch hold of the bird-men (actors dressed as birds) in the four corners of the frame. But these fly away, frustrating the intentions of the monkey-actor, Hun Bátz, like the birds of Hunahpú who did not allow themselves to be caught. This episode, which also has chronological connotations, gave the name of *Palo Volador* to the whole performance. The actor representing Hun Bátz has the chief role and is at one and the same time master of ceremony and the theatrical director. As such, he is the repository of the tradition and charged with preserving it, a responsibility that he shares with his companion who personifies Hun Chouén and will succeed him in the task when he is no longer able. The process of fumigating the base of the mast with incense is the responsibility of a native elder who, after doing it, gets into the hole dug to receive the mast and directs copal smoke to the four cosmic directions. Placement of the mast in the enormous hole symbolizes cosmic union, the marriage of the god of Heaven with the Terrestrial goddess. This aspect of a fertility rite is also clear from the fact that the *Palo Volador* performance takes place before the time of sowing the seed fields as well as during the harvest (April and December, respectively), first on the very date of the ritual blessing of the seeds, and later as an act of thanksgiving. The celebration in December coincides with the fiesta in honor of the tribal deity, an event falling at the winter solstice, anniversary of Hunahpú's birth.

The symbolic relationship between the *Palo Volador* performance and the sowing of the maize is borne out from the fact that the actors must abstain from all sexual contact for fifteen days before the event, the same tabu that is in force before the maize seeds are sown.

In regard to the time-reckoning significance of the performance, there should first be mentioned the value of the cosmic bearer, symbolized by the mast itself, which supports the celestial framework. Heaven is represented by a square wooden frame in the center of which, in Mexico, is placed an actor who turns it while he plays a flute (the instrument of Hunahpú or of Tezcatlipoca), while in each corner of the frame is tied an individual dressed as a macaw. In this manner the cosmic plane is objectified above the earth with its four regents in the corners who with the central god form the diagram of god-Five, the deity of Summer and of the Performance and at the same time the tribal god, a replica of Hunahpú. God-Five's dual character (Hunahpú and Ixbalamqué) is sometimes symbolized, as in the *Volador* of Joyabaj depicted in figure 15, in the dichotomous form of the turning wooden cap-piece that represents the twins or their alter ego, the pair which inhabit the Center of Heaven, i.e., the highest heaven. This cosmic position is figured in the difference in level between the wooden cap-piece and the squared wood frame below it. Formerly the astronomic cross that divides the squared cosmic frame into four quarters was also figured, according to the following reference from Fuentes y Guzman: "To the mast were tied with cord four small ladders which crossed the pole in a cross."[7] The actors

---

[7]*Recordación Florida*, Madrid, 1882.

dressed as macaws simultaneously let themselves fall into space. The ropes that sustain them, unwinding, cause the cap-piece (on which the central actor stands upright) and suspended wooden frame to turn. Each of the four swing-

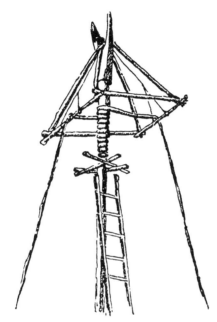

FIGURE 15. Mechanism of the Flying Pole used in Joyabaj, according to a sketch by F. Termer. The dual deity in the center of the highest Heaven is portrayed in the forked cap-piece. The cosmic quadrangle is represented by the four-sided, pyramidal frame suspended from the cap-piece.

ing individuals makes thirteen turns in his descent, symbolizing the cycle of 52 years with its cosmic divisions and connections. In Mexico the performance of the *Palo Volador* was part of the ceremony held to celebrate the renewal of the cycle.

The Mayas do not know the *Palo Volador*, although

they preserve elements related to it. For example, in Chan Kom the ritual of fructification is executed by an individual dressed as a simian (as a coati, says Redfield, from whom we obtain this datum; the coati is very much like the macaque), who climbs a ceiba tree. That monkey-man entertains the audience by his clowning and throws seeds to the winds to show that the tree has produced fruit.

We must ask: Why is it that, in light of the fact that the Mayas and the Quichés shared a common mythology and tradition, the *Palo Volador* which expresses them is not found among the former? On the other hand, it is a typical feature of peoples such as the Huastecs, Otomís, Totonacs, and Quichés, who represent the contemporary state of Toltec culture, as well as of the Nahuas, acculturated by the Toltecs.

Such a phenomenon is explained in terms of historical causality. We know that the 52-year cycle formed the longest time period of Toltec culture. On the other hand, for the Mayas, who had in the Long Count possessed a practically infinite computation of time, the wheel of 52 years had only a very relative importance and was incorporated into larger cycles which cannot be projected by means of the *Palo Volador*. The stela for recording time divisions, characteristic of the Mayan theo-cosmogonic system, is the functional replica of the *Palo Volador*. The material itself from which the stelae were constructed, perishable in the *Volador*, durable in the stela, is expressive of the different conceptions of the cosmos and life that were held by Mayas and Toltecs. While the latter thought that the world could end at the close of each cyclical wheel, the former conceived of the eternal duration of the cosmos.

Both the raising of the mast and of the stela contained the same symbolism of union of heaven and earth. This explains the etymological relation among the words for base, seat, fundamental support, and vital organ that Flavio Rodas has pointed out in his excellent work on Quiché and Maya symbols. Therefore, from the procedures attending the raising of the *Palo Volador* mast, we can infer the nature of ceremonies carried out at the raising of the Maya stone stela.

The Drama of the Giants and the game of the *Palo Volador* complement each other, offering in dramatic form a synthesis of the mythical part of the *Popol Vuh*.

9

Youth of Hunahpú and Ixbalamqué

HUN BÁTZ and Hun Chouén having been destroyed by conversion into simians, the Third Age comes to a close and this ends the long cycle of Quiché-Maya prehistory.

We have seen that the disappearance of her firstborn grieves Ixmucané; but Hunahpú and Ixbalamqué console her, pointing out that they will now take their older brothers' place, an improvement inasmuch as they will now provide for her.

Then the twins declared what they would do to maintain their prestige with their grandmother and their mother. They will cultivate the *milpas:* "Only we shall sow the seed," they tell the grandmother emphatically. "We are staying here to support our mother, Ixquic, and you our grandmother, Ixmucané. We will substitute for our older brothers," they said. Then they picked up their hatchets, hoes, and clubs, and went off with their blowguns on their shoulders. When they left the house, they requested their grandmother to bring them their meal when the sun was at the zenith. "Very well, I will do this," the old woman told them.

Here we have a change in the division of labor within the family, marking a decisive step toward the patriarchal regime. During the former age men remained idle while women busied themselves in providing for them. Now it is the man who works to provide for the family, reducing woman's role to the domestic chores, and chiefly to preparation of the meals to be carried to the fieldworkers. Women became more subordinate to men, since Hunahpú commanded that the twins' meal be brought precisely at midday and the grandmother docilely consented to this by replying, "Very well." These expressions, "Very well" (*está bien*) and "It is not well" (*está mal*) which are so frequently repeated in the Quiché text, embody conceptions of what is according or contrary to the laws of religious morality.

We have another change in the family operation in the declaration that "only we shall sow the seed" and in the exclusive use by the man of the hoe or sowing stick, which had been the undivided functions of the woman during the earlier cycle. The origins of this social revolution go back to the time when, besides the members of maternal descent, those of paternal descent were accepted into the family. Thus Hun Bátz, Hun Chouén, Hunahpú, and Ixbalamqué were found under one roof. The two latter were descendants of the seven Ahpú and in terms of their maternal line belonged to a foreign clan.

Development of the Social, Economic, and Religious Practices as Explained by the Quiché Document

Few if any historical sources reveal in such a precise manner the mediating form in the passage from descendance through the female line to that through the male, this being something that happened centuries before our era. Naturally this process did not occur without friction. The animosity of the eldest cousins and the struggle they wage to assert their rights reveal this condition of things, the precursor of the patriarchal regimen. It is logical to think that at first the descendants through the maternal line continued to enjoy greater privileges than the others, on whom devolved the responsibility to work, it being then considered that in a certain sense labor was demeaning. Two accompanying factors emerged with the expansion of the nuclear family: the economic because of an extension of means of subsistence, and that of the increase in population in consequence of life in permanent settlements. During the matriarchal-horticultural cycle human migrations occurred on an increasing scale over vast portions of the hemisphere; these came to an end under the influence of the two developments noted. The need for increased labor on the one hand, and the growth of population on the other, made modification of the family arrangement necessary. This double circumstance explains why at the beginning those of masculine lineage, such as Hunahpú and Ixbalamqué, were reduced to the condition of serfs.

Such conditions of relative inferiority accelerated the coming of masculine predominance by virtue of the same principle by which the woman gained her privileged legal position following the earliest hunter-gatherer cycle.

In effect, the teachings in the *Popol Vuh*, confirmed by the ethnographic reality, established the fact that masculine or feminine dominance in the structure of the family invariably derives from the economic factor, since the ones who assure the group's subsistence are those who predominate in the social order. But this ascent in the social scale begins with an earlier condition in which the socially strongest were to be found in relatively inferior conditions of servitude vis-à-vis the others. The social predominance of one or the other sex depends, then, upon the role each plays in the regular provision of food guaranteeing group survival; and this varies throughout the course of the ethnic cycles in accordance with the increase in sources of subsistence. To illustrate this proposition, which has come to form a law of development in American society, we will give examples taken from the ethnographic facts themselves. These agree with the principles offered in the *Popol Vuh*. Peoples such as the Fuegians, who live by hunting and fishing and are nomadic, depend upon the labor of the men and therefore are governed by patrilineal descendance. Among them the woman is truly a beast of burden assigned the most laborious tasks. D'Orbigny says of them that among all of the women of primitive American tribes their lot is the hardest. In addition to other chores, they must collect fruits, herbs, and roots and, when plant life is scarce as it is in Tierra del Fuego, they must collect small shells, while the men occupy themselves in hunting.

Unfavorable geographic factors prevented the development of Fuegian society, which never rose above a rudimentary condition. When the nomadic tribe moves into a geographically more favorable tropic, collection of fruits and roots takes on an increasing importance until it becomes the principal source of subsistence, thanks to the discovery of new plants by the women and to the beginnings of horticulture. The passage from collection to horticulture is gradual and comes about when the women observe that cast-off parts of plants take root and grow, and improve with cultivation.

When horticulture supersedes hunting as the chief means of subsistence, the family group depends upon the labor of the woman, who assumes the directive role while the man sees the dread of his hunger disappear and no longer has to devote all his energy to supply each day's meals. He has time then to devote himself to other things such as cultivation of the arts. The basic problem of the native American man was hunger, and the *Popol Vuh* vividly portrays the life of the primitive hunter who had to go days on end without eating (the episodes concerning Zipacná and Caprakán). In contrast with what took place in the Old World, American culture had to develop without passing through the pastoral cycle which in Eurasia was the continuation and natural consequence of that of the nomadic hunter because animals susceptible of domestication abounded, a condition that did not exist in the Americas. Thus passage from the hunter-gatherer cycle to one of horticulture was a logical consequence of the economic development imposed by the milieu, and life then centered about the woman. Later, development of agriculture demanded masculine labor; but, as with horticulture, the beginnings of that new state of things occurred in circumstances in which labor was regarded as demeaning. Those who performed it, then, belonged to a lower social category, the situation to which in the beginning Hunahpú was reduced. But when the group came to depend upon the labor of the man, a reaction took place and life became centered upon him.

This basic socioeconomic principle of American development is expressed in Hunahpú's declaration that "we shall remain so as to feed you." Thereby masculine preponderance is affirmed, and the man assumes responsibility from that time forward for the maintenance of the family. Hunahpú's statement, coinciding with the disappearance of Hun Bátz and Hun Chouén, makes one think that the privileged legal position of the man within the family occurred at once with the displacement of children of maternal affiliation. All this opens new perspectives for sociology in its attempts to uncover the causal relations involved in the progressive development of native American society, since now it has useful testimony from a historical source of the first order.

The change in conceptions related to work brings with it change in social forms and new concepts about the regulation of property by virtue of the principle that the land belongs to those who cultivate it, and any alteration or modification in territorial status must be reflected in that of inheritance. From this we can see that the type of society goes hand in hand with the customs for the handing on of possessions. Nevertheless, change from maternal to paternal line of descent takes place imperceptibly, modifying without destroying the structure of the communal clan that formed the social unit during the matriarchal period. This we deduce because of the legal position of the grandmother, implying the existence of the macrofamily and therefore of the exogamic clan, strongly knit by the triple ties of consanguinous unity, community of interests, and spiritual union in a common religion.

Such a socioreligious unity is moreover reflected in the theogonic system of the Camé and the Ahpú, the latter representative of a cooperativism contrasting with the simple monotheism of the earlier period, denoting out-and-out individualism or egoism. Now we are dealing with a conception of religious and social brotherhood that extends to the gods themselves. In other words, the Third Age was marked by hamlet cultures based on matrilineal clans whose family structure was built on the same foundations as the actual Mayan family, with the sole difference that descendance followed the female line rather than the male, and authority as head of household belonged to the grandmother. Its essential features were: respect for the elderly, the role of the grandmother as the mother of the whole family (later the grandfather as the paterfamilias), equality of brothers with their first cousins, division of labor, existence of private property, and conferment of social and religious rank by hereditary right. All these passed over into the Fourth Age, but now in the patrilineal clan.

Continuing this very interesting etiological exposition, we see Hunahpú demonstrating his condition of "industrious man" (*hombre trabajador*), a term used ever since to designate the agrarian gods. The technique for cultivation of maize is exemplified by Hunahpú as follows: the twins go into the seed field (*milpa*), pick up their digging sticks or hoes lying there (note the use of the possessive here), and make furrows with the implements. With their hatchets they cut and split logs, branches, sticks, and creepers covering the trees. Then they burn the cuttings, after collecting and piling the underbrush and cuttings together. Because of their divine nature they did all this in a moment, just as they had cleared the field of the overgrowth with one blow of the hatchet.

As the twins had ordered, the grandmother came to the field at the proper moment (when the sun was at its zenith) bringing them their meal. But because the twins did not want to be surprised by her, since they had not only cleared the fields but were busy using their blowguns (expressing in this allegory Hunahpú's dual function as Solar and Agrarian deity), when they had finished the fields they instructed a bird called Ixmucur — which they posted in the top of a tree trunk — to watch for the grandmother's arrival. "When she appears," they told it, "you will call out immediately, and we'll pick up the hoe and hatchet." Ixmucur agreed. From that time the carpenter bird, which likes to sit high in the branches of trees, continues to carry out the mission given it by Hunahpú, which is to

warn workers in the fields of the presence of persons they
cannot yet see. In this way they have warned of the
approach of enemy troops, just as geese did in ancient
Rome.

The twins' stratagem had a purpose, since by their own
example they were setting the pattern for the "industrious
man"; but because of their divine nature their work was
done magically and without any effort. So, as soon as they
heard Ixmucur's call, "they returned to work, one taking
the hoe and the other the hatchet. They covered their
heads and spread earth upon their hands, like those with
perspiring faces who have really been working hard. And
so the grandmother saw them. They ate the meal she had
brought as if they had indeed developed an appetite from
their labors in the field. Then they returned to the hut.
'Truly we are very tired, grandmother,' they said. 'We've
ended our day,' and they stretched out to rest in front of
the old lady."

This paragraph from the *Popol Vuh* summarizes the
conduct of the perfect field-worker which the Chortí elder
continues to encourage through his own example, since in
his role as representative of the Agrarian god he must be
the best husbandman of the group that he leads, following
the standard set by Hunahpú. The latter was in fact "a
man fit for all work," as the elders continue to exclaim
with admiration. Disguised as a true worker of the seed
fields, dirty, covered with debris from the trees, mud, and
pieces of moss, just as one sees the Indian amid the activity
of his work, Hunahpú extols the role of the husbandman
who through his work alone gains the right to eat, because
this is the reward of all work according to the customs of
the Maya as decreed by Hunahpú. The one who does not
work forfeits the right to eat and rest. The posture of rest
taken by the twins following their return from the field is

still observed by the Chortís, and is reproduced in the picture of a figure in the Dresden Codex, where god B, the homologue of Hunahpú, is seated with legs and arms stretched out.

Assiduity in labor is expressed in the following sentence: "Before the next day dawned the twins returned to the seed field," a custom that the Mayas have observed ever since. Just as Osiris taught the Egyptians the cultivation of wheat and barley, Hunahpú by his own example teaches the operation of the seed field in all of its ramifications. The life of the farmer is one of effort in which nothing is accomplished without constant work. Hunahpú manifests the attitude the Indian must assume toward the difficulties that face him. The man of the tropics must especially struggle against two elements: nature itself, whose vigor threatens the fields not kept clear of undergrowth; and animals that are harmful to agriculture. Both factors combined to destroy Hunahpú's seed field "in a single night."

Far from being dismayed by such a misfortune, the twins again sowed the field with maize and considered what they must do. "Now we will keep watch over our *milpa*, and we shall see what we do with those who would surprise us," they agreed. Then they returned to their house (note again the use of the possessive), telling their grandmother of the loss incurred, explaining that their field had become one big patch of undergrowth (which happens when the work of clearing the ground has not been done in time). "We are going now to watch over the field, because what they are doing to us is bad." They returned to the seed field and hid themselves in the shade, "waiting without movement, like the lizards, remaining concealed without speaking."

This picturesque description, showing the hero-gods

lying in ambush for the marauding animals that came by night, can be applied to the present-day Indian who, following the pattern they established, guards his property at night. "By being merely seen and surprised," the animals are vanquished and unable to carry out their destruction of the crop. Here is the origin of a curious custom of the Chortís based on the fact that an animal (or an enemy) that is surprised, and whose name and features are known, is already overcome by virtue of the principle that to know a person or his name gives one dominance over him. Thus, when the Chortí husbandman goes around his fields at midnight (the hour instituted by Hunahpú), he speaks aloud to the visible and invisible animals as follows: "Now I see you, now I know you, you are so-and-so, and now I pronounce your name," with certainty that this magical formula will cause any real or supposed marauding rodents to flee the field.

All these details on the way to carry out the serial steps of cultivation (sowing, resowing, cleaning, and guarding the seed field) make one think that in the earlier age there was no such work-regimen governing the *milpa*. It is plausible to think that women did not go out to guard the fields at night and that lacking proper methods of cultivation, the maize plantations did not produce as much as when horticulture gave way to agriculture. Confirming such a hypothesis is the fact that maize did not become divine until Hunahpú and Ixbalamqué incarnated the mystery of the germination and growth of this plant, which ever since has been held sacred and representative of Hunahpú, the Maize god.

Before its deification, maize was no more than one among a number of food plants that, like the bean, yucca, and other vegetables, were combined with hunted food in the diet of the matriarchal family. The divinization of maize occurred when the kernels had attained some degree of development, to judge by contemporary customs which only regard the largest kernels as the residence of spirit or the Maize god.

From the time of its deification, the maize *milpa* is something so sacred for the Indian of Quiché-Maya culture that he dedicates all his time to it, caring for it with painstaking attention, as he would a treasure.

The *Popol Vuh* then recounts the struggle made by the twins against the animal marauders who, because they "have been seen and surprised," are finally subdued and must take flight while the twins try to catch them by hand.

The puma, the jaguar, the mountain cat, coyote, wild boar, and coati refused to be captured, but the deer and rabbit ran with their tails between their legs (a sign of fear) and their pursuers seized them. But the tails broke off, and Hunahpú and Ixbalamqué were left holding only the ends. From that time rabbits and deer have stubby tails. The twins also caught the rat, squeezed its body and burned its tail, "and since then rats have hairless tails and bulging eyes because of the way the twins dealt with them."

This curious etiological legend explaining the form of the tails of these three creatures reminds one of another and similar tradition obtained by Dr. Jesús Aguilar Paz in Chamelecón, the old territory of the Hicaques, which runs as follows: in the time of Hun Bátz, who fed on beetles and spiders, when witches flew and owls spoke, the rabbit had a tail like a cat's, the rat a tail like the horse's, and the deer one like that of a sheep dog. But the day came when by a work of magic these three tails were transformed — and here the informant gave a story similar to what we transscribe from the *Popol Vuh*.

In its difficulties, the rat exclaimed, "Don't kill me as you think to do, because sowing the seed field is not your work." "Well, then, have you anything to tell us?" the twins asked it, because they inferred from what the rat had said that it possessed great knowledge. "If you let me go free I will tell you, because I have truth in my belly; but first give me something to eat," said the rat. The wise rodent demands "payment" in food first before making its statement. But such demands are not acceptable because the twins are laying down the new patterns of conduct, and according to these any reward of nourishment must first be merited.

"We will feed you afterwards, but speak first," they told the rat. Then the rat revealed the secret hiding place where the seven Ahpú had placed their insignia of splendor before leaving for Xibalbá. "Spears, gloves, and ball were left hanging under the eaves of the house. Your grandmother doesn't want to show them to you because these had brought about the death of your fathers," said the rat.

Since the rat had spoken, they gave it a meal of maize, dry pepper, beans, cacao, and *pataxte* seeds. "This now will be your food; hereafter you will search for refuse to gnaw upon for sustenance," the youths told the rat. Their list shows the food plants of the time. These composed the sumptuous meal given the rat in exchange for its service, but from then on it would have a different way of feeding itself. Thus the rat lives on garbage, and men must carry out Hunahpú's sentence by preventing the rat from touching foods reserved only for humankind.

Because it had revealed its secret — a serious and punishable thing that is contrary to the rules of Mayan ethics — the rat fears to appear before the grandmother; but the twins offer to protect it.

After having thought together during the night and reached agreement, Hunahpú and Ixbalamqué went to their house at noon (the hour corresponding to the sun's zenith as well as that of the Agrarian god embodied in the twins, the position determining their moment for action). They carried the rat with them, hidden from view. One then entered by the door and the other through an opening in the wall, and together they let the rat go. Note this example of a plurality in a single act; it is a turn of language constantly found in the *Popol Vuh* and signifies a monotheist conception, based on the idea of a plurality within unity.

The twins asked the grandmother for something to eat. "Grind our meal" (the use of the *metate*). "We wish a chili dressing, grandmother," they said (A. Recinos translation). The grandmother complied, placing the soup and meat before them (note how the twins request their meal and the old woman obeys).

By quietly emptying the water jars and then asking the grandmother for drinking water, they get her out of the house, since she must fetch the water from the fountain — just as do present-day Indian women in observance of the norms established by Ixmucané. Hunahpú and Ixbalamqué, their grandmother thus absent, begin the project they had thought about and agreed on during the night.

In order to keep their grandmother away from the house longer, they send a mosquito to bore holes in the water jar (the act of throwing the magical dart that we encounter so often). Ixmucané tried in vain to prevent the water from leaking out of the jar. Then, mentioning the grandmother's delay and their great thirst, they sent their mother Ixquic to look for the old woman.

Now alone, they took their fathers' ball, lances, gloves, and pelts and hid them by the road leading to the ball court. These were brought down by the rat through a hole in the house's roof (the image of the sun, identified with the ball, which at the end of its course across the celestial vault goes under the earth through an opening).

Then the youths set out toward the river where they find their mother and grandmother occupied with the task of closing up the hole *in the face of the water jar.* "What happened to you? We got tired of waiting for you and so came here," said the twins. "Well, look then," replied the old woman, "we cannot close up *the face of my water jar.*" But the two youths closed it up in a second, and they all returned to the house, the twins going ahead of their grandmother. And that is how they recovered their fathers' game ball.

We have emphasized Ixmucané's expression regarding the "face of her water jar" because in it we find the genesis of the glyph for the moon, shown as a large, narrow-mouthed pitcher (*cántaro*) which is the symbol for Ixmucané, the old Water goddess and Lunar deity. The "face of her water jar" is similar to the very face of the goddess, i.e., her starry form as seen in the sky, inasmuch as the Indian conceives the moon as a gigantic pitcher that pours water from the sky. Thus, to this day he refers to the *face* of the water jar, and calls its handles *ears.* The use of this globe-shaped receptacle, which goes back to the matriarchal-horticultural period, is typical of peoples such as the Taoajka who preserve the culture of that time and continue making such pitchers even now. This shows that pottery-making had undergone notable advances since its humble beginnings in the Second Age, and that the kitchen implements of the Third Age included the grinding stone, water jars, vessels made of calabashes, and earthen bowls or large cups in the shape of the half-calabash. In the remote past as well as the present day, those vessels of globular form designed to carry water are used exclusively by women in accordance with the practice begun by Ixmucané. Their function is moreover made known in some places by ideograms painted on their "faces" which have to

do with rain or water. The double character of the goddess, anthropomorphic and heavenly, is expressed linguistically in the Chortí names for the moon: *ka tú* and *uh*.
Compare the Chortí *ka tú* with the Miskito *ka ti*, Arawak
kat bi, and Quiché *ka ati*. The *ka tú* (our mother, our
queen) refers to the anthropomorphic aspect of the divine
grandmother, the rank Ixmucané had in the mythological
family. The other vocable, *uh*, designates the night star
and connotes the idea of sacred, blessed; it is also used to
denote the semispherical earthen bowl used in worship.

The order of march, with the twins preceding their
mother and grandmother, mirrors another present-day
native custom whereby the children walk ahead of their
parents, going "Indian file" in order of importance in conformity to the astro-theogonic model in which the young
sun (Aurora) precedes its father (Sun).

The twins next go out to play ball in the ball court, but
not without first cleaning off this court where their fathers
had played. This requirement, as we have seen, continues
a custom going back to the First Age when primeval man
appealed to his Creator in clean places.

Besides symbolizing the sun's relative position in the
order of its rising and its daily trajectory, Hunahpú and
Ixbalamqué, playing alone for a long time on opposite
sides of the court, represent the position of the sun and
the moon at opposing solstices, just as this continues to
be depicted on Chortí altars. All this unmistakably reflects a gradual progress in astronomic and cosmogonic
knowledge.

Of course, the two players were heard by the Lords of
Xibalbá, just as these had heard their fathers, the seven
Ahpú, since the roof of the Camé's dwelling place is the
surface of the earth whose openings form the auditory
canals of the underworld gods. These Lords became

angry, and again ordered their messengers to notify the twins that within the space of seven days (the ritual cipher) they should present themselves in Xibalbá to play a game of ball.

Taking the road that the youths would come along to reach their houses (note the use of the plural here), the messengers deliver their message to Ixmucané, who replies that the order will be complied with. But instantly the old woman became filled with anxiety, recalling that her sons lost their lives in the same circumstances. "Whom can I find to go and warn my grandchildren?" she thought and, despondent, went into her house.

Then, as if catching her thought, a louse fell into her skirt. She seized it and put it in the palm of her hand. "Would you go and call my grandchildren in the ball court?" she asked the louse. "Then you will tell them I say that the messengers from Xibalbá have arrived and they must be there within seven days."

The louse left lazily to carry out its commission, when on the road it met a boy named Tamazul (toad). "Where are you going?" the toad asked the louse. "I carry a command in my belly and I'm looking for the twins," it replied. Note that as in the case of the rat, the belly is the organ of intelligence, memory, and feelings, functions that are also located in the heart, as we shall see, which explains the symbolic equivalence of the Heart and Umbilicus of Heaven and of Earth, terms by which the Chortís designate the central Deity.

The ambivalence of the toad and the human being is still preserved in Maya worship in the alternate use of persons who croak like frogs or of actual batrachians, for they "implore better than we do" during the ceremony to entreat for rain.

"Don't you want me to swallow you? You will see how

fast I run and we will get there promptly," said the toad. "Good," answered the louse. It was immediately swallowed, and so the two traveled on for a long time, until they met a great white snake called Zakicaz. The same series of questions was asked of the toad, which consented and was swallowed by the snake, so that the message might reach the ball court. Later the three encountered a bird of prey (a sparrow hawk or raven); the scene was repeated, the bird swallowing the snake and flying instantly toward the ball court.

Ever since, birds of prey eat snakes, these eat toads, and toads eat insects. Besides this meaning, and to show the relative velocity of the animals in question, the allegory unquestionably objectifies an astronomic episode, the animals symbolizing celestial bodies whose importance has the same relation as that of their relative speed. First, the bird of prey, representative of the sun; next the white snake which in Chortí mythology represents the Milky Way; thereafter the *chac* (toad) or god of Rain, projected in the star; and finally the louse, whose meaning we do not know.

It is of interest to point out that for the first time mention is made in allegorical form of the Milky Way, whose movements were perfectly well known to the Maya, and which still plays a principal role in Chortí astronomy, inasmuch as it signals the time of sowing known as "the second." Both the central Deity, as well as the Milky Way and the gods of rain, work in close association, just as the group of animals cooperated to carry Ixmucané's message to the twins. They also offer a vivid image of the conception of a plurality of beings enclosed in a unity, as found in Maya monotheist belief.

Reaching the ball court, the bird of prey alighted on the building there and cawed three times: quako! quako!

quako! This defines the origin of the name of the raven, the onomatopoeia of its sound. The three cries have also a ritual meaning, and with them the bird attracted the attention of the players who, seeing it, shot at it with their blowguns, whereupon it fell to the ground.

Then the hawk spoke, saying it had a message in its belly which it would deliver when its eye, wounded by the youths' dart, should be healed. "Very well," they said, and taking coagulated sap from a plant (resin of the rubber tree according to Raynaud; of the pine according to Villacorta), they applied it to the eye, whereupon it was instantly healed.

Hunahpú in this case performs as a healer, one of the attributes of the Agrarian god and of the Chortí elder, its authentic representative. At the same time a formula from the native pharmacopoeia is described for treatment of cataracts or ills of the eye, whose origin is this miraculous operation of Hunahpú. If the latter this time heeds the bird's imperious request contrary to the way he treated the rat, which he made to speak first, it is because now we are dealing with the nahual of Hunrakán, i.e., with an emissary of the Solar deity which since the time of its curing by Hunahpú is the only animal that can look full into the sun (in Mexico it is the eagle).

At once the hawk spits up the snake which in turn ejects the toad; but it doesn't succeed in dislodging the louse, because the insect stayed locked in its mouth. The toad hadn't really swallowed the louse but had only acted as if it had done so. Because of that the twins, treating it as one would a liar, beat the toad, "giving it kicks in the rump, so that since then the bones in its rump and legs are fallen. Instantly they opened the toad's mouth and found the louse caught in the gum, taking the insect from the toad."

Aside from the etiological meaning, explaining the form and movement of toads, this allegory emphasizes another rule of Quiché-Maya ethics: the denunciation and punishment of lying, a vice that is still dealt with in the way Hunahpú began it. Palacio mentions, in fact, that "whoever is found lying is brutally whipped."[1] So deeprooted is the love of truth among the natives that even today those who preserve their traditional social and religious organization continue to respect that elevated principle of ethics.

Ixmucané's herald at last delivers its important message, telling the twins that through their grandmother the Camé challenge them to a game of ball which has to be held within a period of seven days, and therefore they must take with them their lances, gloves, pelts, and ball so that they can "fight for their existence there." This is to be a decisive struggle between two kinds of culture, personified by the twins and the Camé.

Before setting out for Xibalbá, the youths went to take leave of their grandmother, leaving with her a personal keepsake, reflecting another rule of conduct observed by the present-day Indian. And the memento which Hunahpú and Ixbalamqué left as "a sign of their existence" was nothing less than a stalk of maize.

Each of us *will sow* a stalk of maize in the center of our house. If they disappear, it will be a sign that we have died. "They are dead," you will say then. But if they sprout again, "They live!" you will say. "O our grandmother! You, little grandmother! You, our mother! Do not weep, we have left you the mark of our word," the twins told the two women. Then Hunahpú sowed one stalk and Ixbalam-

---

[1] *Relación al Rey don Felipe II*, dated March 8, 1576.

qué did the same; inside the house they sowed them and not in the field, neither in damp ground, but rather in the middle of their house did they leave them sown.

This episode is extremely important from the theogonic point of view inasmuch as it confirms the double function of Hunahpú as god of Maize and as Solar god (*cerbatanero:* shooter of darts), and is moreover a typical example of nahualism, a belief that is still firmly fixed in the native mind.

Because the stalks of maize sown by the twins are their alter egos or unfoldments, by that token they will suffer an identic fate. If the twins die the stalks will die, but if they live then the stalks will sprout and grow. This explains why they were sown in dry soil and in the middle of the house-floor, for they represent the Maize god in the central point of the cosmos, here symbolized by the house, where the plants will remain as the image of the divine youths. The metamorphosis or fate of the stalks of maize no longer depends upon the quality of the soil or of any other natural condition of things, but upon the destiny of the twins, their alter egos, which they reflect. This explains also the etymological relationship between the words center (*inšin*) and maize (*išin*).

Nahualism embodies the belief that there exists between the person and the nahual (animal or vegetable) a fully determined, intimate relationship that begins and ends with the life of the person. In the ethnographic part of *Los Chortís* we have given cases showing that the death of the individual automatically implies that of his or her nahual, and vice versa. This fact explains the great veneration that is accorded the nahual.

The picturesque allegory of the *Popol Vuh* is explained in terms of Chortí theology by the category of brother gods (with the meaning of an alter ego) such as the Maize and young Solar god, functions that are acquired by the twins, as will be seen. This intimate relationship is also expressed by a common denominator, since both the Maize god and Solar god are numeral gods whose number is five. Mexican mythology offers us Xochipilli and Xochiquetzal, Cinteotl and Xilonen, the functional counterparts of Hunahpú and Ixbalamqué in their double character of solar gods (lunisolar) and maize gods. Similarly to the Chortí mythology, Xochipilli is the brother of Cinteotl. This explains why in a Mexican song Xochipilli is mentioned as Cinteotl, as also Seler's identification of Tezcatlipoca (Agrarian god) with Macuilxóchitl (Solar god or god of Summer). In another version Ce Acatl (one stalk) is the name of Quetzalcoatl in his function as a young god, and his hieroglyph in the form of a stalk of maize corresponds with that of Hunahpú.

In short, we find in the very Mayan glyphs the ideographic correspondence with the concepts discussed above, expressed in the signs *kin* and *kan*, both being represented by a spherical form that is objectified in the *Popol Vuh* — the first by the game ball, at once the symbol of the sun and the equivalent of the sign *kin*; and the second by the grain of maize, the equivalent of the *kan* glyph. Their single genesis could not be better expressed — as we shall see below — than in the fact that both signs correspond to the head of Hunahpú. Finally, the positioning of the maize sprouts in the center of the house, coinciding with the descent of the twins into the underworld, expresses another custom of the time, consisting of burial of the dead within the house, a custom that is widespread in the Americas.

Before going to the next chapter, we should mention the custom preserved by Quiché Indians of sowing two maize stalks in the middle of the plaza in front of their house, in remembrance of the stalks left behind by Hunah-pú and Ixbalamqué as a memento for their grandmother as they left for Xibalbá.[2]

---

[2]Information furnished by Ovidio Rodas Corzo.

10

Hunahpú and Ixbalamqué in Xibalbá

COMPLYING with their destiny, the twins descend into Xibalbá, armed with their ever-present blowguns and dressed in their "elements of splendor." They traverse the same country described during the earlier journey of the seven Ahpú, crossing the same infernal rivers; "however, they do not go through those rivers but cross over them using their blowguns as a bridge, and when they leave the rivers they reach the spot where four roads come together." This is reminiscent of a passage in Mexican mythology where Cinteotl, replica of Hunahpú as god of Maize, sings, saying to the god of the Flowers: "I reached the place where the roads came together, I the god of Maize" (Sahagún).

Crossing the river by blowguns illustrates another native custom whose origin goes back to this legendary trip of Hunahpú. The Chortís, Lenca, and other peoples of less sophisticated cultures such as the Talamanca, throw light lines made of palm or grass fibers over ravines, streams, or deep hollows across which the spirits of their deceased have to pass, so that they can overcome the obstacle more easily.

Knowing the symbolic equivalence of the blowgun to the sun's ray and its correspondence to the divine hair and elements such as thread, rope, and serpent, we understand that the light line, thrown across the cracks in the earth so that the soul of the defunct may pass, corresponds to the blowgun that Hunahpú stretched across the underworld rivers. And this symbolic equivalence is made plain in the Quiché dress on which the solar rays are represented by threads, and in their language by use of the same term (*batz*) to designate the words thread and monkey (as Solar god).

In Mexican mythology the same symbol is expressed in a different form: by the figure of a dog that swims across the Chignaguapan carrying the dead person on its back, and for that reason a golden-colored dog (colored like the sun) was interred with the body and accompanied the dead person, as Xolotl accompanied the sun during its underworld journey. In the Mayan codices, the dog is a symbol of the solar fire or ray; that is, the equivalent of Hunahpú's blowgun. Nevertheless that mythological element appears in a relatively late period of Toltec culture, and of the Maya which was influenced by it, and is not known in Maya culture of the Old Empire or in Chortí mythology. Neither does the *Popol Vuh* mention the dog employed as a temporary bridge for crossing the underworld rivers, and this fact has historical implications.

Unlike their parents who went astray at the underworld crossroads, Hunahpú and Ixbalamqué "knew very well which were the roads of Xibalbá; the black, white, red, and blue roads." It is clear that the twins, conceived in Xibalbá, were perfectly familiar with the place and, having inherited the experience of their fathers in accordance with the biological laws already mentioned, they had knowledge beyond that of their progenitors who had paid for their inexperience with their lives for the benefit of their children.

The twins sent out a Xam (mosquito) as a spy to collect information about all that he might see and hear. "Sting each one," they told it. "First, sting the one who shall be seated, and then sting all of them; from now on the blood that you suck from people will be solely for you." "Very well," replied the mosquito.

Through this tactic Hunahpú and Ixbalamqué will learn the names of the Lords of Xibalbá and so get dominance over them, since each person will react on being bitten by the mosquito, and the others will ask him what has happened, calling him by name, and all this the mosquito will communicate to the twins. But, adds the Quiché account, "in reality it wasn't the mosquito that bit and went to hear all the names, but rather a hair that Hunahpú plucked out of his shinbone, and it was this that stung them and obliged them to say their names."

This clearly defines the magical technique of affecting events from a distance, through invisible darts that sting like the mosquito but which really express the personal magical power of the sender. That method, invented by Hunahpú, a sage par excellence, explains the origin of an interesting magical practice employed by one class of Chortí wise men, who "foretell by means of the calf of the leg," imitating the pattern laid down by the god-hero who found out the names of his adversaries by means of a hair torn from his shin. An identical procedure, consisting of throwing out magical darts, is also used by Chortí elders who declare they "have shot the god-Seven" when by magical art they succeed in making the Agrarian deity descend to the center of the earth. A similar method is also mentioned in Mexican sources which say that the sun, having come to a halt, was stung by a mosquito in its leg. Ixtlilxóchitl says of this that

> during the Third Age [equivalent to the Age in which the *Popol Vuh* places the invention of shooting out such magical darts], the sun stood still for one full day without moving from its place; and as the mosquito saw the sun so still and pensive, it said, "Lord of the World, why are you so still and thoughtful and why don't you carry out your duty as you are ordered? Do you want to destroy the world, as you are now doing?" And seeing that the sun was silent and did not answer, the mosquito approached and bit it on the leg. Feeling itself bitten, the sun began to travel its usual course again.

In another version it is Citli who shoots an arrow at the sun but, the arrow having missed its mark, the sun kills Citli.

In the Chortí dramatization of the *Popol Vuh*, the actor playing Hunahpú swiftly throws himself upon the Black Giant representing the Camé, giving the giant a blow in the chest with his fist, during the scene that symbolizes the mosquito's mission against the Lords of Xibalbá.

Thanks to Hunahpú's tactic, the twins gained full knowledge of the names and, thus, the persons of the underworld. Therefore, instead of addressing the wooden puppets as their incautious fathers had done, they pass them by and direct their address to the Camé Lords themselves, calling aloud the name of each one of them.

"This did not please the Lords, that they should know their names. 'Sit down,' the Xibalbans told Hunahpú and Ixbalamqué; but the twins did not obey the order, declaring they knew the seats were red-hot stones."

"All right," the Camé replied resignedly, making the twins enter the Cave of Darkness at once, thinking that they would be overcome there. Then they sent their servants to give the twins cigars and sticks of torch pine, just as they had done with the seven Ahpú. But the youths, prepared against the deceptions of the Xibalbans thanks to their fathers' experience, decided to "change the nature of the torch pine, soaking it in red water so that the watchers would see that it was like the feathers in the tail of the macaw. And as for the cigars, the twins placed fireflies on their tips which lit them up as if the cigars were really burning."

Thanks to these stratagems they did no damage to the torch pine sticks or the cigars, and when their Xibalban watchers thought they were overcome, the twins really were quite all right (note the equivalence of the macaw feathers with fire and the mention of the properties of the female flying beetle which emits a phosphorescent light).

"Then the twins were brought into the presence of the Lords. 'Who are you and where do you come from? Where were you born and whose children are you?' the Lords, suffused with anger, asked the twins, 'Because what they are doing to us is not good,' they told each other. 'Their manners are strange, too.'"

But the twins do not reveal their names, and they reply to the Camé in the same way and using the same frustrating words the Indian of today will use to reply to indiscreet questions put to him by investigators: "Who knows?"

The Grand Council of Xibalbá now places its hopes in the ball game where it thinks it will defeat the youths. But a controversy arises over which ball will be used, that of the twins or of the Camé, the latter having finally to give in and use the ball of Hunahpú, signifying another defeat for the Camé. Because of the symbolism of the ball game, it was a matter of vital importance to the Xibalbans that their ball be used since, as has been explained, the ball represents the head and the players the body of a theogonic entity, and these elements must be perfectly homogenous, which would not be the case if Hunahpú's ball were used, since that would symbolize the youth's ascendancy over the Camé.

The latter then said, "Let's begin, only we will contend together." "Naturally," replied the twins. In the Dance of the Giants the idea set out in this textual reference is expressed in the cruciform dance where the contenders intermingle when they come to the central point of the cross. This allegory reflects the social situation in that ancient time of the transition from the matriarchal to the patriarchal cycle. Its meaning is similar to that of the introduction of the descendants by the paternal line into Ixmucané's family.

Before beginning to play, the chiefs of the Quiché Avernus ask for a short time period, which they use to execute an act of bad faith. They throw out their own ball which knocks over the lance in front of Hunahpú, wounding him. The Camé's intention was to kill the two youthful guests and they desisted only in the face of the twins' vehement protest. "What is this?" said Hunahpú and Ixbalamqué, "Do you want to kill us? Didn't you ask us to come here, and didn't your own messengers come for us? Really we shouldn't have come; we will go back immediately," the youths told them.

Once more the Xibalbans are mastered by the twins, because now they have to entreat them to stay.

"Don't go away, children; let's continue to play ball, and we will use your ball," they told the twins. "All right," said the latter; and using their own ball Hunahpú and Ixbalamqué defeat their adversaries.

This contest between the team of the true and of the false gods, of the white against the dark forces, represented in the struggle of the white Gavite against the Black Giant in the Chortí drama, symbolizes the strife of good against evil, of civilization against barbarism, light against shadow — as with the *diurnus versus nocturnus* of the Romans — and of knowledge against ignorance. Hunahpú here proclaims other patterns of conduct for the ethical person, who must act always according to his or her duty. During his whole existence the god-hero extols ethics, by both words and example, as the highest expression of human life, aiming to delineate the ideal type of Maya man and woman. He proclaims the fact that it is ethics alone which leads to a plane of salvation and that exalts the human being. He proclaims that such qualities will be obtained by means of education based on the principles of the Hunahpú code that is preserved in native traditions. This code consequently embodies the principle of justice, and as such it is invoked by the Chortí in the name of the Child King of Justice (*Niño Rey de la Justicia*) in his role as Chief of the Tribunal of Justice.

The treacherous action of the Xibalbans, a mark of beings of undeveloped ethical stature who are equated with evil-natured entities, accords with the belief that natural death does not exist and that death is produced through the power of evil. The name of Mictlán itself — "the place of those who have been *killed*" — the Mexican equivalent of Xibalbá, reflects that idea.

Perplexed by their repeated defeats, the Camé ask themselves, "What will we do to overcome them?" Then they promptly tell the twins, "We want four jars filled with flowers." "Very well, what kind of flowers do you wish?" they replied. "A handful of red flowers, one of white flowers, another of yellow flowers, and another large bunch of yellow flowers." "All right," replied the youths. Note in this mention of the ritual colors the preponderance of yellow, the color of the flower of death.

Then the Xibalbans rejoiced with the thought that this time they had defeated the guests, since "Where will they get those flowers?" they asked each other. "If you don't bring us our flowers, we will sacrifice you," they told Hunahpú and Ixbalamqué. (Observe here the constant reference to human sacrifice during the Third Age, the characteristic practice of a barbaric culture but one not permitted by Mayan ethics.)

Putting into motion this new trial which the Camé thought would be decisive, they made the twins go into the Cave of Flint Knives, the second place of torture in Xibalbá. But the youths did not die there inasmuch as Hunahpú and flint were consubstantial. In fact, Hunahpú was created from a piece of flint, the very material that embodies Hunahpú's functions as Lord of the Cold — the equivalent of Ixtli in Mexican mythology[1] — and Hunahpú found himself in his proper element. Obsidian, symbolic of the young god during his stay in the underworld, still serves as an amulet against evil conjurations. In addition to what we have said about this, it is worth recording that in Mexico the actions of the sinister owl-men, dangerous black magicians, are warded off by contrary actions. A plaque of obsidian, placed in a cup full of water beside the door, reduces the most powerful sorcery to nothing.[2]

While they were in the Cave of Flint Knives, Hunahpú and Ixbalamqué told the flint knives, their jailors, "the meat of all animals will be yours." At once the knives became motionless.

How much meaning there is in these few words! The twins here reaffirm the law prohibiting human sacrifice set forth in the religious principles of Maya culture, opposed

---

[1] Girard, *Los Chortís*, "Religion."
[2] Beuchat, *Manual de Arqueología americana*, Madrid, 1918.

to the laws of the cycle of barbarism personified by the Lords of Xibalbá. From then on the flint knives would not feed upon human flesh but on that of animals, since it was their flesh that Hunahpú gave them in place of his own. For that reason the twins were neither wounded nor killed by the now immobile flint knives.

Taking advantage of the hypnotic state of their flint wardens, the twins call upon various kinds of cutting ants, telling them: "Come *all together;* now go and bring us the flowers the Lords have asked for." The ants assented and went to get the flowers from the gardens of Hun Camé and Vukup Camé.

Here we are given an explanation of the origin of the ants' communal feeding and living habits: Hunahpú endows them with a social order based on the Maya model. These insects, formerly the followers of Zipacná and used by Hun Bátz to torture Hunahpú, are now the faithful allies of the twins just as the Tukur became servants to Ixquic. All this manifests the progressive evolution in the terrestrial sphere toward a new order of things.

Evading the vigilance of the sentinels of Xibalbá in the garden, the ants cut the flowers requested by the twins. The sentinels uselessly called out among the tree branches where they maintained their vigil: "Ixpurpugüek! Pujuyu!" (night birds, whose names are onomatopoeic, imitate their song).

Quickly the ants carried away four bowls of flowers. Thus the twins once again overcame the Xibalban Lords "whose faces became purple because of the theft of the flowers." The Camé rebuked the keepers of their garden for their misfeasance, but these said they had not even felt it when their own tails were cut along with the flower stems. The Camé lacerated their mouths in punishment for permitting what was under their care to be stolen.

Then once again the Camé played ball with the twins and the match was a draw, all agreeing to continue to play at dawn the following day.

The twins were then sent into the Cave of Cold "where it was so cold that it made one sick. In this House of Cold a thick ice whipped about, which the twins dissipated by burning old tree trunks," so they did not die there and were quite hale and hearty when dawn arrived.

When the messengers from the Xibalban Lords came, the twins went out with them and stood before the Camé, who were amazed to see them alive. "How is it that they did not perish there?" they asked each other.

After another ball game the Camé made the two youths go into the Cave of Jaguars, a grotto full of these animals. But the twins spoke to the cats, saying: "Do not bite us, we have something to give you." They threw bones to the animals who seized them to gnaw upon. The noise they made cracking the bones caused the Xibalbans to think that their opponents had finally perished and the idea "made their hearts drunk with pleasure." But next day the twins emerged from the cave unscathed, which is easily explained by the fact that the jaguar is the nahual or alter ego of Hunahpú's mother and is also consubstantial with Ixbalamqué (*balam:* jaguar).

Thenceforth the jaguar, formerly an instrument of the evil forces, becomes an instrument of the true deities; and we have here the explanation of the phenomenon whereby the jaguar, a demon for peoples of low culture, is a god in the Quiché-Maya theogony.[3]

The astonishment of the Camé now passed all bounds. "What kind of people are you? Where do you come from?" they all asked. They speedily put the two into the Cave of

---

[3]Girard, *Los Chortís*, "Ethnography and Religion."

Fire, where there was nothing but flames. But the twins were neither burned, suffocated, nor roasted, and they emerged in excellent condition next morning. Saved by their mother in the earlier trial, this time their father, the old Fire god, saved them, the element of fire being consubstantial with Hunahpú, Solar god and god of Fire. The Xibalbans were "disheartened" by the failure of every one of their stratagems. Nevertheless they made a last effort, forcing the two youths into the Cave of Bats. Only vampire bats filled this cave, the lair of the great Camalzotz, the one which was like Chakitzam, who immediately killed and consumed all that came into its presence. But the twins slept there protected by their blowguns (the blowgun or solar ray protected them magically), and the vampire bats in the cave did not bite them.

The twins were thinking and talking together amid the great noise of all the bats when suddenly another Camalzotz flew down from the sky. Then there was a profound silence, all the bats ceasing their chatter and flying about, and clustering over the open ends of the twins' blowguns. At that moment the celestial vampire cut off Hunahpú's head with its talon, leaving the head lying there separate from his body. "What happened was done solely to make known its power and function as Celestial god."

This happened when Ixbalamqué asked Hunahpú whether it was already sunrise, and Hunahpú, stepping outside, "feeling a keen desire to look through the mouth of his blowgun to see if the sun was up," was suddenly decapitated by the celestial vampire. Ixbalamqué, frightened, exclaimed, "At last they have beaten us."

Immediately, on orders of the Camé, Hunahpú's head was placed atop the building above the wall forming one side of the ball court, while all the Xibalbans rejoiced to see the lopped-off head of their adversary.

This is one of the most difficult episodes to interpret, and yet it is one of great importance since, on the one hand, it symbolizes the death of the maize grain — equated with the head of Hunahpú — in the bosom of the earth preparing to transform itself into the plant; and, on the other, the death of the sun before it surges forth triumphant, as occurs in the resurrection of Hunahpú after he has destroyed his foes. Ixbalamqué, alone in the midst of the infernal beings, exemplifies the functions of the Lunar goddess who unaided defends humanity against the monsters of the night when the sun has disappeared below the horizon. From that time on the jaguars (*balam*), nahuals or alter egos of the female deity, watch over the Indian's village and his roads and lands during the night.

To our way of thinking it seems illogical that after triumphing over the most difficult trials and defeating his fearful opponents all along the line, Hunahpú should be beheaded by a vampire which comes down out of the sky. But for the mystical mentality of the native American, this allegory explains the causes of a natural phenomenon by the intervention of a supernatural one, agreeable with the instinct inherent in man which drives him to learn the causes of things. The vampire, in fact, symbolizes the divine spirit that descends from heaven and manifests in the maize, it being necessary that the grain — the equivalent of Hunahpú's head — should die to become transformed on germinating within the earth.

The depiction of the descent of the celestial vampire, or divine nutriment, and the subsequent death of the god of Maize is an ever-present theme in native art and denotes a fundamental article of faith of Quiché-Maya culture. Elsewhere we have amplified in all their details Mayan conceptions regarding fertilization of the earth, the death of the grain, its germination and metamorphosis into a food plant, as well as the way these are depicted in Mayan art.[4] The enormous importance given to each one of the phases of the creative and germinative process of maize indicates that we are dealing with a matter of vital interest for Maya culture, one that must have been the object of prolonged and detailed observation by the Indian. We have established comparisons among the diverse artistic expressions of these ideas during the archaeological period and in the present day, and have also referred to the monumental sculptures of the celestial vampire placed high up in Maya temples in the part representing the center of the sky or heaven, from which the divine bat descends vertically to earth as do the sun's rays when the daystar goes through its zenith.

The theme of the descending god — which goes back to the period before the *Popol Vuh* — is represented in the most varied forms. But none in the Quiché text is so suggestive as the figure which follows, from the Tro-Cortes Codex, showing god B with the face of a bat throwing itself from heaven, carrying in its hand the hatchet whose sharp edge will lop off the head of the Maize god. Its look corresponds with the *Popol Vuh's* description of this being "which immediately kills, consuming all that comes before it," and accords with native beliefs that all contact with the sacred is dangerous. The parallel between the Quiché version and the figure of god B converted into the Vampire god is clear and, moreover, establishes their theogonic identity from the very name given the deity figured in the Maya codex, which is identical with that given in the *Popol Vuh:* Chakitzam (according to the Rodas-Villacorta translation). It is well known that god B is the figure of the Agrarian god called Chac or Itzamná.[5]

---

[4]Girard, *Los Chortís*, chapters on science and religion.
[5]Girard, *Los Chortís*, "Religion."

The cut-off head of the Maize god or Hunahpú, corresponding to that most precious grain, is represented with frequency in Mesoamerican iconography. Inverted heads of Ahau, symbolizing the grain that falls from on high, can be seen both in the Mayan codices, where it usually appears in the form of a breastplate of god B, and on the statue which present-day Quichés near Chichicastenango venerate, while in Zapotec and Huetar art those severed heads are held to be the Agrarian deity. On Mayan stelae the same motif is alternatively figured by either a head or the sign *kin*, its equivalent.

Below is reproduced a figure taken from page 42 of the Dresden Codex, showing god B with hatchet raised to cut off the head of the young Maize god. To the right can be seen a bowl with the sign *kan*, *crowned* with the headdress of the Maize god, a symbolic sign of the sacred kernel, equated with the separated head of Hunahpú. It is most significant to find this scene placed under one (in the frame above it) that represents the acts which immediately precede germination of the kernel. God B, exempli-

FIGURE 16.

fying the elder's standard of conduct, is seen in the attitude of entreating the descent of divine grace, and then in that of sowing the maize which falls into the interior of the earth where it will germinate. Its germination is reproduced in the lower drawing, which symbolizes the underworld, that very Xibalbá wherein Hunahpú is de-

capitated.[6] In another drawing in the Dresden Codex, one
can see the head of the Maize god upon a pyramid, a posi-

FIGURE 17.

tion that recalls the placement of Hunahpú's head on top
of the Camé's house where it symbolizes both the maize
kernel and the game ball, i.e., the sun.

[6]For more detailed information, see Girard, *Los Chortís*, chapters on
religion.

The scene described in the *Popol Vuh* and so vividly portrayed in the Dresden Codex is objectified with cruel realism, proper to the Aztecs, in Toxcatl (the moment of the sun's passing through the zenith). At that instant the victim who represented Tezcatlipoca was sacrificed at the top of the pyramid, but his body was carried down to the foot of the structure where its head was cut off, to symbolize the falling of the maize kernel — equated with the head of Tezcatlipoca — from heaven to earth.

This mimetic rite is illustrated in a picture in the Borgia Codex showing an anthropomorphic god that falls, head first, down a stairway. In a drawing of a *tecpatl* (flint knife) on page 54 of the Vatican Codex, the obsidian blade opens into two, with another blade coming out of it, a vivid demonstration of the unfoldment of the Agrarian deity which comes down from heaven to fecundate the earth and, once within it, becomes the germ of the maize.

Within these allegories lies the monotheist idea whereby the young Maize deity is conceived as a hypostasis of the Agrarian god, and the idea is expressed in the most varied ways. Elsewhere we have given the picture from Mexican codices of the mythological separation of Tezcatlipoca's foot, swallowed by the earth-monster in order to become a stalk of maize. From the leg wound flows a swelling of blood, the colorful pictorial representation of the divine sacrifice whose double object is to fertilize the earth and give itself utterly for the nurturing of humankind. These concepts, illustrated in the sacrifice of the seven Ahpú and in the scene of Hunahpú's beheading, remain very much alive among the Chortís who assert that Saint Manuel (the Agrarian god) gave his blood for the nourishment of his sons. Knowing the symbolic equivalence of the divine blood and maize, we understand the esoteric significance of the allegory in which the god pours its own life into human life. But it was not possible to develop such a conception except after man had gained perfect knowledge of the plant's growth process, and especially of the mystery of germination.

This development in the economic and religious process, the fruit of human experience, has to modify the conceptions of sex regulating the regime of family and society, as well as the doctrines of the ultimate purpose of things and the way of conceiving the world, matters which are related because the former are necessarily linked with and subordinated to the latter.

We have seen that Hunahpú exemplifies the operations of the *milpa* to the last detail, and that his teachings in themselves form a veritable agricultural code that to this day guides the practices of the Quiché-Maya farmer. But, after the sowing, all information ceases since the youth departs for Xibalbá, leaving planted a stalk of maize whose growth is linked with the fate that will befall him in the underworld, where he dramatizes the mystery of germination. The length of the text describing the trials undergone there by Hunahpú and Ixbalamqué reveals the importance of the germinative process. The struggles that the youths make — like the maize grain — are set out in all their smallest detail until we reach the fifth place of torture, that is, the center of the cosmic plane. In his function as Maize god, Hunahpú must occupy the center of that plane — as much in the underworld as on the surface of the earth, symbolized by the house in whose center were sown the maize plants — in perpendicular position to the center of heaven from which the divine spirit will fall vertically as do the sun's rays when the daystar goes through its zenith, the position that determines the sowing of the grain.[7] Mi-

---

[7] Girard, *Los Chortís*, "Tzolkín."

nute details are given regarding the conditions that favor its protection against evil beings: the help of the god of Fire which produces the heat in the earth's womb to give life to the infant; the constant aid of the Lunar goddess and its direct influence upon germination, expressed in its incitement of Hunahpú to "go out and see if it dawns"; the marked wish the latter felt to look through the mouth of his blowgun, which could not more eloquently express the impelling force of the germ and its will to grow toward the earth's surface.

All these scenes, repeated in different forms in Mayan art and glyph, form the theme of the theogonic complex known as the Lords of Night, which the Chilam Balam of Chumayel describes as beings having "pointed helmets," with which they bore through the roof of their subterranean abode to come out on the surface, as does the maize grain.[8]

The germination of maize was without doubt the most difficult mystery for the primeval mind to understand, and only after a long process of domestication, when the grain had taken a form that allowed it to be equated with the divine head, game ball, or solar sphere, was the miracle of germination conceived as an effect of supernatural forces because beyond human comprehension. Until that time the discovery of wild maize was not really a major one; but the application of knowledge gained through long experience in dealing with the plant was actually the real beginning of agriculture. Because concepts of fertility of the earth and fecundity of woman are inseparable, any new interpretation of the one produced its secondary effects on the other concept. In this case, discovery of the laws of

---

[8]For details and illustrations, see ibid., "Religion" and "Esotericism of the Monuments."

germination had to modify the idea held about human fecundity, since they obey the same causal principle.

During the matriarchal cycle the woman is the center of the procreative act as well as of society; but now it is Deity itself which intervenes in the production of the being, becoming the efficient cause of the phenomenon of reproduction in which man places the semen in the woman's womb. But the metamorphosis of the semen or seed can only take place thanks to supernatural action. The male's role now is no longer merely accidental but of primary interest, and this is projected in the act of sowing which from now on will be the man's exclusive task, the reverse of the situation prevailing in the earlier period when the man prepared the orchard but the woman planted it, just as she alone reared her children. It is interesting to relate the primordial concepts of native American women with those of the Papuans, who believe that pregnancy can be caused by the rain falling upon them from above and are unaware that it takes place through sexual penetration (Malinowski). Sowing the fields is incumbent upon the man only, because the introduction of the sowing stick into the earth and placement of the seed in the hole it makes symbolize the role he plays in the sexual act, from the time when he gained awareness of his role in the reproduction of the species. From being the center, the woman has now become a mere agent. Parallel with this the man is conceded rights that during the matriarchal period were reserved exclusively to the woman, and the new order of things becomes reflected in the mythology.

The supernatural fecundation of Ixquic by the seven Ahpú signals the beginning of new sexual conceptions; Ixquic's role is overshadowed by that of Hunahpú, which reflects the norms of masculine conduct. And thereafter, work in the *milpa* is properly "the work" and the farmer "the worker," the same judgment that Aristotle will express at a later date.

We have underlined the fact that both the procreative act and the activity in the *milpa* are expressed by a common verb: *trabajar*, to labor. This emphasizes once again the close interdependence and interaction of religion, family, society, economy, sexuality, work, property, and government in the dynamic process from which come forth the social forms and institutions of Maya culture. In fact, the evolution of its religious thought goes hand in hand with that of its maize cultivation, as well as with a general transformation in all aspects of the culture, which indicates the necessary interrelation among its structural elements. A genuine revolution took place in conception of the cosmos, of life, and of death. Discovery of the laws of maize germination is accompanied by these new perceptions of being and cosmos, and the indivisibility of these three elements is seen in the fact that Hunahpú personifies them all at one and the same time.

Besides symbolizing the process of the maize kernel that, falling into the earth, dies only to convert itself into the germ of a plant, Hunahpú exemplifies the destiny of the human being who, like the maize grain that dies, goes to the underworld and returns gloriously, as the young god-hero returned. In this allegory is proclaimed the belief in the immortality of the soul, the supreme consolation of humankind. Thus the fear of death, which darkly shadowed life during the previous racial period, was lost. Without doubt such fear was the motivating cause of the system of secondary interment, in the belief that the soul's life was subject to the duration of the material remains of the deceased, which one therefore attempted to preserve. Now man is immortal like the gods, a principle which ele-

vates him to a superior spiritual plane and resolves the
problem of the relations of the material with the spiritual,
at the same time defining the nature of the soul, whose
essence is divine. In the future, fears about the end of the
cosmos will be the great problem of Quiché-Maya thought,
since the universe is susceptible of being destroyed at the
end of each cycle as it had been at the end of each prehistoric Age; and this idea was what led to the creation by
the Mayas of a practically infinite cycle. Fear of personal
death had disappeared after Hunahpú taught man how he
must live so as to free himself from afterdeath perils.

We have elsewhere described the hardships the Chortí
had to undergo during his passage through the underworld, where he had to cross the nine parts of Avernus
wherein constant dangers threaten.[9] Those sectors are the
same as the ones made known to us in the *Popol Vuh* in the
course of Hunahpú's and Ixbalamqué's extraordinary odys-
sey. But they overcame all difficulties and taught man
how to free himself from them. If the deceased has observed the rules of religious ethics instituted by the hero-
god, he will emerge triumphant from the test of Xibalbá.
Like Hunahpú, he will cross the infernal rivers on threads,
untouched by their waters. To ward off the ice in the Cave
of Cold he will build a fire using the flint and steel his relatives will not fail to include in his mortuary outfit. The
flame of the fire symbolizes the old Fire god who so oppor-
tunely sustained the twins when they lit tree trunks in
that cave, the origin of the Chortí's custom of providing
the dead with a striking steel. The Cave of Darkness will
be illumined by pouring water on the grave. To cross the
Cave of Flint Knives, where one must walk over sharp
flints, the dead person is provided with a pair of new

---

[9]Girard, *Los Chortís*, "Ethnography."

sandals; and to protect him from the dreadful animals, he is given a cord or rosary symbolizing the divine serpent, who will be his defender.[10] At the end of this dread journey, the deceased ascends to heaven.

Similar customs were observed by the Mexicans, who prepared their dead for overcoming the dangers of the postmortem experience and reaching the mansion of Mictlantecutli, to whom they must offer, among other things, pine torches (recall those the Camé demanded of their victims).

But if the Indians of Quiché-Maya culture did not fear death, they feared the dead, because these are accustomed imperiously to demand their rights if relatives do not fulfill their obligations to them, since both living and dead form one single community having reciprocal rights and duties.

Such a well-grounded knowledge of what takes place in the afterdeath world implies a new scientific vision of correlated astronomical and cosmic phenomena, and this development is made evident in the contrast between the conduct of the seven Ahpú and that of the twins during their journey to the underworld. We have already emphasized that at the start the universe was conceived of as being formed of only two cosmic planes, heaven and earth, in accordance with the logic of primeval man for whom cognition of the visible was easier than intuition of the hidden. The mechanism of the heavenly bodies was then unknown, and discovery of the principles of scientific astronomy came about only as a result of the triumph of Hunahpú and Ixbalamqué, parallel with creation of the sun, moon, and the Pleiades and integration of the third plane into the cosmic system. From the point of view of anthropocentric theory, the sun at the end of its daily pas-

---

[10]For details, see ibid.

sage goes into the bosom of the earth where it continues its journey in an inverse sense, illuminating the kingdom of the dead, crossing through the nadir and reappearing in the east. The working of its underworld trajectory is identical with the course pursued by the daystar in the celestial vault; and this is expressed in the ball game which symbolizes, both above as well as below, the same divine proceeding.

The seven Ahpú were able to play ball while on earth, but they could not do so in the underworld. Their innocence and ignorance of the nature of Xibalbá reflect the ignorance of the period, and because of it they were easily overcome. But from their failure is born the experience that they will pass on to the twins by virtue of the law of heredity that we have referred to: an eloquent image reflective of the efforts man made to garner experience and transmit to his offspring a knowledge and a tradition that would steadily grow with the passage of time.

Hunahpú and Ixbalamqué "already knew about the four roads" of the lower plane, and they descended into Xibalbá invested with all of their "elements of splendor." Familiar with the stumbling blocks in the infernal region, and having perfect knowledge of its dwellers whom they defeat, they render harmless the roadways of that world so that in future the sun as well as the deceased can travel along them safely. Hunahpú alternately symbolizes the triumph of the daystar, when he plays ball and defeats his opponents, and the role of the maize grain and of death in the caves of torture, making known the respective destinies of the maize plant and of humankind.

Quiché-Maya culture has now run through its entire life cycle and has a conception of the world that reflects its scientific-religious philosophy, resting in germ during the previous cycles. Perfect cosmic harmony is now established, and this order of things projects itself in the family and theogonic order which now reflect that harmony. Since man learned how to work and to take the social role intended for him, conjugal harmony is absolute because husband and wife are blended in an indivisible whole.

This very close relation between husband and wife, the consequence of the new sexual and religious conceptions, denotes the principle of duality within unity whose beginning is found in this epoch, and the same principle is projected into the world of the supernatural, since the goddesses are no more than hypostases of the gods. This manner of conception is so difficult for the Western mind that some students of sacred traditions interpret it as hermaphroditism.[11]

The contrast with conjugal life of the Third Age is emphasized in the paragraph from the Chumayel scripture, already cited, in which the men (or gods) of that Third Age who believed that they were gods but were not, are termed evil because *they did not sow seed* (sexual concept) and, although they are connected *fragment to fragment* (but do not blend as one single being), did not say what they loved.

Before continuing with the Quiché narration, we should observe that Hunahpú establishes the work norms for one single *milpa*, corresponding to the first or the one called "*milpa* of fire," whose sowing is determined by the first passing of the daystar through the zenith. That correspondence appears in the episode of the descent of the celestial vampire, which according to Chortí theology can occur only during that first transit by the sun through the line of the parallel. This explains the great religious importance of the first *milpa*, until this day regarded by the

---

[11]Girard, *Los Chortís*, "Religion."

Indians of Guatemala as the most sacred and obligatory in character. At the same time, it supports what we have said elsewhere that at first this was the only sowing made by the Maya's remote ancestors, and that their existence depended upon it.[12] It was not until astronomical and meteorological knowledge was perfected that two or more sowings of the *milpa* were made by the Indians.

---

[12]See ibid., "Tzolkín."

11

The Deification of Hunahpú and Ixbalamqué

FINDING herself alone in the midst of the underworld beings (like the moon amid the monsters of the night), Ixbalamqué conceives a stratagem to prevent Hunahpú's head from being used as the game ball by the Xibalbans. She brings together the animals of all categories, great and small, asks what is their manner of feeding themselves, and charges each to go and fetch its particular food. There follows the description of what the various animals eat. Among the remains of their meals, Ixbalamqué picks up a shell of a bottle gourd (*Cucurbita ficifolia B.*) which very easily simulates a head in form, cutting two holes in it as eyes. Thanks to the divine inspiration fallen from the Center of Heaven into the nether world where the Cave of Bats was, she and the animals succeeded in devising a convincing "replacement" for Hunahpú's head.

Every creative act must take place during the night so as to be concluded by dawn. When the horizon was tinted with red, the smile of the dawn came to shine upon the artificial head of Hunahpú, which was perfect, since the bottle-gourd shell really looked like the bone of his skull.

We note here once more the equating of the shell with bone, as in the case of the gourds identified with the skulls of the seven Ahpú. This part also illustrates the procedure for making idols or "semblances of the gods," an exceedingly delicate operation whose execution requires all kinds of precautions on the part of the maker. The latter must take himself into the thickets of the woods where the sun's rays do not penetrate, or any profane sound whatever, being required to be in a state of purity so as to lift his spirit toward the divinity that inspires his actions, as it inspired those of Ixbalamqué.

Ixbalamqué then goes out to play alone, confronting the Xibalbans and, as expected, the game begins at dawn. The Camé, vainglorious over their apparent triumph, demand that Hunahpú's head be used as the ball during the game they will play against Ixbalamqué (note the clear correspondence of the head of the Solar god with the game ball).

> Then the Xibalbans threw their ball. Ixbalamqué stopped it in front of her lance and then kicked it high over the house by the ball court, where it came to rest in a hole in the roof. Then a rabbit, having been previously instructed by her in what to do, came out and began to run about and leap. All the Xibalbans took up pursuit of the small animal, "shouting and running after the rabbit."

This intimate cooperation between the Lunar goddess (Ixbalamqué) and the rabbit is most clearly expressed in the lunar hieroglyph illustrated here, taken from the Borgia Codex. It shows a large, narrow-mouthed pitcher — symbol of the moon — inside of which is a rabbit.

In this way, says the *Popol Vuh*, Hunahpú's head did not disappear and the sowing of the bottle-gourds by Ixbalamqué did not terminate. In fact, the bottle-gourd was substituted for the game ball, and because Ixbalamqué threw the ball onto the roof, a custom began of placing bottle-gourds under the ceiling of houses. Aside from its etiological meaning, this legend expressly mentions that discovery of this new plant is due to a woman.

FIGURE 18. Lunar glyph in the Borgia Codex, according to Seler.

Because of the clever disappearance of Hunahpú's head, the evil intentions of the Xibalbans were thwarted, and when they struck the substitute game ball it broke into a thousand pieces, "splashing their flesh with white blood like unto tears." Note the equivalence of fruit sap, blood, and tears, and that it is expressed in the semantic connection among these words, whose etymology is defined by the legends from the *Popol Vuh*. This was how the Lords of Xibalbá were once more defeated by the twins, and how Hunahpú recovered his whole body.

After such pitiless struggles between the forces of good and those of evil, in which the latter were continually overcome but not reduced to impotence, the twins foreknew that they must die, since this was their destiny as redeemers of humankind. Intuitively they knew that their implacable enemies planned to burn them in a fire in a stone oven, but that they would not die in reality, because they were immortal. This mention of the stone oven is interesting because it appears to be similar to the *temascal* or steam bath wherein the Quiché Indian offers his sweat to the sun, doubtless in that way commemorating the sacrifice made by Hunahpú.

The twins get help from Xulú and Pacám, great sages and seers who "see all." This repeats the appearance of supernatural counselors on the scene, such as took place in the earlier episode of the struggle against Vukup Cakix.

Hunahpú and Ixbalamqué say to these counselors:

> The Lords of Xibalbá will ask you about our death, which they are planning and preparing for, because we have not died nor have we been sacrificed in the places of torment. If they consult you about the kind of death they should select for us, asking, "Wouldn't it be well to throw their bones into the ravines?" you will say, "That won't do because then they will return to life." If they say, "Shouldn't we hang them in the trees?" you will reply, "Under no circumstances, because they will only continue to exist." And when, for the third time, they ask, "Then shall we throw their bones into the river?" you will reply, "By all means. It will be well that they should disappear; and first their bones should be ground up like maize flour — each one ground separately. Then throw them immediately into the river where the fountain gushes forth so that the bone-dust will be scattered through forest and hill."

"That is what you will reply," the twins told the sages as they said their farewells, knowing beforehand how they were to die.

Such instructions describe three different ways of disposing of the dead which pertained in all probability to successive eras: burial in caves or gorges in the first; and the practice of placing the cadaver in a tree; and finally, the secondary burial practiced during the matriarchal cycle, described in an earlier chapter.

With regard to the last form of disposal, cremation is meant. This is the method chosen by Hunahpú, which is remembered by the Quichés on the day named Hunahpú by the lighting of a bonfire on the tomb of their dead while they pray for them.

In the method favored by Hunahpú for reducing his bones to dust, like maize flour, we also have the origin of the *cernada* (a mixture of earth and the leaven of cooked maize), a specific still used by the Chortís to prevent fires by lightning or celestial fire. Water cannot be used to put out such fires, because water like fire is a celestial element that must be countered by earthly elements. In the same way, the maize kernels intended for the sowing are sterilized by mixing them with ashes, that magical substance into which Hunahpú and Ixbalamqué have to transmute themselves, and which has the virtue of destroying malign spirits. Such procedure, originating in myth, corresponds to a practical application in the native agriculture which employs ashes to protect the maize kernels against the rot and damage these can suffer when placed in the earth.

The Xibalbans make a great bonfire, a kind of oven, feeding the fire with tree trunks and branches, and at once the twins arrive escorted by their guards. Hun Camé by trickery tries to make them go into the red-hot oven, offering them of his drink if they will then go through the fire four times. This is the origin of the curious custom, observed in Ocotepeque and Jocotán during the festivals of the patron saint, consisting of throwing a person four times over the flames of a bonfire lit beneath a ceiba tree in the public plaza.

But the twins are alert and are not fooled by the Xibalban. "Do you think we don't realize that we will die in the fire?" they reply. And rejecting Hun Camé's overture, "they face each other and holding hands, the two siblings throw themselves into the bonfire, dying there together."

All the Xibalbans were filled with joy and climbed upon the hills, whistling, shouting, and lifting clasped hands over their heads. "Now we have indeed won because finally they let themselves be vanquished." Centuries later the Aztecs would copy this mythological account when they composed their own version of the creation of the sun and moon.

Just as the twins had planned, the Xibalbans consulted Xulú and Pacám about the best way to dispose of the remains of Hunahpú and Ixbalamqué, and, following their advice, ordered the ashes thrown into the river. The ground-up bones were not picked up by the current, however, but sank to the bottom of the water where they became transformed into two handsome adolescents having the same appearance as Hunahpú and Ixbalamqué who, like the Phoenix bird, are reborn from their ashes (the dead return to trouble the living so long as the latter still owe them something). On the fifth day they made an appearance and were seen in the water by the populace, but now they appeared to be fish-men (*winak-car*).

Here we have a fact of great interest, insofar as the young Solar and Maize god is identified as the numeral god-Five, according to the selfsame Chortí method by which the number of days falling between the sowing of the maize (symbolized here by the throwing of the ashes into the river) and its transformation into a tiny shoot of maize with its first leaf, determines the number that characterizes the Maize god. This is supported by what we have said elsewhere with regard to the original area of maize cultivation, which had to be located in a fertile land having a hot climate in which the grain could convert itself into a small shoot and leaf five days after the sowing.[1] All

---

[1]Girard, *Los Chortís*, "Tzolkín."

this corroborates once more the historical character of the *Popol Vuh*, written in a region where maize needs twice that number of days to sprout.

Another important feature of this episode is the twins' transformation into fish, which is to say that they took the form of their zoological nahual. From the most remote archaeological horizon and in the various cultures imitative of the Quiché-Maya, to the mythology of present-day Indians, the fish is in fact the nahual of the young Maize god. The merit of the Quiché account consists precisely in the fact that it gives us the mythic origin of this aspect of that deity. Again there is emphasized here the beauty of the young god and his companion, an aesthetic ideal which Quiché-Mayan art always strove to reproduce.

On the following day the twins disguised themselves as beggars, and were seen as such by the Xibalbans. The two did a number of amusing things, dancing the dances of the Cux, the Iboy, and also the Ixtzul and Chitic (the one walking on stilts). The dance on stilts is still performed among the Cakchiquels of Antigua and was known to the Maya of Yucatán, according to references in Landa, and appears on page 36 of the Tro-Cortes Codex, as reproduced here.

In the four dances mentioned above, Hunahpú, as the god-Five, and his inseparable companion, formalize the diagram of the twenty-day period or uinal with its subdivisions by teaching for the first time dances of a ritual and time-computing character that the Indians of today continue to perform, such as the Dance of the Giants.[2]

The twins did many remarkable things, says the Quiché epic. They seemed to burn themselves as if they had really done it, and then returned to their original

---

[2]Girard, *Los Chortís*, chapter 13.

condition. Then they cut each other to pieces, one killing the other, the one killed being immediately revived by the other. The Xibalbans looked with amazement upon all that they did, and the twins repeated these things as the prelude to their coming victory over the Camé.

Those details of the prodigious technique of magic invented by the twins are faithfully reproduced in the Chortí Drama of the Giants. We find them also in the following description which Sahagún gives us of the magical practices of the Huastecs:

> They were adept at creating illusions by which they tricked people, making them see the false as true, such as believing that houses were burning which were not, or causing to appear a fountain with fishes when there was none, nothing except an illusion to the eyes; and that they killed themselves, cutting their flesh into pieces, and other things that were only appearances and not real.

That quotation could be a page torn from the Quiché codex as well as a colorful description of the scene dramatized by the Chortís, all of which shows the intimate cultural connection among these peoples and the great stability of their traditions which have endured without variation in groups separated from the common cultural trunk centuries before our own era.

FIGURE 19.

All of Hunahpú's triumphs spring from his knowledge of magic resulting from divine revelation or inspiration. Magic, inseparable from ceremonial action and from science, is the knowledge which conquers ignorance, the intelligence that overcomes force — or the clumsy methods of deception practiced by the Xibalbans.

Now a particular aspect of the magical sciences comes into play: imitative magic, which Hunahpú and Ixbalamqué teach for the first time, a science that will in future form the fundamental basis of Quiché-Maya ritual. The twins "repeated and performed over again" the same acts so that the Xibalbans would imitate them. We have reached the point in this dramatic poem at which the main action is developed.

The Camé sent their messengers to call upon the twins with flattery. "We would that you come and perform again your extraordinary dances before us, since we wish to see how you do them."

But the twins beg off, alleging that because of their very ugly faces, with such large eyes (an allusion to the use of ceremonial masks), they are not fit to appear before such great lords. "What will the poor people say, our comrades who also wish to see our dances and entertain themselves by them?"

In a concise but accurate and beautiful way, as with all Mayan literary forms, there is expressed in this quotation the principle of social ethics that governs the indigenous community and preserves a stable social order based upon an equality of rights and obligations. It is a wonderful proclamation of the fundamental principles of Mayan democracy wherein neither poor nor rich existed.

Faced with the insistence of the Camé's messengers, Hunahpú and Ixbalamqué decide to go, but with such reluctance and ill will that their ushers have to whip them forward in order to hurry their arrival before the masters of Xibalbá. Hiding their faces they arrived full of humility, prostrating themselves in reverence and humbleness, showing an exaggerated respect before the Lords. "They definitely arrived in an attitude of poverty and misery," says the *Popol Vuh*. This pathetic picture is a defense of humility, resignation, and poverty in the face of the Camé's pomp and arrogance. A like conception is found at the heart of the legend in Mexican mythology of the poor god and rich god who compete for the title of Solar god, the poor god winning out.

The Xibalban chiefs ask Hunahpú and Ixbalamqué to tell them the race *and the mountain* from which they come. They ask them also for their genealogical connection, querying them about their mother and their father. "Where do you come from?" the Camé asked. "We do not know, my Lord. Nor do we know the faces of our mother or our father; we were very young when they died," replied the twins. The series of questions put to them reveals the type of social organization of the time, linked with territorial status and based upon the matrilineal culture of the hamlet, in which the "mountain" is the fatherland (*patria*). The preeminence of mother over father is seen in the order of the questions.

The twins do not reveal their identity, for the reasons given in previous chapters. Then the Xibalban chiefs said, "It is well. Now perform for us so that we may marvel, and we shall pay you to see it." "We want nothing, because in truth you will be frightened when you see us," they replied to the Lords (reward for work performed had already been the rule during the Third Age; but the twins will accept nothing).

"Don't be embarrassed, you won't frighten us. Now, dance! And do first the part where you kill each other and cut each other up; and next burn our house. Do everything that you know how to do; we want to witness it," the Camé told them.

As they began their dance with shouts, all the people of Xibalbá crowded around to see what they did. This passage exemplifies and evokes the clamor that precedes the performance of the Chortí Drama of the Giants and quickly commands the attention of the audience. As in the staged development of "The History" of the Chortís, the scenes follow each other and offer various episodes whose sum forms a complete theme. Establishing the guidelines for the native theater, the twins successively perform the dance of the Cux, the Pujuy, and the Iboy.

At the request of the Great Lord of Xibalbá they cut up his own dog and then revive it immediately, and "when it definitely returned to life, it wagged its tail in pleasure."

Notable here is the religious importance of the dog, associated with the figure of the Camé, which appears as a motif in the mythology of the protohistoric cycle but is not mentioned again during the period corresponding to Quiché-Maya culture, when the mythical coyote also disappears. This has historical implications that are discussed elsewhere.[3]

Then the Xibalban chief, Hun Camé, says to them, "Now burn my house." The divine twins burn his house with the whole Council inside it, but no one is burned and the house quickly resumes its former condition without being lost for even an instant.

All of the Lords marvel at this performance. Then Hun Camé said to Hunahpú and Ixbalamqué, "Now kill one of my people, cutting him up, but so that he shall not die." "Very well," they replied, and taking hold of a man they quartered him and tore his heart out, holding it up for the Lords to see. Immediately they brought him back to life,

---

[3]Girard, *Los Chortís*, chapters on "Ethnography" and "Comparative Religion."

and as a result his heart was exceedingly happy once again. The Xibalbans were amazed. "Now cut yourselves up, because really our hearts yearn for that," they said. The twins immediately cut each other into pieces. Hunahpú was cut up by Ixbalamqué (this role corresponded to Ixbalamqué, who is the nahual of the jaguar, the carnivore par excellence of American animal life). She cut off each leg, then the arms, and when the head was severed she placed it at a distance and then removed the heart, which she wrapped in leaves, all of which delighted the Xibalbans beyond measure. Only one of the dancers was now visible: Ixbalamqué. "Get up!" she commanded Hunahpú, who instantly revived.

Then because of what was in the Lords' hearts, the twins' dances aroused their desires, and Hun Camé and Vukup Camé broke into words (the effects of imitative magic): "Now do the same with us, cutting us into pieces," they demanded of the twins.

"Very well, Lords," they answered. So then Hunahpú and Ixbalamqué cut off their heads, first Hun Camé's followed by that of Vukup Camé; but they did not revive them. When the Xibalbans saw that their chiefs had suddenly died, they all ran away.

Reproduced here is a typically native scene that has not varied from the time of the most remote horizon to the Colonial era: the death of the chief causes the disbandment of the group he led. This is because the chief is the "head" of the group, which is equated with a body, and just as a headless body cannot live, neither can a group exist without its chief. In native American languages, generally speaking, the same word is employed to designate chief and head. Following this line of thought, the Chortí community compares itself to a serpent of which the elder is the head, and that is what his title indicates: *hor chan* (head of a serpent).

But the twins are not satisfied with having beheaded the chiefs, and pursue all the Xibalban Lords until they have been destroyed. Nevertheless one of them, who had not been found, presented himself before Hunahpú and Ixbalamqué, humbling himself and asking for mercy. "Take pity on me!" he said, surrendering himself to them.

The children and slaves of the Xibalbans fled to a large gorge and hid themselves under a steep cliff; but hordes of ants discovered and dislodged them, forcing them to return along the road. When they came up, they all prostrated themselves before the twins. And so the Xibalbans were conquered. Hunahpú and Ixbalamqué were able to gain their victory only by means of the magical arts that they possessed.

Then the two disclosed their names to all of the Xibalbans:

> Listen, then, to our names and also the names of our progenitors: we are Hunahpú and Ixbalamqué, these are our names. The names of our fathers, whom you killed, were Hun Hunahpú and Vukup Hunahpú. We whom you see here, then, are the avengers of the sorrows and sufferings of our progenitors. You are going to suffer the same hurts that you caused us. We shall make you also to disappear, killing you, so that none of you shall remain [the law of an eye for an eye].

Then all the Xibalbans fell to their knees, crying, "Forgive us, Hunahpú and Ixbalamqué! We were definitely to blame for what we did to your progenitors, who are buried in Pucbal-chaj." Thus the twins brought vindication to the memory of their fathers; and this episode signals the end of the era of barbarism. Now is proclaimed veneration of one's father and one's ancestors through the male line, in contrast to what took place in the earlier period when veneration of the grandmother was extolled. This indicates a radical change in relative rank within the family and society: the passage from matrilineal to patrilineal descent, and consequently a change of rules of property, division of labor, and of government.

In light of the Xibalbans' opting to surrender, the twins pronounce this sentence:

Very well; these are our words. Listen, you of Xibalbá. Your offspring will no longer worship you, and therefore you will have nothing to eat [in future no one will venerate them, and so they will be neither invoked nor fed: the gods of the Third Age become the demons of the Fourth]. Neither will you have the ball game [they will no longer be solar gods]. The civilized human progeny will no longer belong to you, and intelligent people will draw away from your presence. Sinners, evildoers, mean persons, the cowardly, those given to vice: these are the ones who will resort to you. No longer will you be able to injure people — now hear it well — by means of the blood of those heads. For that is what brought your loss and your ruin, as well as worship of you, since you were not being adored as formerly. In truth you were not gods, and you frightened everyone by your ugly faces and horrible appearance, since you were evil-intentioned like the owls. You incited people to evildoing, to excesses, and to discord. And in your hearts you cultivated the bad feelings in place of the good feelings, setting an example of ignorance and bad faith. You painted yourselves and greased your faces, thereby losing the admiration people had for you, because you did not possess lofty feelings either.

This pronouncement and sentence is a true exposition of Mayan ethics, setting up against the vices of "barbaric" people those qualities that should characterize the enlightened human being. Thenceforth those qualities will constitute the law and code of rights of Maya culture. At the same time, physical deformity is compared with bad or *black* feelings, an allegory accompanying the one that compares physical beauty with ethical beauty. The vice of bad or black feelings is attributed to the ignorance and stupidity exhibited by those of an inferior cultural level; thus, folly and ignorance are equated with evil mentality, a postulate that we shall see confirmed further on. For that reason the truly enlightened not only ceased to pay homage to the false gods, but were also horrified by them and utterly detested them when they became evil beings. Here we have a clear explanation of the transformation of the Third-Age gods into the demons of the Age of Culture or Fourth Age, a fact fully confirmed by comparative ethnography, as we saw with regard to the character of the Quiché Hunrakán versus the Carib Camé.

During the matriarchal cycle people painted their faces, according to the inferences found in the Quiché text, but that custom was later given up. Nevertheless, facial painting as a distinguishing mark of the warriors comes back into vogue in a later period of Maya history. As said elsewhere, this war paint inspired fear, and according to Father Avendaño facial blackness was compared to wickedness of heart. Following the same order of ideas, the Chortís call unlucky days of the calendar "dark days" and these correspond to annotations in black in the codices.

Concepts about barbarism and related notions remain unchanging through time. And it is to be noted that under pressure from foreign influences the Mayas are obliged to return to the practice of face painting in order to distinguish warriors from the ordinary people. But they declare this a barbarous custom, thus identifying the aggressive mentality of the warrior with that of evil beings, because to them such pertains to the Third Age and is contrary to Mayan ethics.

There is a fact that should have been noted by the reader. Hunahpú and Ixbalamqué could have completely eliminated both the dark forces as well as the people of evil custom; nevertheless they did not do this, because the preservation of those forces, put to the service of the true gods, was a necessity from many points of view. In the first place, they were needed to establish the derivation of evil feelings and of all perversity that comes to pass in human life and in the bosom of nature itself. The Indian has always aspired to know the causes of things and, to explain the options in his life, pictures a world populated by good and bad spirits which influence his existence. Night is when the malevolent beings go into action, protected by the darkness that is their environment and has the color characteristic of evil feelings. All the evils afflicting humanity as well as phenomena which work against society's well-being are attributed to such perverse beings and so have their causal explanation, inasmuch as those calamities cannot be attributed to Deity which is essentially good.

After Hunahpú won the unconditional surrender of the forces of Xibalbá, the action of these evil beings is restricted to the field which Divinity assigned them, and limited by its express decision. To test human virtue or castigate offenses against religious ethics, Heaven allows action of evil spirits by temporarily or permanently withdrawing its protection from particular individuals or an entire group. Then the elder intervenes, the one possessing the magical formulae for conjuring the evil that will be overcome in the long run, just as were the forces of Xibalbá by the twins, following a long-drawn and tremendous struggle. Evil, according to the popular saying, endures for as long as Divinity wishes. In these cases of crisis, religious fervor recurs, expressed in self-sacrifice, offerings, and the observance of special ceremonies designed to gain the good graces of Divinity. The existence of evil potencies explains the eternal antagonism of the messianic forces, without detracting from the concept of divine omnipotence. The triumph which good always gains over evil in the long run expresses a principle of free will by which man must ever contribute with his actions and constantly exert himself in order to merit the help of Providence against those forces that oppose him. As said elsewhere, there is no dualism, i.e., no opposition between a good and an evil god, in native theogony, inasmuch as the Supreme Being is omnipotent and the dark forces are, in essence, no more than an instrument of its purpose.

This view of good and bad is also applied to rate one's own culture with respect to that of the rest and is the reason why each ethnic group believes itself superior to the others, regarding itself as chosen by Divinity because composed of true men in contrast with the others who are barbaric. Such concepts flow from the very constitution of indigenous society as a closed circle centered about the figure of a god which exemplifies the communal unity. Maya religion is a tribal religion and as such is not a religion of conversion; and this explains the curious phenomenon of neighboring peoples who really live in distinct worlds, as revealed by archaeology and ethnic cartography.

According to the Mayan, Chortí, and Mexican mythologies, the malefic beings reside in the northerly region of the underworld. Deity does not allow them to come up from there, affirm the Chortís, who call the underworld "the other State," the same as their designation of barbaric peoples. Thus it is that for them all the evils that afflict

mankind, such as heavy rains and winds injurious to agriculture, evil intentions and inclinations, etc., come from
the north. This corresponds to a climatic and historical
reality, since in fact it is from the north that come the
winds harmful to the *milpa*, and it is also from there that
waves of barbaric human hordes have come down in a
constant stream.

The Maya traditions agree perfectly with those of the
Quiché with reference to creation of the underworld as a
result of the destruction of Xibalbá. The Book of Chilam
Balam of Chumayel says in that regard: it was on the day 9
Cauac that the underworld was prepared for the first
time, but it was not until 10 Ahau that "bad men" went
there. In this sequence, which is expressed in terms of the
katún wheel, is seen the relation between the mystical
number 9 and the 9 underworlds of Quiché-Maya and
Mexican mythology. The existence of the underworlds is
necessary as the appropriate place for the punishment of
evils, particularly those that result from recantation of
religious faith. The black magician (*brujo*), who is the
representative of the evil entities within the community,
will without fail go to the underworld; he is the eternal
adversary of the elder (*chan*) who embodies the forces of
good and defends "his children."

The existence of underworld beings is necessary to encourage the virtues in the Maya people. By the same token
incorporation into the native pantheon of the false gods,
converted into demons, answers to an authentic conception of history proper to Maya culture. The Mayans take
into their body of beliefs elements from the previous ethnic
cycles through which they have passed, their culture being
a product of their historical experience. Of course, the
elements from the prehistoric period are reinterpreted
according to the latest norms. In that way earlier forms

that go back even to the most remote horizon are projected in the theogonic system as well as in their economy and society. The final product is, then, the result of a long evolution which gave Quiché-Maya culture its high degree of maturity.

These conceptions are also expressed in the very history of Hunahpú and Ixbalamqué who are exponents of that culture. But before being able to personify those conceptions, they have progressively to overcome and put to their service all of the opposing forces which symbolize the cultural characteristics of the first three Ages in toto, brought together in the figure of the Black Giant of Chortí tradition. This succession of periods contained in the history of the seven Ahpú, of Hunahpú and the Camé, and which appears as a reconstructed whole in Quiché-Maya beliefs, is eloquently objectified in the following figure from the Tro-Cortes Codex showing god B sowing a forked stick which is immediately destroyed by god A but then restored by the young Maize god, a suggestive image of the work of the seven Ahpú (fathers of the young god) who attempt to implant Maya culture only to have their work destroyed by the Camé (depicted as the god of Death), and then reestablished by Hunahpú (the young god).

We have said that the end of the Third Age saw a radical change in all aspects of the culture. Further on we shall see how the Quiché manuscript relates the advent of the patriarchal era and the termination of female hegemony decreed by Ixmucané herself, who embodied it, instituting at the same time the worship of the Maize god and its corresponding ritual.

Ixmucané wept, calling to her grandchildren, standing before the maize plants that they had sown. She saw them sprout, and later dry up when the twins were consumed in the bonfire; but they sprouted once again. Then the grandmother lit her fire and burned copal incense in front of the maize plants in memory of her grandchildren. The change in the maize plants, which undergo the same metamorphoses as the twins, illustrates the conception of the nahual, while the offering of incense marks new ceremonial patterns whose object is to ward off evil entities and protect the twins. The old woman's heart was made

FIGURE 20.

happy on seeing the maize shoots sprout a second time. Then she blessed and worshiped them, and called them "the center of the house." "Living stalks on the plain of the earth" is the name given by the Indians to the maize plants sown in the center of the patio.

After the interlude in which the twins' struggles and victory command the reader's attention, the grandmother makes her reappearance for the exclusive purpose of inaugurating worship of the Maize deity and its ritual, symbolized in her prostration before the maize stalks — the images of Hunahpú and Ixbalamqué — placed in the center of the house or yard, her offering of copal incense, and her blessing by pronouncing their names: that is, proclaiming their divinity.

The plain surface in whose center are placed the maize sprouts symbolizes the altar with its idol as well as the cosmic plane whose center is the temple. Elsewhere has been established the symbolic equivalence of the altar, the *milpa* or sowing field, and the earth-plane, an idea that goes back to this scene in the *Popol Vuh.* Ixmucané "names" the new theogonic entity that arises in the Quiché-Maya Parnassus, and in this act makes divine the most important plant of Mesoamerican culture. This ceremony will be observed in future by the Maya elders who, imitating the ritual patterns laid down by Ixmucané, must "name" the Agrarian deity, clearly specifying its names and qualities each time they direct their invocations to it, accompanied by generous burning of copal incense.

Of all the names by which the Maize god is known, the name Ce Acatl of Mexican theogony is the one that best expresses this scene of the divinization of maize by Ixmucané, since Ce Acatl (one maize stalk) is the day of the Maize deity's birth. For the same reasons, given above, the center of the earth was called Nepantla by the Mexicans and was expressed pictorially by a maize shoot breaking through from the heart of the earth.

With regard to the name Ixmucané gave her grandchildren, see what was said in earlier chapters about the word *imix* (name of the First Regent, the equivalent of Ixmucané) and *ixim*, its metathesis, as also the name of the maize kernel in Mayan languages. Although the divine twins are the authors of the agricultural code, it is the grandmother who must be credited with discovery of maize as well as its primordial cultivation; and with this we are given to understand that the finding and first domestication of that plant was the work of woman and took place during the matriarchal cycle. This same tradition survives among the Huastecs who, according to R. Shuller, ascribe to Ixcuinána, the first woman, the origin of maize cultivation.

Both names (Ixmucané and Ixcuinána) contain the

roots of the words for mother and maize, whose close genetic connection goes back to the era of the Ixmucané myth.
The same is true of the word *imix*, synonym of Ixmucané,
the First Regent, which is etymologically related to maize
and mother. As shown in former chapters[4] *imix* (or *imox*)
is also the mother tree, and its figure represents that of a
pregnant woman. The same theme is expressed in its
anthropomorphic aspect, in archaic statuary, by an extra-
ordinarily fat being which symbolizes Mother Earth and
her offspring, maize, in a state of gestation. The figure of
the Agrarian god is placed upon the umbilicus of the Earth
deity, objectifying in this way the conception of the theogonic trinity in a single symbol which the Chortís continue
to represent by a single idol (a cross). In other representations of the mother-offspring theme these appear sculptured together in a single statue. In proportion as the
culture evolved, masculine gods began to predominate over
feminine.[5] The close linkage of mother-son (or mother-
maize) expressed in Mayan art and language is also seen in
the glyphs. In codices and monuments we find the glyphs
kan-imix in frequent association; sometimes *kan* replaces
imix, and the sign *kan-imix* is glyphically related with the
west, the homeland of maize. *Imix* is still a word that
designates the earth among the Ixil, who speak one of the
oldest Mayan languages among the southerly group.[6] Thus
in the *Popol Vuh* we have not only a historical explanation
of the evolution of Maya culture and language but also the
history of its artistic development.

The mother-son theme, so strongly present in the art,
language, glyphs, and the myth that explains it, is not

---

[4] In Girard, *Los Chortís*.

[5] Girard, *Los Chortís*, "Archaeology and History."

[6] Ibid., "Linguistics."

exclusive to Quiché-Maya culture and languages. Even a rapid comparative examination of the terms for maize — or the food plant — and mother in all of the genetically related Mayan languages will show the parallelism. The genetic connection is confirmed by the very phenomena of displacement of meaning and of phonetic mutations, such as *im* becoming *am* and its metathesis, that operate in the root for maize. In languages that generally represent a more advanced cultural stage, the word for mother — always related to that for maize — becomes the word for designating the father or the grandfather. This book cannot possibly include an exhaustive series of comparative words. Nevertheless, those given in Appendix B are enough to demonstrate the genetic relations among the terms applied to the primary authority in the family or the group, and those that designate the principal food plant in the languages stemming from a common linguistic subsoil. Among these words, we have included the related term *poo* (moon, white hairs), whose etymological relation is well defined in the Quiché codex which presents us with the grandmother or house-chief — equivalent on the theogonic plane to the Lunar deity — as an old woman having white hair, the distinctive color of her function as the First Regent.

But, to return from this long digression to the *Popol Vuh:* on making the maize stalks divine and marking out the patterns of a new worship, the grandmother also proclaims the new family and social order which will prevail thenceforth, founded on descent through the male line owing to the veneration of masculine ancestors and of the Maize god. But that distinction is not made until the twins have gained full knowledge of their origin and paternal ancestry. Here is what is said in that regard: at first they found out about their names in a vague way only, and spoke of them as though this explained their origin; but the title of

Cerbataneros (solar gods) was not applied to them until their solar nature had been revealed to them. In this way they inherited the grand consciousness which their fathers over there on the Pucbal-chaj were to leave in their hearts.

These norms still govern among Quiché descendants who do not have the right to the title of Achi ("companion of the sun": translation of F. Rodas) or to the use of the corresponding symbols until such time as they gain consciousness or awareness of their divine origin, their duties, and innate qualities; that is, until they become fit to discharge the functions of the perfect human being. Besides illustrating those patterns of filial conduct, the paragraph above has connotations of an ethnological character. The twins were born and grew up during the matriarchal period without knowing their fathers, of whom they had a very confused notion. On the other hand, they knew their mother and grandmother at first hand. Nevertheless they did not inherit the names of these but rather those of their fathers, which would thereafter be transmitted through the masculine line in the same way as a man's function in life and his possessions would be inherited. Those conditions are listed in the following paragraph:

"You [their fathers] will be invoked," said the divine twins when they felt that great consciousness in their hearts. "You will be the first to manifest, the first to be reverenced by the enlightened and civilized. Your names will not be lost. You will be the beginning of our line. We are only the avengers of your death and of the sufferings that they caused you." This was their farewell to their progenitors, the Ahpú, when they had finally vanquished all in Xibalbá.

Then they departed from there at the moment of the sun's zenith (*en el medio de la luz*), and immediately raised themselves to heaven: one to the sun and the other to the moon; instantly the celestial vault and the face of the earth were illumined, the two remaining in the heaven.[7] Then there also rose up the 400 boys whom Zipacná had killed, and these became the companions of the twins and were transformed into stars in the heaven.

Thus it was that after being deified as maize gods, Hunahpú and Ixbalamqué became solar gods, so as to illumine the Dawn of the Fourth Creation which corresponds to the beginning of the Quiché-Maya cultural era.

As said earlier, the twins' victory over the forces of evil symbolizes the triumph of light over shadow, of civilization over barbarism, good over bad, day over night, explaining moreover the mechanism of the sun's daily appearance.

In Mexican mythology Chicomecoatl, "so called because he pretended to have prevailed against seven snakes" (Durán), brings about the defeat of the seven Camé whom the Mexicans like the Chortís equate with snakes (*culebras*), a pejorative term used to designate the hellish beings who are in opposition to the serpents (*sierpes*), which are divine nahuals.

Like Ahuramazda, Hunahpú personifies the aurora,

---

[7][Because of its direct bearing on a fuller insight into the meaning of this episode, we include a footnote that Dr. Girard appended to the text of his *Origin y Desarrollo de las Civilizaciones Antiguas de América*, Editores Mexicanos Unidos, S.A., Mexico, 1977; p. 168. — TRANS.]

"It should be noted that the myth's text does not say that the twins are the sun and moon, but that they raised themselves to these lights. This is congruent with the Chortí judgment which clearly establishes that the celestial figure is merely a tangible manifestation of the intangible which resides in it. There is no confusion between spirit and matter, inasmuch as the objective of worship is the divine force that causes its sanctity. This difference is expressed in the distinct names which designate the sun as a star, and the sun as a god."

light, the brightness that dissipates the shadows of ignorance. Hunahpú, having taken the power away from the false gods, replaces them in the universal reign; and, like Ahuramazda, does away with human sacrifices. The aurora or dawn forms the most beautiful theme of Quiché-Maya mythology, as it does of the Aryans of Asia. As much in the Vedas of India as in the *Popol Vuh*, the dawn has inspired the best stanzas of their poetry, describing human longing for the awakening of the light of day — a moment in which the Indian "weeps for joy," as will be said farther along in the Quiché codex.

Xochipilli, god of Dawn in Mexican mythology, is the functional replica of Hunahpú. In other versions he is called Macuilxóchitl, Tlahuiscalpantecutli, "The Lord of the House of Dawn," or Ce Xóchitl (One Flower), child of Chicome Xóchitl (Seven Flowers), as Hunahpú was the child of the seven Ahpú.

This function as *sol invictus*, which implies that of tribal god or protector of the tribe, is dramatized masterfully in the Chortí theater when the actor who embodies Hunahpú uncovers his face after having defeated and beheaded the Black Giant, exhibiting then his countenance, resplendent and radiating light through all of his being. In his double character of Solar and Maize deity, Hunahpú rises triumphant and ascends to the heavens, symbolizing at one and the same time the appearance of dawn and the shoot of maize breaking through from the underworld onto the earth's surface, where it is crowned by a crest of green leaves, identified with the magnificent feather headdress of the young Solar deity. In terms of spiritual doctrine, this ascension symbolizes the conversion of the dead person into a divine spirit that rises to heaven, like the 400 boys who are transformed into the souls of the stars and enter into partnership with the sun.

Both in his function as Solar god and that of Maize, Hunahpú performs the role of a savior. As Solar deity he defends humanity against the forces of evil which he annihilates with his magical rays. In Chortí theogony this function of his is distinguished by the name of Child Redeemer given to the god of Dawn whose appearance is announced by Venus, called "angel Saint Martial and herald of the world." As Maize god, he gives his life to feed his worshipers.

In a very late epoch of its history, Maya theogony had to have recourse to a god of War, a role that the Solar god itself was to fill. That is the way the Chumayel manuscript expresses it, saying that "the sun was a warrior and had its hair in long locks." The god of War will overcome the enemies of the Mayan nation, which are his enemies also, employing the same magical procedures that allowed him to defeat the giants and the forces of Xibalbá.

Because Hunahpú is the paradigm of all the virtues and superior qualities that the great Maya chiefs must have, he is the wisest of the wise, the best farmer, and the bravest among the brave. In accordance with these norms, the elder (*chan*) or the general must always be at the front of his followers so as to set the proper example, the elder as the most able farmer and prototype of perfected human conduct, and the general as the bravest warrior. This explains the reason why the native chiefs always walk at the head of their troops, as an example of valor.

But this is not all. The esoteric doctrines of the resurrection and ascension of Hunahpú and Ixbalamqué express the magnificent ideal of Maya culture which says that the human being cannot raise him- or herself up to the perfected state of Hunahpú except when the whole community shall also have attained to divine perfection. That objective is gained by following the rules of conduct exem-

plified by the son of Divinity, a condition to which are
correlated those members of the Mayan fraternity whom
the *chan* calls his "children." As Max Scheler says, the
highest and purest conception that is possible within the
limits of monotheism is one which sees all men as children
of Father God. The intermediary in this relationship is the
"Son" who partakes of the same divine essence and reveals
it to men, and at the same time prescribes with divine
authority certain beliefs and commandments. With these
sublime teachings, which give to man the consciousness of
being part of divinity, Mayan metaphysics attains its highest degree of development. Founded on these tenets, its
theology, which contains philosophical principles and is
inseparable from law and ethics, is developed. These
norms resolve the spiritual problems of the Indian, fix the
duties of the people in general, assure human rights as well
as institutional stability, and elevate work to the category
of a religious obligation. They teach that the eternal
happiness to be enjoyed after death should be sought and
gained as a reward of sacrifices made during life on earth,
inasmuch as the civilizer-hero has firmly established the
links that unite Divinity with humankind and transformed
himself into a man in order to demonstrate to men how
they can become gods.

   Although Hunahpú's code, which satisfactorily resolves
the problem of social justice and human relations in life,
was not written on stone monuments, its unchanging doctrines endure in the native consciousness as an undying
monument to that great religious leader. That god, whose
epic fills the pages of the *Popol Vuh*, must have been a
great leader of the Quiché-Maya people, deified after his
death, as were Quetzalcoatl, Xolotl, Camaxtli, and Huitzilopochtli in Mexico; Tammuz in Babylonia, Osiris in
Egypt, Adonis in Phoenicia, Attis in Phrygia, Orpheus

in Greece, and Jesus the Christ in the Western world. Of these god-men, those that pertain to Mexican mythology have well known historical antecedents and were, before becoming gods, great leaders of peoples. We know the story of Quetzalcoatl, the oldest of them, just as we know the great deeds of Huitzilopochtli, the most recent of the series. This latter god lived on the Coatepeque hill, near Tula; of him Sahagún says that "they held him in high regard when he lived and after his death they honored him as God." In the same way the Mayas deified Kukulcán, following his departure from the Yucatán peninsula. From all of this we infer the process of deification of Hunahpú, whose actual life story has not come down to us because he belonged to a very remote past.

12

Cosmogonic, Astronomic, and Chronological Meaning

A S IN THESE PAGES we have been following the
development of the Quiché text, together with the
progressive evolution evident in all aspects of the
culture, we have also been pointing out the advance of
knowledge in matters of astronomy and cosmogony that is
given out in allegorical form in this famous codex. In those
sciences progress follows an ascending trajectory and culminates when man has gained full knowledge of the universal configuration. Astronomy is inseparable from the
cosmic mechanism, and both are foundations of the calendar. From then on cosmic harmony reigns and man has
complete consciousness of his metaphysical position and
his relation with the universal principle. This new conception of the world and of life makes possible his dominion
over the forces of nature for the purpose of utilizing them
to benefit all people, since control of supernatural forces —
to which natural forces are now linked — is achieved
through new techniques of magic combined with methods
of a scientific character.

But such knowledge does not reach its maturity except
when Hunahpú, after overcoming the forces of Xibalbá in

the dark and strange regions of the underworld and
destroying Hun Bátz and Hun Chouén, takes their place in
the regency of the world and personifies the Dawn of
Quiché-Maya civilization whose distinctive color is red.

In terms of the Maya calendar, this brilliant image of
Hunahpú corresponds to Cib (light, torch) and, according
to the Book of Chilam Balam of Chumayel, the epoch that
it opens up is the 4 Ahau, the equivalent of the Fourth Age
of the Quiché codex.

Recapitulating the series of Regents given us in the
Popol Vuh, and comparing it with the lists of the Maya
and Quiché calendar of the classic period, we get the following picture:

Chilam Balam	Popol Vuh	Color	Quiché	Maya
1 Ahau	Ixmucané	white hair	Imox	Imix
2 Ahau	Camé	black	Camé	Cimi
3 Ahau	Bátz-Chouén	yellow pole	Bátz	Chuen
4 Ahau	Hunahpú	red	Ajmák	Cib

We have already established the correspondence between the cultural marks of the Third Age of the *Popol
Vuh* and those of 3 Ahau Katún of Maya terminology. The
4 Ahau has the same parallelism with the Fourth Age of
the Quiché document. The Chumayel manuscript in fact
says that when the 3 Ahau Katún shall have ended, there
will appear the line of the noble Princes and that of their
descendants, who were insulted by the rabid of their time,
the madmen of their Katún, by the son of evil (note that
both sources, Maya and Quiché, equate insanity with ignorance and barbarism).

Likewise the point of departure of Maya chronology is
a date 4 Ahau at the end of a Baktún 13, and this date,

which is the equivalent of the zero point of the Long Count — and is confirmed because the following Baktún is 1.0.0.0.0. — has had no satisfactory explanation until now. The agreement of Maya and Quiché sources in assigning 4 Ahau, the beginning of the Fourth Age, as the initial date of the cultural era or historical period of the Quiché-Maya peoples, which the Long Count places at the end of the fourth millennium B.C., brings a solution to the problem.

According to Maya chronology, before that age-date there had elapsed 13 complete Baktúns, or a span of 5,200 years, which embrace the prehistoric period, making their beginnings go back to the ninth millennium or approximately 10,500 years before our era.

Although this figure is probable and adjusts itself in principle to information supplied by other disciplines,[1] we cannot regard it as exact but rather as approximate, taking into account the fact that such a definite notion of time did not exist during the prehistoric epoch. Therefore we must consider the 13 Baktúns which possibly embrace the three ethnic cycles of Quiché-Maya prehistory as hypothetical.

On the other hand, there is no reason for rejecting a priori the validity of the age-date 4 Ahau 8 Cumku, which serves as the point of departure of Maya time-reckoning, since it must not be forgotten that in those times the Indian had attained a high intellectual level, formed throughout the three preceding ethnic periods. Moreover, the native is characterized by an extraordinary memory and does not forget even small details over the course of many years. If his ability to reason is not unusually brilliant, conversely to remember information is an innate habit with him, and these mental peculiarities mirror the sources of his educa-

---

[1] Girard, *Los Chortís*, "Archaeology and History."

tion: established doctrine and tradition. It must also be kept in mind that since time immemorial the Indian has known how to use mnemonics, which did and still does enable him to keep accurate accounts.

The Mayas always took great care to link their historic epochs chronologically, with no break whatever, and we have a good proof of this in the continuity of the katún wheels during the Maya-Toltec period in Yucatán, consistent with the system used during the Old Empire, notwithstanding the calendric reforms that altered the timekeeping system.[2] When their time-computing method reached its perfection, they fixed the beginning of their historical era in terms of Katúns and also recorded the prehistoric period in the same way so as to indicate that it is incorporated into their chronology as well as their history as part of a continuing process. For that reason the Mayas compute time elapsed, taking into account their prehistoric past — the same system that the Chortís still employ when at the end of each year they add one more knot to their *quipu*.[3] This method is reflected in the twists and turns of their language; as discussed in the linguistic part of my larger work,[4] the Chortís do not employ the present tense to refer to an action taking place, but rather express it by means of the gerund. Agreeably with the same order of ideas, they tied together the successive ethnic periods, uniting them by means of the Regents which governed each Age, it falling to Hunahpú — the equivalent of Ahau — to close the series.

In no other native American source do we find such detailed information concerning the mythological origin of

---

[2] Girard, *Los Chortís*, "Tzolkín."
[3] Ibid., "Ethnology."
[4] Ibid.

the cosmic Regents and the explanation of their order of
succession. The Mesoamerican tradition has faithfully preserved the recollection of this succession of Regents and of
its relative importance, holding the first of the series to be
the principal one, even when in their computation they do
not use the primary category corresponding to Imix, Cimi,
Chuen, Cib. Thus we have the Mexican tradition telling us
of the white jaguar — the characteristic color of Ixmucané
or Imix — as the captain of the four cosmic jaguars; while
for the Mayas the white Bacab is the principal of the four
bearers of the sky and the "dominical letter" corresponding
to it is *ix*, the equivalent of jaguar[5] and the integrating root
of the name Ixmucané. In the same way the Chortís begin
their static Tzolkín with the sign Imix and follow it with
the Second and Third Regent as in the order given in the
Popol Vuh. It falls to these two to cover the winter (rainy)
period of the Tzolkín, that is to say the dark part of the sky
which, historiographically speaking, corresponds to the
shadowy period of barbarism. The wheel of the Tzolkín
closes with the arrival of the new sun, Yaxkin, which
inaugurates the summer season, the time of clear skies, and
which corresponds to the coming of Hunahpú.

But there is even more: the Chortí winter series that
begins with Imix, continues with the Second and Third
Regents and closes with Imix, the same sign that opens and
closes the period of the Tzolkín, finally relinquishing the
charge to the Solar god.[6] These norms of Chortí ritual correspond admirably with the patterns set down in the *Popol
Vuh*, by which Ixmucané is the First Regent and, after an
interlude during which the Second and Third Regents are

---

[5] As shown in the chapter on theogony, Girard, *Los Chortís*.

[6] Cf. details in chapter on Tzolkín, ibid. [Imix, represented by Ixmucané, is the first to inaugurate the worship of the Solar god, her grandchild. — TRANS.]

active, reappears at the end for the purpose of extolling worship of the new sun, just as the Chortí elder continues to do every year in his role as First Regent. In that way the cyclographic score of the *Popol Vuh* is continually dramatized in the Tzolkín, which invariably begins with Imix and ends in the summer season with the summoning of the Solar deity (Hunahpú). The most surprising thing in this matter is that it is not the Quichés — who wrote the *Popol Vuh* — but the Chortís who have followed the dictates of the famous codex to the letter, from the beginnings of their culture until the present day.

This affords a brilliant proof of the veracity of the ethnographic reports contained in the chapter on the Tzolkín[7] as well as of the common genesis of the Quichés and Mayas, and at the same time shows that the ritual norms preserved by the Chortís have not varied since the most remote times; therefore, they are the same that took place in Maya ceremonial during the Old Empire.

As explained in the chapter "Theogonic Mechanism,"[8] the rainy season is compared to a period of struggle and battle, like that through which Hunahpú passed before declaring himself Regent, New Sun or Yaxkin. And this coming forth of the daystar and of the individuality of Hunahpú at the end of the Third Age, after a period during which he did not reveal his name and so did not exist, in the astronomic order symbolizes the awakening of the god-star following its lethargy during the winter solstice. This explains the curious Maya and Mexican legends telling of the halt in the sun's course before it begins its trajectory, legends that mutually support each other. In this regard the Chilam Balam of Chumayel says that in

---

[7]Girard, *Los Chortís.*
[8]Ibid.; see also chapter on religion.

Katún 3 Ahau, the equivalent of the Third Age, the sun was halted in its journey for three months. For his part, Ixtlilxóchitl relates that during the Third Age the sun remained for one full day without moving in its course and resumed its movements when bitten by a mosquito. The Aztecs had a sun ceremony on the day "Four Movement" to commemorate the date on which the star began to move again. And this astronomical phenomenon determines the initial date of the Tzolkín, following the days without name which, as explained elsewhere, symbolize the sun's lethargy. The sun will resume its course because of the magical arts of the elder who throws his darts at it just as the mosquito bit it, pricking the sun to make it wake up and continue its march.

All those legends explain allegorically the origin and initial point of departure of the Tzolkín together with the civil year, at the end of the winter solstice and the un-named days, the same position preserved for it by the Chortís.[9] That calendar could not operate during the pre-historic epoch since its framework rests on the complete series of regents, and only when Hunahpú confirmed himself as Fourth Ahau was the formalization of this perfected timekeeping system possible. From this it follows that the beginning of the Quiché-Maya calendar coincides with that of the historical era. At that time all of the arithmetic elements required for its assembly had been acquired. As noted elsewhere, the baseline of the Tzolkín is determined astronomically by the sun's zenith during its first passage through the parallel, as verified by the position of the Plei-ades. The simultaneous ascension to heaven of Hunahpú (sun) and the 400 boys (Pleiades) corresponds with those astronomical events, mythologically expressed by Hunah-

---

[9]Girard, *Los Chortís*, "Tzolkín."

pú's association with the 400 youths. Concomitantly we have the invention of the vigesimal system of computation (embodied by Hunahpú) and its maximum expression in the number 400 (embodied by the 400 boys), which was at that time the highest exponent of mathematics and timekeeping.

It is well known that Hunahpú, the Solar deity, embodies the primary unit (the *kin*, sun) or the numeral that forms part of his own name (*hun* = one, *ahpú* = sun or blowgunner) which is translated as either sun or day. This number is expressed pictorially by means of a small circle or a sphere, an ideophonetic sign that reproduces the figure of the sun.

But the Solar deity also personifies the cycle, i.e., the greater unit, in the same way as in the cosmic drama it symbolizes the day, the year, or time units of greater magnitude. For this reason cycles, eras, or ages are compared with suns, as is the day or the year. In his very anatomy the Solar deity also embodies the vigesimal unity by his extremities, which total the 20 fingers and toes of his hands and feet, forming *One Man;* while a single one of his extremities, or better his entire body placed in a cruciform position, expresses the number five, the equivalent of the Solar deity's name.[10] This equivalence stands out better in the names of Ce Xóchitl (One Flower) and Macuilxóchitl (Five Flowers), Mexican deities which as we noted are functional equivalents of Hunahpú. This shows that the mathematical or timekeeping system reflects the native monotheist principle, which is the concept of plurality within unity.

We have moreover seen that Hunahpú symbolizes the figure twenty in the dances that he performs before the

---

[10]Girard, *Los Chortís*, "Theogony."

Lords of Xibalbá, in accordance with norms that he exemplifies for the first time and which continue to be observed today by the natives who dramatize their arithmetical and chronological system in dances.[11] The Book of Chilam Balam of Chumayel (in the "Book of the Month") places the invention of the twenty at the end of the account of the creations: simultaneously with the appearance of the four Regents, called Ah-Toc, "was the Month created," says this Yucatecan source, giving the list of the twenty names of the uinal which "went to the middle of the sky and took each other's hands. And each getting to know the others, the days said: 'thirteen and seven in a group.' This they said so that their voice would be heard." The text adds that "the relation of the days, day by day, must be read beginning from the east, according to the order in which they are." This natural order is that indicated by the course of the sun, following Hunahpú's triumph.

In both the Maya and Quiché sources, concretely in the first, allegorically in the other, we find the elements of the mechanism of the Tzolkín with its internal articulation based on the numbers 20 and 13, whose origin is attributed to the Solar god. We have also a record of this in the traditions collected by Fray Gabriel de San Buenaventura in his *Calepino*, where he says that the first to find the letters of the Maya language and to make computation of the years, months, and ages and teach all this to the Indians, was an Indian called Kinchahau (Maya Solar god) and by the other name of Tzamná (Maize god). Both these functions are brought together by Hunahpú, the prototype of the True Man. This connection between the civilizing hero and the invention of arithmetic and agriculture appears as well in the system of measurements of the *milpa* which is based on the

---

[11]Ibid., chapter 13.

unit called *hun winik* (one man), derived by multiplication of the figure 20 (20 x 20 = 400). Here we see the method used by the Mayas for obtaining the cabalistic cipher 400 which intimately links the Pleiades to the Solar deity. In the Book of Chilam Balam of Maní there is a list of the twenty days of the month, with their attributes and prognostications. Each day is a dawn or *yahalcab*, which A. Barrera Vásquez translates literally as "the awakening of the world." The same expression appears in the Chumayel document which says that "the Month was created when the earth awoke." These are eloquent references to Hunahpú's double function as god of Dawn and symbol of chronological unity.

In the Maní list, which is astrological in character, we find references that can only be explained in terms of the *Popol Vuh*. Let us take for example the day Cimi (equivalent of Camé) — whose sign is an owl (the messenger from Xibalbá) — whose augurs are dullness, the assassin, and the destiny of a very bad man — characteristics descriptive of the cultural state of the Third Age (ignorance, human sacrifices, wickedness). Conversely Chuen, whose sign is an artisan in wood (recall the Age of wood) and of weaving (female industry invented by woman during the matriarchal cycle), has as its prediction: to be Master of all the arts (Hunahpú's older brothers are described in the *Popol Vuh* as great artisans).[12]

The numbers 13 and 9, associated with the 20, are inseparable from the Tzolkín. Thirteen already appears in the list of the 12 gods which in union with the central deity form the thirteen-complex. With regard to the 9, we know that this number represents a feminine concept.[13] The

---

[12]According to information supplied by A. Barrera Vásquez.
[13]Cf. Girard, *Los Chortís*, "Religion."

Book of Chilam Balam of Chumayel confirms this in the following terms: "These nine gods manifested themselves in nine faces of king-men of the mat of the second time, which arrived within the 3 Ahau Katún. The nine gods will close the cycle of 3 Ahau Katún." The relation of the 9 with the Third Age could not be more clearly expressed. Furthermore, we cite the transcription of Juan Martínez Hernández (mentioned by Genét) regarding the 9 gods: Bolón ti kú (god-Nine) created women who had no parents (*ix-maymob*), and who, with no husband (*ix-machiamob*), give their lives to the *ah-numeyaob* (the people who suffer).

Basing ourselves upon the teachings of the *Popol Vuh*, we can reconstruct the history of development of the Maya calendar as follows:

Ixmucané and Ixpiyacoc, equivalent to Oxomoco and Cipactonal of Mexican mythology, create the lunar calendar during the matriarchal-horticultural cycle. Both because of the legal position of the male who had not then become a "true man" and the description of the imperfect creature of that epoch who had no extremities, we are unable to think of a calendar based on the vigesimal system, the paradigm of the great True Man with his twenty fingers and toes which were a center of interest.

This can be proven by recourse once again to comparative ethnography, inasmuch as peoples who preserve the Third-Age culture govern themselves by lunar computation. Aside from the information collected by the author among the Taoajkas Indians of Mosquitia, we know that the Talamancas used the system of lunations to measure time, and the period during which the cadaver had to remain in the air during the initial phase of the secondary burial consisted of nine moons. Lunar mythology characterizes the culture of Arawak peoples. Among certain groups of the Tupi-Guaraní family the mourning period lasted for one lunar cycle.[14] We could add to these references, but the above suffice for our purpose. The linkage of the cabalistic number 9 with the lunar calendar, an association that is carried on in Maya computation, should be noted. The number 9 was the beginning of the framework of the tun, divided into 2 series of 9 uinals.

This was because, as we have several times repeated, Maya culture incorporates and reinterprets elements from previous epochs. On formalizing the Tzolkín, just after the coming of Hunahpú which corresponds to the advent of agriculture and the patriarchal regime, the ancient calendar combines itself with the solar count to form the new system of lunisolar computation. Thus the primary form of the calendar continues to maintain itself throughout the whole of Maya history and comes down to our time. We have powerful testimony of this in the inscriptions in stone, in the lunar series in the Dresden Codex, and in the actual practices of the Chortís.[15]

As happens during the first phase of all great discoveries, the lunar calendar was an imperfect system for determining the time for preparation of the soil, the burning of the fields, and the date for sowing — operations that were the practical cause for the invention of the calendar and of astronomical observations. With creation of the Tzolkín, a great step forward was accomplished because this instrument allowed prediction with complete exactitude of the dates on which those serial operations had to take place in the *milpa*.

But the Tzolkín has its roots buried in the deep subsoil of Maya prehistory and, when it appears in its initial form,

---

[14]Arthur Ramos, *Las Poblaciones del Brasil*, Mexico, 1944.
[15]See Girard, *Los Chortís*, "Tzolkín."

it already possesses its essential features as an instrument with which to calculate the time for preparing the fields and to perform an astrological function. This is demonstrated by the preservation of those features in cultures corresponding to the prehistoric horizon. We have already noted that the Talamanca Indians, like the Chortís, believe in days of evil shadow, those that in the Maya calendar are represented by black numbers.[16] Among peoples that preserve Third-Age cultural practices concerning foretelling the future, astrology and curing the sick are the business of wizards or medicine men. These same functions are carried out by the Maya or Chortí elder, the sole interpreter of the Tzolkín as well as the doctor (chac) of the community. Thus it is that the primary forms of the calendar as well as the Mayan institution of elders (chan) go back to the cycle of their prehistory, which is that of history for those peoples that did not progress along with the Quiché-Maya.

The Tzolkín is the point of departure of the complete time-recording system of Mayan and Mexican chronology. And that system is founded upon the method of combining and elevating to greater power the series of this religious-agrarian calendar.[17] Such time periods were conceived as closed cycles like those of the prehistoric epoch which always terminated with an apocalyptic catastrophe. For this reason it was believed that the end of the world could come about at the end of the cycle, an idea that has endured until this day in some Mexican quarters. Only the Mayas freed themselves from this fear by creating a practically infinite cycle.

In the same way, the system of changing calendric

---

[16]Girard, Los Chortís, "Ethnography."

[17]See demonstrations given in the chapter on the Tzolkín, ibid.

Regents to mark a historic point of change had its inspiration in the function of the first Regents, which pertained to distinct ethnic periods. We have seen elsewhere that the successive slippage of Regents that occurs in the Maya calendar of Yucatán expresses distinct historical situations.

The series of Regents that the *Popol Vuh* gives us is, as said, the one that corresponds to: Imix, Cimi, Chuen and Cib of the Maya count, whose cycles invariably terminate on an Ahau day and therefore begin on Imix, the day that follows Ahau. Those Regents marked the divisions of the Maya and Quiché calendar, while these peoples shared a common culture and did not have to record any historical event of importance to one or the other of them.

13

The Fourth and Final Age: Era of Quiché-Maya Culture

SURROUNDED by the brilliant solar rays, Hunahpú had to illuminate the scene of the new creation, and this must be concluded before the dawn. To that end, the divine council once more came together to form a new humanity and "'consecrate the nutriments which will sustain our civilized progeny, making their existence on the face of the earth divine,' they said among themselves."

Then they sent their prayers amidst the darkness of the night (exemplifying the norms of the agrarian ritual celebrated only during the night, like the coitus); then those shadows scattered, and they were filled with gratitude. In that way the purifying sentiments of their progeny were coming to birth, and they found what would form the flesh of the new humans (maize). Only a short time remained before the sun, moon, and stars would appear.

Note that now the creative gods treat their creatures as their own offspring, comparing them with Hunahpú, the very term the Chortí elder — as representative of the agrarian gods (which are also the creative gods) — applies to his flock. Thus the humankind of the Fourth Creation will be formed in the same way as Hunahpú, from which it follows that the divine spirit now enters into human life, lights the flame of knowledge in the soul, and gives to the being its new ethical physiognomy. Therefore man's feelings will be pure and elevated and, having an awareness of being part of divinity, he will know how to discharge his real duties, paying tribute to the Creator in the same way as do the creative gods to the Supreme Being to whom "they give that which is its just due." Such is the view of the Chortí theologians, and upon it is also founded the law of obligatory offerings to the elder.

Because of this the creative gods "are filled with feelings of gratitude," since they will now be able to subsist by virtue of the principle that they cannot live without man's veneration, nor can man live without divine protection: the advent of both these conditions is implied. But in Maya mythology the coming of Deity into the soul as well as into the body is naturally related only after maize becomes the material employed to mold the beings of the Fourth Creation.

The relation between Deity and mankind is linguistically expressed by the use of a common root. For example, in Zapotec *vi* or *bi* means vital breath, wind, and enters into the composition of the name of the divinity, *vi dó*, and of man, *vi nih* (compare this with the *winik* of languages in the northern Mayan group, *inik* in Huastec, *vinak* in Quiché, etc.). This is the real meaning of this latest creation, which no longer relates to the universe or the human species as such, but rather to the formation of beings that are perfect, like gods, and who possess the Quiché-Maya qualities of culture.

To emphasize the beginning of their cultural era, the Mayas have it begin with the latest creation, which is also the creation of the great luminaries and of the stars. All

that came before the Fourth Creation has little importance, as if it had not existed, since in the Maya conception
the world begins with the coming of their historic era. The
Chumayel document confirms the Quiché text, declaring
that "then the stars awoke and from that moment the
world began." Referring to the humanity of the earlier
cycle it says, "those creatures had no fathers [a specific
mention of the matriarchy], lived a life of misery, and
were living beings but had no hearts." The annals of the
Cakchiquels speak to us in similar terms of life before the
latest creation: "Formerly man lived in misery, fed on
wood, had no blood or flesh, and lacked anything fit to eat
until maize was discovered."

This allegory of a miserable humanity that lived in
shadows before the existence of the stars is typical of native
American myths, since we find it everywhere, from the
country of the Red Skins to that of the Urus. The traditions
of the latter, recently collected by Dr. A. Vellard, exhibit
surprising similarities to those of the *Popol Vuh*. Everywhere, the native American peoples make known the inci-
sive division between the prehistoric cycle and the beginning of their history.

> From Paxil and Cayalá, so named, came the yellow corn
> ears and the white ears. These are the names of the animals
> which provided them with news of the new foods: *yak* (the
> Mountain Cat), *utiú* (the Coyote), *quel* (the Magpie), and
> *joj* (the Crow, or Bird of Prey). Four, then, were the ani-
> mals who gave the news of the existence of the yellow ears
> and the white ears, which were found in Paxil; and they
> pointed out the road to Paxil. In this way the gods found
> the elements that would become the flesh of the people they
> were going to create and form, and the liquid of their blood
> would be the blood of the people, and this liquid Alom and
> Cajolom caused to enter into the maize ears.

And so the gods were filled with joy, having found that place full of good and delicious things where the yellow and white maize ears abounded, where were abundant also the *pataxte* [*Theobroma bicolor*, a variety of cacao] and cacao, and groves of zapotes, annonas [custard apples], apples, cherries, and honey. Full of succulent foods were the places called Paxil and Cayalá. There were foods of every kind and shape, produce of great and small plants, and the animals showed them the road they were to use to get them. Then they shelled and ground the yellow and white ears, and Ixmucané made nine drinks whose ingredients entered into the substances destined to give life, strength, and vigor to the people.

Immediately afterwards they made and formed our first fathers and our first mothers; of yellow maize and white were made their flesh, their arms, and their legs. Only maize dough became the flesh of our first fathers, the four men which were created.

These were our first fathers, named Balam Quitzé, Balam Acap, Majucutaj, and Iqui Balam, our first seed.

They had no mother or father; they were just called *Men*. They were not born from woman, but were sons formed by Ajtzak and Ajbit, by Alom and Cajolom. Their formation and creation was wholly brought about by the supernatural and marvelous work of the gods, who gave them the appearance of men. They then spoke, reasoned, saw and felt, walked and grasped things; they were men perfect in face and of good and beautiful form.

Equally with the Romans, Greeks, Chinese, Japanese, and other Oriental peoples, the Quiché-Maya regarded themselves as direct descendants of the gods.

14

The History of Maize and of the Quiché-Maya Civilization

WE HAVE come to the conclusion of the *Popol Vuh*'s long exposition describing the slow evolution of Maya culture and its successive transformations from the lower level of the hunter-gatherers until it reaches the agricultural-patriarchal stage. The cultural horizons of the Quiché-Maya classification are established when a new element of prime importance arises to modify the type of life and the cultural circumstances; but the successive development of means of subsistence and the parallel course taken by the evolution of family and society, division of work, types of living quarters, as well as of arts and sciences, embraces a continuous process, allowing us to grasp the structure of its historical totality. When a high degree of evolution was attained in all phases of the culture, the basic patterns of Quiché-Maya civilization were thereby firmly established.

As for the degree of artistic advance at the beginning of the Fourth Age, it suffices to compare the beings whose arms and legs are formed of maize with those which in earlier epochs lacked all extremities. The emphasis now

THE HISTORY OF MAIZE

given those parts of the human anatomy reveals that the native artisans, imitating the gods, had markedly progressed and could sculpture anthropomorphically complete figures.

In the economic and social order, the Third Age is characterized by the horticultural-matriarchal regime, with the bean as its essential food, since humanity then was formed of that substance. Conversely, the Fourth Age is that of maize cultivation by men and by a patriarchal regime. This distinction is fully established in the references to the fact that formerly men had only mothers; now, however, they are not born of mothers but through a supernatural act, as Hunahpú, the Maize god, was born; moreover, the gods created only men — women will come later — and this determines their lawful position.

Maize has become the principal source of life, allowing man to share in the divine nature; it is the very essence of divinity that enters into the formation of humankind and from then on will sustain it both materially and spiritually, since by eating of maize man makes himself consubstantial with Deity itself.

But before acquiring its divine condition and becoming that basic food, the maize grain had to undergo a long process of cultivation until it gained its spherical form, full and hard, which will assimilate it with Hunahpú's head. That there then existed fully developed maize ears with their rows of grain is attested by the repeated mention of the white ears and the yellow ears. Those repetitions form part of the very technique of native literature for emphasizing every far-reaching event, and it has its linguistic correspondence in the phenomenon of reduplication. Such repetitions become tiresome and unpleasant to the ear habituated to European literatures; but if we penetrate into the native mentality we understand that they have a

profound meaning and, because of that, justify their seem-
ing monotony.

The history of maize starts in the Second Age, i.e., in
exceedingly remote times when the earth produced only
scarce and inadequate foods and — quoting Torquemada
— "the foods and fruits of the earth did not grow well,
causing people to die from eating various dangerous
things."[1] Among the wild grasses that were then included
in the diet was "the grass *centeucupi* and the grass *achian-
tli*," according to the account in the Thévet manuscript
and the Vatican A and Franciscan Codices. These latter
say that *cintrococopi* (the *centeucupi* of the Thévet) is a
certain kind of wild maize (called *atzitziutli* in the Vatican
Codex). Since the Mexican and Mayan sources belong to
the same mythographic horizon and make reference to the
same process of historical stratification, we have in the
Mexican, then, excellent complementary information to
the *Popol Vuh*.

There is additional historical and botanical evidence
that makes it impossible to think that the Mexican sources
refer to peoples of the altiplano and causes one to suppose
that they pertain to those who then inhabited the Central
American region, their cultural homeland. For example,
wild maize does not figure in the diet of the Chichimecs,
who ate "prickly pear leaves, various roots, palmetto,
honey, and yucca flowers," according to Sahagún. On the
other hand, in Guatemala there are two wild relatives of
maize, the only ones known, which are native to the
western part of this country (two kinds of teosinte and
various species of tripsacum).

Besides that, it must not be forgotten that the *Popol
Vuh* describes for us allegorically the evolutional process of

---

[1]Juan de Torquemada, *Monarquia indiana*, Mexico, 1934.

maize through the matriarchal age up until it acquires a character more or less like what it now has, with ears and grains perfectly developed. From the *Popol Vuh* we know that during the Third Age maize is already under cultivation and is found in the family garden. In those times men cleared the land and women sowed and reaped on a small scale, regulating their operations by the lunar calendar. This cultivation, pursued during many centuries of time, improved the quality and quantity of this grain, whose discovery is attributed to Ixmucané. But during that Age it was not yet "the food," the bean and root-plants (yucca and manioc) having the preferred place in the native diet. That its divinization occurred at the beginning of the Fourth Age shows that maize had not achieved its full development until then. Maize is the typical exponent of Quiché-Maya culture, as wheat and sorghum is of the Egyptian, and rice of the Hindu and Chinese.

The *Popol Vuh* specifies that the first kind of food made from maize took the form of a drink — the 9 drinks of Ixmucané. This could mean that at that time neither the earthenware pan for cooking maize cakes nor the knowledge of preparing tortillas existed. This would support S. Linné's observation that use of the earthenware pan is typical of a relatively recent epoch, it being unknown in what he calls "primary cultures." In support of this Swedish expert's conclusion, we have the linguistic peculiarity that there is no original word to designate the tortilla (see Appendix A).

The 9 drinks of Ixmucané became the sacred food par excellence, reserved exclusively for offerings to the agrarian gods, and they preserve their original name (*boronté*) among the Chortís, even in places where use of the vernacular language has been lost. This custom, whose origin goes back to the episode described in the *Popol Vuh*, would seem to confirm that maize as food was first employed in a liquid or paste form and that that form was incorporated into ritual as a result.

Another piece of evidence supporting this postulate lies in the fact that the peoples separated from the common cultural trunk at an early stage — such as the Andes culture — still consume maize preferentially in liquid or paste form, and in many places the earthenware pan is unknown. Similarly, it was not known among peoples who represent Third-Age culture, as the author was able to verify among the Taoajkas of Mosquitia, who use the grinding stone but are ignorant of preparation of the tortilla.

Mesoamerican culture is founded upon utilization of the following plants: maize, beans, calabash, cacao, the rubber tree, tobacco, and cotton (and in a minor degree upon sweet manioc), which make up its economy. Therefore the origin of the culture should be found in that people which discovered the use of these plants. In this regard the testimony of the Quiché manuscript is most eloquent in telling us about their discovery, it being the only American source to explain the mythic beginnings of all of them as well as their religious and practical usage. We have in fact followed the process of formation of maize, fabrication of cigars, the origin of the calabash and the place where it was first known, incense, the ball game, the beginning of the potter's art, the use of the grinding stone, the evolution of the calendar, etc. As for cacao, we learn that two varieties existed. Besides the names of rubber, maize, the cigar, cacao, etc., of Mayan origin, we have additional information in the Quiché manuscript of Francisco García Calel Tzunpán, which mentions that a king, Hunahpú, was the discoverer of cacao and of cotton.

These are the decisive arguments regarding the origin of agriculture in the New World and, besides the botanical facts to which we have referred in the chapter on the Tzolkín,[2] they rest upon the testimony of the *Popol Vuh*, the single native source which accounts for the evolution of maize and the phenomenon of its germination. It contains the code of the perfect farmer and also refers us to the social or astronomical events related to agricultural development, giving the time and place of the beginning of its cultivation. It locates this place in Paxil and Cayalá, a region that, as we shall have an opportunity to see when we discuss Tamoanchan, corresponds in its geographic, botanic, and zoologic aspects to the Pacific coast of Guatemala where all of the botanical and zoological species referred to in the *Popol Vuh*, and which were made divine by Quiché-Maya culture, are native.

The proof that Mexican traditions emanate from this same place is seen in the preservation of religious symbols such as the quetzal, tapir, lizard, cacao, rubber, etc., all of which imply an essentially southerly origin and are absent from the Mexican plateau. We repeat here the case of wild maize, mentioned in Mexican sources but unknown to the Chichimecs.

Raynaud translates Paxil as "houses upon pyramids." For reasons that we now give, a more appropriate translation is "hill (which later on was compared with the pyramid) of food" (*cerro del alimento*), the homologue of the "hill of subsistence" (*cerro de los mantenimientos*) on which the *Legend of the Suns* locates the finding of maize by Quetzalcoatl, disguised as an ant.

The root *pa*, by antonomasia, in fact means food, but its true meaning has not yet been uncovered because we are dealing with an archaism. This place-name, inseparable from maize or food, has in the linguistic order the

---

[2]Girard, *Los Chortís.*

same close etymological relation with these elements, a fact that can be proven by comparing the various languages stemming from the same linguistic and mythographic subsoil. There follows a short list of words meaning maize or allied concepts, related to Paxil or Cayalá (*pa* means tortilla, food, in Chortí):

With the root *pa:*

opa	maize, in Cuna
patta	food, in Miskito
ba cal	corncob, in Maya
pak cá	tortilla, food, in Paya
pacač	tortilla, in Maya
ipac	maize kernel, in Popolaca
pac	bean, in Matagalpa
ta pa	maize, in Araua
as cá	*milpa*, in Paya
ba cá	to sow, in Paya
tapxni	maize, in a Totonac dialect
buca	boiled barley and beans, in Chontal
noo-pá	corn ear, in Chorotega
kiz pa	corn, in a Totonac dialect

With the root *ta:*

t'a	corn, in Otomí
ta	*milpa*, in Chibchá
ta na	*milpa*, in Lenca

With the root *yal:*

aya	maize, in Miskito
nal	green corn ear, in Maya
c'ucjal	green corn ear, in Quiché
huayá	*milpa*, in Xinca
kan jal	large maize, in Poconchi

ijá   corn ear, in Tlapanec
hya   sun, in Otomí

With respect to the root *xi* of Paxil, one should consult the list in Appendix A dealing with *ixim* and related sounds, where there also appear names having the root *pa*. In the Memorial of Tecpán-Atitlán we have an informative supplement of great interest with respect to locating the geographical area of the homeland of Quiché-Maya culture. It says:

> Two animals knew that there was food at the place called Paxil: the Coyote and the Wild Boar. But the Coyote, when it pushed aside the maize looking for seeds to knead, was killed by an animal called Hawk. And from within the sea the Hawk brought the blood of the Serpent and of the Tapir with which it kneaded the maize, and from this the flesh of the people was formed by Tzakol and Bitol. And these knew well who was born, who had been begotten, since they made the people as they were. There were thirteen men and fourteen women. These married and one had two wives [polygamy for the lords; compare with the situation of the earlier cycle in which the seventh of the Ahpú had no wife but was single, a civil state at variance with the Maya family regime]. Therefore the race mixed, this race of ancient times, as they say [an allusion to the change from the matriarchal to the patriarchal regime which caused one clan to mix with another].

Here we have, completely explained, the etymological origin of Tamoanchan, a word which like that for maize, rubber, cacao, etc., is an exponent of Maya culture and can be correctly translated only from the Mayan. The name Tamoanchan breaks down as follows: *ta* = place; *moan* or *muan* = hawk or sparrow hawk; and *chan* = serpent, all in Chortí. Its meaning, then, is the Place of the

Hawk and the Serpent; in other words, the region where the Hawk brought the blood of the Serpent from the sea, the material that was kneaded with maize and entered into the formation of man. This means, then, a maritime region.

Although apparently differing, the Cakchiquel, Quiché, and Mexican versions tally in essentials regarding the anthropogenetic myth, with the single difference that in some versions anthropomorphic gods intervene, while in the Cakchiquel manuscript the same gods are represented under the disguises of their zoological nahuals, the bird and the serpent, which respectively symbolize heaven and earth. For the Mexicans it is Quetzalcoatl, the Creative deity, whose name embodies the mythical bird and serpent, who creates men with its own blood and cares for them by feeding them with maize.

The hieroglyphic of Tamoanchan is expressed by the rebus-sign of a bird of prey in the act of drawing blood from a serpent with its talon, such as appears in the following figure, taken from the Dresden Codex. This symbol, omnipresent in Mesoamerican culture, represents also the mystery of fertilization of the earth, which is no more than a constant repetition of the anthropogenetic myth. The Chortís recall the drama of the Fourth Creation each time that a babe is born, mixing its blood with maize at the moment the umbilical cord is cut, and that maize is given it to eat.[3] The Totonacs use a different method since, according to R. de la Grasserie, they make a kneaded mixture of the first fruits and grains of the harvest, mixing them with the blood of three children who were sacrificed. And the Mexicans allude to this symbol in the following line of the song to the Earth goddess: "The eagle is painted

---

[3]Cf. details in Girard, *Los Chortís*, "Ethnography."

with blood of the serpent." But nowhere do we find this idea so forcefully depicted as in the San Agustín monolith from Colombia (Figure 22, p. 258), which again makes the common genesis of American cultures clear.

The hawk and the serpent are still Huastec totems, according to observations of R. Shuller. The same theme was later copied by the Aztecs and even comes down to us in the coat of arms on the Mexican flag. But until now the indirect causes of the Aztec myth were unknown, and even though the legend of the founding of Te-nochtitlán is in the pub-lic domain, until now no effort had been made to go back to its far-past origins and to learn pre-cisely why it was that a serpent and a bird of prey should be poised on a prickly pear tree. We shall return to this mat-ter when we explain the symbolism of that tree, which does not belong to Maya mythology.[4]

FIGURE 21.

The importance of the Cakchiquel version lies not only in giving us an exact etymological definition of the word Tamoanchan, which until now no one, and no source, had succeeded in explaining satisfactorily, but also in locating

---

[4] Girard, *Los Chortís*, "Comparative Ethnography."

FIGURE 22. Theme of the Bird of Prey and the Serpent in the art of San Agustín, Colombia. This statue is in the Berlin Museum of Ethnography.

it firmly in history, time, and geography. Besides referring to a maritime region, the presence of the mythological tapir — whose habitat is purely Central American and does not extend beyond Chiapas — shows that the coasts to which this source refers must be sought south of Chiapas, that is, in the very zone in which the calendar was invented.[5]

Tamoanchan, a word that is translatable only in Maya and whose etymological explanation is found solely in Quiché-Maya sources, has been adopted by the Mexican

[5]Cf. Girard, *El Calendario Maya-Méxica*, Mexico, 1948.

tradition which also adopted the symbol of the bird and the serpent. We therefore find that the hymn to Cinteotl begins with this stanza: "The god of Maize has been born in Tamoanchan, in the place where there are flowers, in the place where there is water and moisture." Moreover, in Mexican myths Tamoanchan is the "house of birth," the place where man was created and where he delights himself. The Mexicans were aware that their mythical paradise was found in Central American lands, inasmuch as Sahagún informs us on the basis of native testimony that the original Tamoanchan is found in Guatemala, an affirmation that Henning also makes in declaring that Tamoanchan must be located in the south of Guatemala, where the first Tula was also located.

The description of both the legendary Tula or Tlalocán and the mythical Tamoanchan or Chortí paradise tally with Paxil and Cayalá, and appear as different names for the same place.[6] This place is referred to in all the sources as the homeland of maize, a garden of abundance, Xóchitl icacan, the country of flowers (one thinks of the Xuchiate River, "of the flowers," that divides the Mexican state of Chiapas from Guatemala). This idea is well expressed in the Vatican A Codex picture representative of the Fourth Creation that shows on a red-yellow background (color of the dawn and of the Fourth Regent according to the *Popol Vuh*) the young god (or god of the Flowers)[7] descending or falling from heaven and grasping the braided tresses in which very large flowers are hanging. Flowers also adorn

---

[6]Cf. chapter on Tzolkín and chapter 13, Girard, *Los Chortís*.

[7]The flower or Flower god is the emblem of beauty, a mark proper to the god of Maize. The relation between the god of Flowers and the Maize god, in addition to what we have said on the matter, appears in the Quiché word *cotzij* (flower) which is applied to the Agrarian god of the Zapotecs (*cocijo*).

the red field as well as the hands of the personages that are on the earth (see the accompanying figure, taken from the Vatican A Codex, plate 7).

The same motif, the Maize god falling from the sky and grasping cords in which he entangles himself, can be seen

FIGURE 23.

on statuary at Copán where in this form the descent of divine grace is represented, the essence which fertilizes the earth to produce maize or which fecundates woman to produce creatures.[8] This idea, illustrated for the first time in the immaculate conception of Ixquic, is expressed in the Chilam Balam of Chumayel in the following words: "There will fall girdles, cords, on the day when the Foam [the divine essence] of the Book [the Word] and the Fish [nahual of the Maize god] descend [see the text of the

[8]See Girard, *Los Chortís*, chapter 18.

katún wheel]." The theme of the cord by which gods or the generations descend to the earth, or men ascend from the underworld, is a common one in many American myths.

Moving on to another concept related to the Fourth Creation, we find that Quiché and Cakchiquel sources attribute the discovery of maize to animals who then pointed out the road to Paxil. In this allegory, in which the raiders of the *milpa* figure, it was doubtless their wish to record that wild maize was in the beginning considered inedible, until those animals by their example showed man that he could eat it without risk. That was a matter of vital importance for the primeval Indian "who died through eating various damaging things," as Torquemada said.

Those animals, discoverers of maize, are perpetually evoked in Chortí and Quiché rituals during the moment when the elder throws four grains of maize to the four cosmic directions, assigned to the coyote, the bird or crow, the bird of prey, and the mountain cat.[9] Very significant is the intimate relation among the coyote, the bird (the only animals mentioned in the Cakchiquel manuscript), and the wild maize or teosinte which the Chortís call *nar mut* (bird maize). They consider this plant to be the "grandfather of maize,"[10] while in the region of Bado Hondo and Santa Elena in the Chortí area itself, teosinte is popularly called "tail of the coyote."

The killing of Coyote by Sparrow Hawk, when the former was collecting maize seeds for kneading, is exceedingly interesting from the theogonic and cultural point of view. In another way, the *Popol Vuh* corroborates this passage of the Cakchiquel legend when it replaces Hunah-

---

[9]Girard, *Los Chortís*, "Ritual."
[10]Cf. ibid, "Ethnography."

pú-Utiú (sun-coyote) by Wak-Hunahpú (sun-sparrow hawk) in the list of the gods and does not again mention the Coyote god, who disappears from the mythographic scene from the beginning of the Fourth Creation. Aside from the testimony of the sources already cited, the existence of a Sun-Coyote god in the primeval religious stratum is confirmed by the preservation of the figure of the Coyote god, correlated with a Solar god, among some northern peoples who pertain to the hunter-gatherer cycle. But Sparrow Hawk killed Coyote when the latter tried to collect seeds to knead; that is, the animal that symbolized the prehistoric cycle is annihilated by the one representing the Quiché-Maya culture. This killed that, as Victor Hugo would say.

The dawning of the new culture is related as follows:

People were aware of their intelligence. They understood what they saw, and finished by learning and knowing everything that is under heaven. They could see through the shadows without the need to walk to the object of their vision. They projected their wisdom into the trees, stones, lakes, the sea, the mountains, and the coasts (note again mention of the sea and the coasts of the primeval homeland). They spoke the same language as the gods and understood the gods perfectly. Great was the wisdom that they possessed.

We see here a linguistic homogeneity described with the color and poesy of Quiché literature. This contrasts with the situation in the first horizon of the Mayan cycles when people could not understand one another. The Quiché traditions faithfully register the evolutional process in all aspects of the culture, including language development. They also mention the differentiations that took place within the Quiché language itself beginning with the departure from Tulán, noting that later on language became confused and people could not communicate. After the gods had formed the four first true men, to whom they transmitted their knowledge, they said to them: "Take possession of your mountains and your coasts." From then on, the earth, that divine inheritance, becomes the indivisible enjoyment of the native community and will be passed down through male descent.

Immediately the four creatures show their gratitude to the gods by "giving thanks two and three times," something their predecessors could not do, and thereby mark a new pattern of ethics and agrarian ritual, since a sense of gratitude is an innate quality in the Quiché-Maya Indian.

"Thanks then to you, Ajtzak and Ajbit, for having given us being; you are our grandfathers." This they said, when they gave thanks for their life and manifested existence.

They finished by learning all, searching out the four corners of all that is in the spaces of the heavens and on earth. In imitation of the gods the men established the squaring of the earth, to which they remain intimately linked since they themselves represent the four cosmic gods, one of them — Iqui Balam — being sterile like the part of the universe that it embodies. As cosmic gods they acknowledge the central duo as their grandparents and therefore affirm it in their words. Thenceforth the Quichés invoke that divine pair as their grandparents, a title that the elder who is their genuine representative (*chuch-kajaú*) will keep. The four first men establish the four-quartered division of territory and political organization. In a word, that first civilized generation was the equal of the gods because it was perfect.

But this did not please Ajtzak and Ajbit because there was then no difference between the creators and the created; and to overcome this difficulty the theogonic

council comes together once more and agrees to limit the
vision of the god-men, "blurring their eyes as the breath
dims the surface of the mirror; thus their eyes remained
cloudy and they could see only what was near. The eyes
that men now have continue to be blurred because even
yet their consciousness is not good." This explains the
Chortí elders' belief that Deity does not permit them to see
the suns and stars close up, and they can be contemplated
only from far away.[11]

At the heart of this allegory is a principle conducive to
ethics and wisdom, qualities that are inseparable. Thus it
is that in the Chortí view the most virtuous are always the
wisest, and true men nurture a continuous aspiration to
excel in virtue so as to be able to realize the ideal of divine
omniscience and so regain the condition of god-men that
they originally possessed.

After creating the four first civilized men, Cabahuil,
"by his word," creates four beautiful women, giving them
as wives to the men and so completing their conscious
awareness. This creation took place while the men were
asleep so that on waking they experienced the pleasant
surprise of finding at their side their respective companions
and therefore "their hearts were filled with happiness."

From then on man should awake at the side of his wife
and carry out the sacred law of reproduction, promulgated
in the above paragraph by implication. To that end Deity
has placed in man's heart that feeling (the sexual instinct)
which causes him to become full of happiness on finding
his partner who will be his other inseparable and accom-
modating half.

"They begat the people of the great and small tribes
and were the origin of us. Many were those who obtained

---

[11]Girard, *Los Chortís*, chapter on Tzolkín.

the ability to be sacrificers and adorers (elders), but only four were our progenitors."

This verse explains the origin of the caste of Mayan elders, instituted following establishment of ritual practices. The office of elder will be hereditary within the line created by Deity itself. Only those of that pedigree will be able to exercise the double office of spiritual and political chief of the tribe. From this comes the importance of the genealogical tree of the Maya or Quiché dynasties whose origin goes back to the beginning of the agricultural-patriarchal era, that is, to the opening of the Fourth Age.

"Balam Quitzé is the grandfather or father [note the equivalence of the terms father and grandfather, formerly applied to the mother and grandmother] of the house of Cagüek, Balam Acap of the house of Nijaibap, and Majucutaj of that of Ahau-Quiché, there being formed three descents, and no one forgot the name of his grandfathers and fathers who begat them there where the sun rises."

Only Iqui Balam had no descent, inasmuch as he was sterile. He becomes the patron of married persons who do not produce children and forfeit the right to use the solar symbols on their apparel, inasmuch as the male who is sterile does not give life as does the sun and is regarded as a son of Iqui Balam who left no succession or symbols to the race (F. Rodas).

Parallel with the inauguration of the Quiché-Maya elder caste, the tribe comes into being as an administrative unit which, like territorial demarcation, is patterned on the quadripartite model of the cosmos. This is a notable advance in political institution: for the first time the tribal society is organized on the basis of the federation of clans, in contrast with the earlier epoch when the clan formed the largest social unit composed of family groups. In like manner, the religious fraternity has become the tribal religion. One of the originating causes for the beginning of the tribe or clan federation was doubtless the shift from the matriarchate to the patriarchate "when the races mixed," as the Cakchiquel source puts it. The meaning here is that, in spite of the change effected, the same groups of families continued within another larger unit; this new condition is embodied by Hunahpú when he joins his grandmother's clan, later proclaiming the rights of the male, and he himself becoming the first tribal god.

We now have a complete picture of the development of Quiché-Maya society from the horde to the tribe, the largest unit of state. The tribe was the form of government during the classical period of Quiché-Maya culture, and is today among the Chortís.[12]

The clan continued as the basic unit of tribal organization, as it still is in the Chortí state which has a rural population scattered over a large territorial area. Given these antecedents, the next evolutional step toward a superior form of government can only be that of a tribal confederation as an extension of the federation of clans.

---

[12]Cf. Girard, *Los Chortís*, "Ethnography."

15

The Original Maya, Quiché, and Lenca Tribes

T HE NEXT paragraph in the *Popol Vuh* has great historical interest because it gives the names of the peoples which, besides the three Quiché lines of descent, proceed from the same cultural trunk and probably occupied the same country, beginning with the Fourth Creation. The Quiché text says:

> None of the three lines of descent forgot the names of their grandfathers and fathers who begat them there where the sun rises. Likewise there come those of Tamup and Ilocap with their thirteen generations, according to the tradition: the thirteen of Tecpán: the Rabinals: the Cakchiquels: those of Tziquinajá and those of Zacajip: there follow those of Lamakip, the Cumatz, those of Tujaljá and of Uchabajá; those of Chumialá with those of Aj-Quibajá; of Batenajá; the people of Acul, of Malamijá, of Canchajelep, and of Balam-Colop.
>
> This is, then, the origin of the *great tribes*, as we call them; we will speak only of the principal ones. Many others came out from each group of the people, but we will not write about them, except only about the place where they were begotten, where the sun rises.

Nineteen tribes, including the Quiché, composed the ethnic group that was then settled in the common cultural homeland. Of these the Pocomams and Poconchis have been identified, according to Brasseur de Bourbourg; also the Rabinals and Zacajip as branches of the Quiché group, and the Cakchiquels and Tzutuhils (Tziquinajá). But as A. Recinos observes, until now it has not been possible to identify the remaining tribes.

Of those unknown tribes our attention is especially drawn to the Cumatz and the Balam-Colop. The first name means serpent in Quiché and Cakchiquel, and is the equivalent to *chan* in the languages of the northern group in the Maya family. Here we have the etiological definition of the Maya tribe inasmuch as Chan is the original name of this people, and is preserved today by the Chortís whose elders title themselves Hor Chan (chief of Chan) and call the group under their jurisdiction, *chan*.[1] This documentary proof, firmly supported by ethnographic information, is also upheld by the relationship that is evident between the Quiché and Maya peoples who for long periods shared a common language and culture. The reference in the *Popol Vuh* is of the greatest importance because it establishes the community of origin of the Quiché and Maya groups and their geographic contiguity in a remote epoch of their history, data corroborated by archaeology and linguistics.[2]

Chan, the generic name of the Mayas, is derived from their cultural totem, the serpent. This figurative ancestor gave its own blood to form the true men of Quiché-Maya culture. This is the reason why the serpent is an omni-

---

[1]Girard, *Los Chortís*, chapters on Chortí religion and sacerdotal caste.

[2]Ibid., chapters on linguistics, archaeology, and history.

present motif in Maya art as a symbol of the divine nahual, and protector of the tribe and, by extension, of the whole nation derived from this original tribe. It passes by heredity from generation to generation to each group separating from the primeval tribe, so that all feel themselves joined together through their common belief in that totem. As said elsewhere, the Chortí community led by its elder regards itself as a serpent whose head (synonymous with chief) is that elder and whose body is the communal group. This idea is expressed pictographically in Mayan codices by the figure of a serpent with the head of god B, whose representative is the elder of the agrarian religion.[3]

All members of the group carry in their veins, by atavism, the blood of that common mythical ancestor of which they are descendants. This is why the Mayas consider the preservation of the purity of that divine blood an indispensable requisite for the very existence of the group, rejecting the introduction of any foreign element that might disturb its perfect homogeneity. It explains the hermetic character of the native community and the reason why the Chortís, and the other Mayan peoples who preserve their traditions, still regard as a public calamity — capable of receiving celestial punishment — any infraction of that basic law of their constitution. It is absolutely clearly put by the Chilam Balam of Chumayel: "The cause of our death is bad blood."

This aspect of Maya idiosyncrasy must be borne well in mind if we wish to understand the isolation and self-sufficient regime of the Old Empire tribes, or formulate adequate judgmental criteria to apply to outstanding problems of native culture, since this perception of the matter on the part of the natives themselves has not varied from

---

[3]Cf. Girard, *Los Chortís*, chapters on religion.

the beginning of the historical era right down to the present day, and the future action of the Indian derives from his past.

Aside from these considerations, the historic Mayas or Chan reveal in the name of their totem itself the geographical location of their original homeland situated in Tamoanchan, i.e., in Paxil and Cayalá.

It seems strange that the Cakchiquel manuscript should explain the symbolism of the totem adopted by the classical Maya group while the Cakchiquels themselves adopted the bat, as the *Popol Vuh* says in a later part. But, as has been said, the vampire is identified with the sacred bird and the butterfly, symbols of the god of Heaven, while the serpent is rather identified with the Earth god. But both animals are inseparable from the anthropogenic myth expressed in the figure of the serpent-bird, of which the Cakchiquels took one element and the Mayas the other. All this helps once again to demonstrate the common genesis of the Quichés and Mayas.

The above brings us to a consideration of the process of branching off and expansion of peoples separated at specific times from the same cultural trunk. Identification of any people in a particular epoch of history is determined by the name of their tutelary god, which is a symbol of their cultural and linguistic unity and the source from which springs their sense of common nationality. Although at bottom the gods of those diverse peoples are no more than distinct names for the same deity, that their names differ is sufficient to make of each a distinct god and therefore each has power and worship only among its own people. When through the passing of time and an extension over ever-widening areas linguistic differences come into play and are projected in the different names for the tribal god, this indicates the formation of a new nation.

Idiom and tribe are coextensive only while there is preserved the same name for the tutelary god. Such is the
process of the extension and separation of peoples which
have emerged from a common cultural horizon but which,
with time, have finally come to differ notably among
themselves.

Further on the *Popol Vuh* gives us a precise datum in
this regard, but there is even more: the famous codex
speaks of the dispersion of "many other peoples separated
from each nation," but these events are so far in the past
that "it does not mention the names" of those peoples
which have become lost to history.

This gives us a clear perspective of that centrifugal
movement of peoples emigrating from a common cultural
homeland in different directions and in differing moments
of time toward peripheral and ever more remote regions,
pushing one against the other, and corroborates the data of
ethnography concerning the distribution of peoples and
cultures over the Americas. Because of the constant increase in population growth, the Quichés themselves emi-
grate from their primeval homeland toward the north; and
this will be discussed below, but before that we must speak
of the Balam-Colop.

As we have demonstrated, Balam-Colop means "Tribe
of the Jaguar," the equivalent of the generic name of the
tau lepa (lineage of the jaguar) known today as the Lencas,
and for whom the jaguar is the cultural factotum.[4] The
root *col* (*op* is the particle for plurality) has remained just
as invariable in Quiché as in Lenca, and in both languages
has kept the same meaning, being translated by tribe,
people, group of people, while in Mayan languages of the
northern group *col* designates the *milpa* or farm. *Col*

---

[4] Girard, *Los Chortís*, chapter 1.

enters into the toponymy of a great number of Lenca villages. Moreover the Colop are identified as the Lencas by Vásquez (1714) and Vallejo (1893).[5] *Tau lepa*, the house of the jaguar, the homologue of *Nachan*, the house of the serpent of Maya traditions, was the name of one of the great Lenca religious centers situated on the lake of the same name (Taulepa altered into Taulabe). Lepa is for the Lenca what Chan is for the Mayas: the totemic designation of a primeval clan, which became the name of the nation formed as a result of expansion of that clan. The civilizer-hero of the Lencas is Comizahual (the jaguar which flies), and the figure of this feline is omnipresent in the rock art and folklore of the Lenca area just as is its name in their regional toponymy. The Lenca goddess named Ixelaca is the same as the Maya Ixel, whose name and function has not varied in either culture, which once more demonstrates their very old relationship. We have already in the ethnographic part of *Los Chortís ante el problema maya* underscored the cultural features that the Lencas and Mayas have in common. The jaguar is a cultural element pertaining to a very old horizon and continues to be a god in Maya theogony.

While the Chortís use the same word for jaguar and puma, in the variation of the suffixes the Lencas establish a difference between the two cats to accentuate the individuality of their totem. It is worthy of note that the Lenca name for the jaguar is used in Mame, one of the oldest languages of the Maya group, to mean serpent (*lepa* = jaguar in Lenca; *lebaj* = serpent in Mame). On the other hand, the Lencas call the earthworm by the same word the Mayas use for serpent (*chan* = serpent in Maya, and earthworm in Lenca). Something similar takes place with

---

[5] Ibid.

the Quiché word *cumatz*, which is applied also to the caterpillar and the earthworm, while the Chortís call the earthworm *lu kum* (literally, earth-egg), the same word that in Chol is employed to designate the rattlesnake. With regard to the word *lu*, we will note in passing that this root has remained invariable in Chortí and Lenca, having the same meaning (earth) in both languages, showing both the great age of this word and the intimate linguistic relation between Maya and Lenca. With respect to the root *pa* < *ba*, from the Lenca word for jaguar, we will find it also in the majority of the tongues imitative of proto-Maya, as can be seen in the following list:

ba lam	jaguar, in Maya
paj ram	jaguar, in Chortí
pa sum	jaguar, in Huastec
com ba	jaguar, in Chibcha
lu ba	serpent, in Aguacatec
amap	serpent, in Lenca
amaro	serpent, in Quechua
lepa	jaguar, in Lenca
pa nam	jaguar, in Coroado
a pa ué	puma, in Jívaro
bua, pua	jaguar-puma, in Hicaque
tza pas cajua	jaguar-puma, in Xinca
je ba	serpent, in Carib
namá	puma, in Matagalpa
lebaj	serpent, in Mame

In this short list can be seen the alternatives of a very old root which came to designate the jaguar in some languages and the serpent in others, a fact that is projected in Mayan and Toltecan art in the hybrid figure of the jaguar-serpent, to which we have referred in previous chapters of

Los Chortís ante el problema maya when discussing Mesoamerican art and its symbolism. The Quekchi seems to be
an exception to the rule, making use of the term *ix* to mean
jaguar, a root that in other languages is the prefix for the
feminine. *Ix* enters into the name of the goddess Ixbalamqué of the *Popol Vuh*, a Lunar deity figured as a feline,
and also into the formation of names for the moon in languages that have preserved their archaisms to any major
degree as, for example, the Mame (*ixjau* = moon) and Uru
(*isis* = moon, *his* = month). We must also note that in the
languages of peoples that pertain to the prehistoric horizon
according to the *Popol Vuh*'s classification, the jaguar is
related with the demon. Thus it is that the Ulua language
uses the same word to mean both these (*naual* = jaguar or
devil) and in the languages of the Sumo group, *naual* or
ulasa means both jaguar and demon, in this case repeating
the conception that the gods of the cultural cycle are the
demons of the earlier period. Therefore the peoples that
deify the jaguar extend back into prehistory.

PANORAMA OF THE PREHISTORY AND
PEOPLING OF HONDURAS

By mentioning the Lencas among the tribes which at
the beginning of the cultural era lived in the common
homeland, the *Popol Vuh* expresses a historical reality
having its full confirmation in the distribution of the native
population. Ethnic cartography in fact shows that the
Lencas and Mayas were contiguous during the whole of
their long histories until the collapse of the Old Empire,
when the Pipil wedge was introduced, which partially
separated them in the southerly area. Both Maya and
Lenca tribes had been developing in such a way that they
began to cover large territorial extensions populated by

hundreds of thousands of their descendants. Their expansive movements began from the Pacific Coast and moved inland, the Mayas occupying part of Honduras, Guatemala, Chiapas, the Petén, Tabasco, and finally all of the Yucatán Peninsula. The Lencas extended themselves through a large part of the Republics of Salvador and Honduras, to the east of the Maya area. The fact that the Balam-Colop should appear last in the Quiché list of tribal names seems to reflect their geographic position relative to that of the Maya peoples; they are a peripheral group in the area in which American culture was incubated.

If the tribe of the Chan and that of the Lepa-Col (Cumatz and Balam-Colop) could increase so much in numbers, we can infer that that process took place over a considerable lapse of time, which gives us an idea about the populating process of the other tribes, as well as those whose names are not mentioned, because they separated from the common trunk in even earlier times. All this helps us understand the way the continent has been peopled beginning with a sparse initial population. The oldest migratory movements seem to have followed the easiest route, that of the Pacific Coasts in a southward-moving direction. Supporting this conjecture is the fact that the Mayas, on moving inland into Chiapas, Guatemala, and Honduras in their slow migration from the Pacific toward the Atlantic, found the interior unpopulated;[6] and those peoples that flowed back toward the north are carriers of the culture they acquired in Central America.

In their advance toward the interior of Honduras, the Lencas pushed aside small groups related to them by language and culture, which had preceded them but which, because they had separated earlier, possessed the cultural

---

[6]Cf. Girard, *Los Chortís,* "Archaeology and History."

conditions the Mayas and Lencas had had in an earlier period of their history.

This explains the difference in social structure between the Lenca and Hicaque: the former are organized in tribes, while the latter preserve the clan as the largest social and political unit, which can still be seen in the group living in the Flor mountain, divided in two "halves" — that of Fidelio and that of Bertrand. The name the Hicaques give to themselves is Torrupán (family), which expresses the arrangement of the people organized by clans based on groups of families. The Payas, also related linguistically with the Lencas and Hicaque, descend from a primeval clan which had the monkey for its totem, today the protector of the whole nation. The Paya economic regime, like that of the Hicaque, is based mainly on cultivation of sweet manioc and maize; and both peoples practice polygamy — features placing them on an older ethnological level than the Lencas. Beyond the Payas in Nicaraguan Mosquitia and in the sector adjacent to Honduran Mosquitia, we find the Sumos whose family regime is governed by a pure matriarchy and whose economy is that of horticulture and the Age of wood. This cultural layer extends from the Atlantic slopes toward the south (the Talamancas) and continues farther into southern America.

Such a mosaic of cultural areas in so reduced a spatial extension gives us a living picture of the history of Mayan cultural development from the prehistoric age in a panorama extending from Copán — the apex of Mayan civilization — to the peoples of the Mosquitia who preserve a primitive mode of life. Each one of these peoples of the Mosquitia is characterized by a culture distinguishing it from the others, in spite of their living together in the same country, a fact that shows their independent evolution following separation from the common trunk. And this phenomenon confirms what was said at the beginning, that the Mayas of the Old Empire did not exercise influence outside the limits of their own territory. The degree of cultural advance of the various peoples is in direct proportion to their geographic distance from the Maya area. In other words the ethnologically oldest groups are the most distant in time and space from that cultural homeland from which they moved out, a fact that makes evident the spreading out of human groups in successive waves from a common center on the one hand, and on the other confirms the historical validity of the *Popol Vuh*. The ethnic panorama of Honduras reproduces on a smaller scale the process of cultural diffusion of the continent itself.

QUICHÉ EMIGRATION

Following the paragraph that deals with the origin of the tribes and the emigrations of peoples, the *Popol Vuh* tells about the migration of the Quichés themselves because of the constant growth in population. "Many men were made and in the darkness they multiplied," says the Quiché text (A. Recinos version). In order to better capture the meaning of those words, we should remember that according to the religious code the procreative act can take place only during the night.

On becoming more numerous, the Quichés emigrated and, coming from the place where the sun arose, found themselves in an isolated region, all together and in large numbers. "They had nothing with which to maintain their strength; they could only gaze up to heaven and did not know why they had come so far."

Farther on, they "heard news of a people, and they went there." Then is related their initial encounter in foreign territory with peoples in a state of barbarism, an account which we quote because of its historical importance:

> There were black people [barbarians] and white people [those of Quiché culture]. The physiognomies [physical types] of those people were distinct and so was their speech, as well as their manner of seeing and hearing. There were many of them under the sky; they were in the forests also, but their faces did not differ nor had they houses [a clear description of a natural grouping of individuals of equal language and culture, proper to the First Age]; they continually wandered about the woods and forests like mad people, like those possessed by folly [note once more that madness is here used as a synonym of barbarism]. This is how the Quichés described these people of the forests, looking down upon them.[7]

The barbarians to whom the *Popol Vuh* refers spoke to those who came from where the sun rises. Here we should say that the "country where the sun rises," mentioned so often, corresponds to the original Quiché-Maya homeland where the sun that lit up the Fourth Creation was born, i.e., the region that saw the dawning of culture.

"Those people had only one manner of speech among them all [important historical information about the existence of only one linguistic group]. They still could not name the trees or the rocks." This, in Quiché thought, reveals that the barbarians they encountered did not worship before figures of stone or wood and lacked proper names for stone and wood, a description applicable to primitive Nahua peoples whose language lacks specific names for designating trees and plants, inasmuch as these names come from the Quiché-Maya language. In this

---

[7]From A. Recinos's translation.

regard see the study of Marcos E. Becerra upon Maya-Mexican linguistic connections in which he points out that all of the Nahua names of plants from hot climes and of southern origin, and whose termination is *tl* and *tli*, are suspected of having originated in Maya etymology with the termination in *te*.[8]

This is also confirmed by the fact that the religion and culture of the Nahuas are patterned upon that of the Quiché-Maya and the very names of their ancient gods derive from those mentioned by the *Popol Vuh* (Cipactli or Cipactonal, from Zipacná; Oxomoco, from Ixmucané; Nanahuatl from Nanauac, etc.).

In contrast with the inferior cultural level of those primitive peoples, the Quichés possessed a culture that had been fully developed as the result of a long evolutional process embracing three succeeding ethnic cycles. They were expert sculptors compared with the barbarians, who could neither "name nor work wood or stone." On the other hand, the Quichés "looked around to find what they might use to sculpt the figure of their gods so they could pray before them."

This valuable information, which points to the direction followed by Quiché emigration, will be corroborated by the *Popol Vuh* itself further on when it refers to the Quiché return from Tula (Mexico) to Guatemala in the following words:

> After that they decided upon their *return* toward the place where the sun rises [an expression alluding, as said, to the cultural homeland]. And, when departing, they said, "We are going there, where the sun rises, *toward that place whence our fathers came*." This is what they said when they set out on their march.

---

[8]Cf. *Rev. Investigaciones Linguisticas*, vol. 4, nos. 3 and 4, Mexico.

But before devoting itself to the episode of the return to Guatemala from Mexico, the *Popol Vuh* goes into detail upon the reinstitution of human sacrifices among the Quichés, which because it was contrary to traditional customs brings about insurrections and serious outbreaks that culminate in the decision to abandon Mexican territory en masse. The text also emphasizes the linguistic differentiation taking effect among the tribes during their stay in Mexico, which gives some idea of the time that elapsed between the epoch of migration to the north and of the return to Guatemala, as well as the degree of expansion of population that was reached, inasmuch as linguistic heterogeneity is a phenomenon paralleling the separation and multiplication of peoples.

The archaeological and ethnographic data show that the Quiché group presents at the time noticeable differences in its customs in relation to those of the Maya culture, and its language reveals a prolonged contact with peoples of Nahua filiation. In the chapters on ethnography and comparative religion in *Los Chortís ante el problema maya*, the aforementioned episodes, and the part of the *Popol Vuh* which discusses the history of the Quichés themselves after their separation from the common trunk, are considered in greater detail.

16

The Dance of the Giants

SINCE time immemorial, ritual dances, farces, or open-air theatrical presentations form an indispensable complement of every religious festivity in Mesoamerican culture. In this wise they perpetuate traditional myths that exalt those ethical principles governing the patterns of life, as well as extol the mysteries of creation, of cultural origins, and of the religious code that is a compendium of all the laws and great deeds of the hero-gods, by putting them in the form of allegory that is within reach of the public's understanding.

But ever since the Conquest, these manifestations of the native spirit carry the inevitable mark of colonial European theology, and this has permitted them to survive under strange formalisms in versions corrected and authorized by the Spanish clergy. Thus it was that "The History," the name the Chortís have preserved for the Dance of the Giants, became transformed in appearance into two Biblical episodes: the beheading of Saint John, and the battle between Gavite (meaning David) and Goliath.

Nevertheless, beneath this superficial disguise the Chortís have known how to preserve the most valuable literary document of their past which, besides being a historical account of great significance, can well be regarded as the most important present-day expression of Mesoamerican theater, as much because of its content as because of its venerable antiquity. And this work's importance acquires even greater merit since it deals with a people about whose past we know nothing, as we completely lack informational sources.

Although the Chortí "History," such as we find it exhibited in the Dance of the Giants, contains traditions common to both Maya and Quiché culture and is found written in the *Popol Vuh*, we see that it is presented only in the exclusively Chortí area and lately is confined to a small part of Camotán. This is the final redoubt where this dramatization of the mythic portion of the *Popol Vuh* can still be observed. It was more or less a century ago that performance of the Dance of the Giants was discontinued in Chiquimula as a result of a cholera epidemic which caused the death of the group of artists responsible for continuing that traditional event.

As said, ritual dances given in the ceremonial plaza of the district capital of the tribe formed the cultural patrimony of specific clans that had specialized in certain artistic presentations, in the same way that industrial firms specialize in a particular product. Thus the Dance of the Giants, with its body of players directed by a master of ceremonies, is a long-time specialty of the village of Tisipe, located a half-league from the town of Camotán. According to the artistic director responsible for carrying on the tradition, that very important dance is slowly coming to its end since the "accounts" of today are already incomplete, it being noted that since the past century part of the text that is recited during the theatrical presentation has been lost.

Responding to one of the imperatives of ethnography — to rescue while still possible all the manifestations of native culture in their multiple aspects — I arranged with the master of ceremonies to put into writing under his verification the actual extent of the "accounts," promising not to divulge the contents of my report to any person in the Chortí area and to give him a copy of what I wrote. As a result of this agreement and after having witnessed the famous Chortí drama many times over in order to compare the spoken record with the written, I delivered to the master of ceremonies the version that today can be found amid the ceremonial paraphernalia of the director of "The History," and which he found completely satisfactory.[1]

We have some idea as to the relative antiquity of this theatrical piece from the fact that its theme forms a cultural inheritance common to both Mayas and Quichés before their separation, i.e., before our own era, the Chortí "History" being the myth of the *Popol Vuh* made into drama. It must not be forgotten that Mayas and Quichés were separated during the whole of the Old Empire period, and when the Quichés returned to Guatemala about the tenth century of our era, according to their own traditions, a long time had already elapsed since Maya civilization had collapsed. The Quichés brought with them a folkloric series: the Dance of the Deer, the Flying Pole, the Dance of the Snake, etc., all of which are foreign

---

[1]That my report was accurate is vouched for in the following paragraph taken from a letter written to me by the mayor of Camotán, responsible for receiving, lodging, and feeding the actors. It says:

The Master of Ceremonies of the Dance of the Giants tells me that the report you sent is very good, and needs no modification whatsoever. Thank you for the photographs. Affectionate greetings to the Very Honorable Don Raphael Girard.

(signed) FIDELINO ROMERO

to Chortí culture. On the other hand, the Quichés do not know the Dance of the Giants or any similar presentation, but they did indeed write the *Popol Vuh*, which we find to be the explanation of the Chortí drama. Considering these circumstances, the famous "History" cannot be attributed to Quiché influence and must be seen as an element that has been preserved from a remote past which allows us to go back to the common cultural origins of both groups.

Its principal *dramatis personae* embody the hero-gods Hunahpú and Ixbalamqué who, with their parents the seven Ahpú, fight against the mythological giants Vukup Cakix, Zipacná, Caprakán and the forces of Xibalbá represented by the Black Giant and his henchmen. This is the theme that embraces the whole of the mythic portion of the celebrated Quiché text. Evocation of the life of the gods in mystical dramas is a typical custom of Mesoamerican peoples; and we have a proof of this in the "Tulanianhululae," which according to the Vatican A Codex condenses the cultural origins of the Aztecs expressed in dances and songs. Despite that, the Dance of the Giants or Chortí "History" is something original and unique in America. What "The History" offers us is not solely a mythical account; it sums up the native knowledge of theogony, cosmogony, and astronomy as well as the arithmetic and time-reckoning procedures employed during the Great Period of Maya civilization. Therefore, every single thing pertaining to its presentation is carried out according to a program that is exceedingly carefully laid out beforehand in harmony with the mathematical mentality that is so characteristic of the Maya.

The Chortís emphasize with great frequency that everything taking place in the world, as well as in their lives, has "its day and its hour," predetermined by Providence. Therefore "The History" must be presented exactly at midday when the sun is at its zenith. The drama is presented three times in the year: June 24, coinciding with the fiesta of San Juan, patron of the town; June 13 on San Antonio day; and December 8, fiesta of the Immaculate Conception, patroness of Camotán.

In each of these presentations the Dance must be given twice on each day on three successive days: the day before the fiesta date; that day itself; and the following day. These numbers are not arbitrary since the total of 18 annual presentations corresponds with the 18 months of the old native calendar that still governs their ritual and economic cycle today. With regard to the dates given and despite a slight variation so as to adjust them to the fiestas of the holy days of the Roman Catholic Church, the day of San Juan corresponds to the old three-day festival which formerly celebrated the summer solstice amid great solemnities and mythological dances. Likewise, that of the Conception coincides with the old three-day festival that solemnized the winter solstice. It is curious to note how in the celebration honoring San Juan two millennial rites come together: one pertaining to the primeval civilizations of the Old World and the other to the Mayan people, but whose original meaning was the same. Actually the fires of San Juan, by which that Roman Catholic date is commemorated now in some parts of Europe, are vestiges of the solstitial festival which was celebrated before the arrival of Christianity. Thus, both commemorations are closely related in the same way as fusion of the birthdate of Christ and the winter solstice came about.

The old rules are rigorously observed down to their smallest details, such as the one requiring that the actors who represent the solar and lunar gods take their places according to the respective positions of those heavenly bodies during the winter solstice. Moreover, by means of the mysteries in which word and mimicry are combined, the gods are praised in public, this being a form of prayer or adoration which every human being should give to his creators.

This detail in ritual stands out clearly in the Chortí drama when the actors, at the start of each allegorical scene and at the end of the presentation, give homage to the sun, saluting it ceremoniously with face turned to the east while they trace semicircles from east to west in the air with their naked swords, imitating the daystar's trajectory symbolized in olden times by the ball game. This game is also remembered in the struggle of Gavite with the Black Giant, in which these stand respectively for the opposing light and dark fields of the cosmic plane. When paying homage to the sun, the actors invariably place themselves in a position that corresponds with the east-west axis, directing their salutes toward the east. One time, when the Indians danced expressly for me, I repeatedly tried to get them to change their position under pretext of getting better photos of them in movement, but they automatically returned to the posts indicated by tradition and, when the ballet took the form of the cosmic cross, the artists glided each to his place, resulting in a perfect image of that cross oriented toward the four cardinal points.

This sun veneration emanating from the whole Dance performance seems not to have undergone any alteration since the pre-Cortéz period, despite the efforts the priests made to change the "pagan" theme into Biblical episodes. Although the earlier names of the principal actors have become Christianized, the substance has preserved all its native flavor, with the single exception that the epic battle between Hunahpú and Hun Camé has become the individual combat between David and Goliath, respectively called Gavite and the giant Golillo, while what is the

beheading of San Juan for those not versed in native matters is in reality the beheading of the seven Ahpú by order
of Hun Camé.

The eight actors, who in addition to the master of ceremonies and the musicians form the cast of the Dance of the
Giants, are divided into two equal groups that take positions facing each other. One group is in the east and the
other in the west of an imaginary quadrilateral that represents the cosmic plane. The east foursome includes the
King who personifies the Father-Sun, the greatest deity of
the native pantheon; two Gavites who symbolize the
young sun and the young or full moon and are the twin
hero-gods represented in the *Popol Vuh* by Hunahpú and
Ixbalamqué; and a "captain" who embodies the role of the
Mother-moon, companion of the sun-King, equivalent to
Ixmucané of the *Popol Vuh*, who completes the east quar-
tet. These take posts in accordance with the position of the
starry bodies during the solstice in the manner shown in
the diagram on p. 288. The western foursome is composed
of the Black Giant, the personification of both the mythical giants and the Camé, which have come together in one
personage symbolizing the malign forces of the universe
eradicated by Gavite and confined to a sector of the underworld; a White Giant, who embodies the role of the seven
Ahpú fallen into the power of Hun Camé; and two "armorers" or "outfitters" whose parts will be explained
below.

Both quartets in their relative positions and their cos-
tumes represent the clear or luminous side of the universe
in combat against the dark side, or the contrast between
day and night, the summer and winter sky, the upper level
of the cosmos in opposition to the lower; and, therefore, of
civilization against barbarism. We shall discuss all of this
symbolism and explain it in terms of native thought.

The actors place themselves as follows:

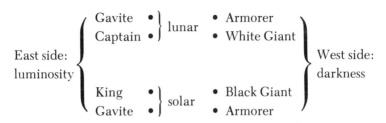

Before explaining the action of the dance, we shall describe the apparel of the actors. The King wears rose-colored trousers whose two cuffs have each been cut in four triangular points to make eight "solar rays," a feature we also find in the dress of figures sculptured on the stelae at Copán which have the lower legs adorned with belts of triangles whose meaning of sun rays is well known. Also the cuffs of the shirt sleeves, tied up like bracelets, terminate in yellow pointed festoons, the typical color of the Solar god. It must be noted that whereas one cuff has ten festoons, the other exhibits only seven. The shirt is sprinkled with blue points on a light background and, in terms of its cut, the front flap is longer than the rear, and the area of the umbilicus is bordered by thirteen points having yellow borders each ten centimeters long. The collar is cut into five triangles. As for the adornments of the cuff, armlet, and anklets, we find they are also typical of those found on the sacerdotal personages depicted in Maya statuary; there they figure not only as simple adornments but as arithmetic and time-reckoning elements, as we shall explain. Upon the rose-colored background of the trousers, along the outer seams, run two vertical yellow bands sown with a double line of red thread; each band finishes in a figure of three elements (reproduced below), also yellow, which are the graphic expression of the trine and dual conception of native theogony.

The King is the only personage who wears a crown, made of cardboard and covered with brilliant gold paper, terminating in ten points. In form it is similar to the head-dress worn on certain crowned heads in ancient Meso-american statuary. A blue bonnet, symbol of the celestial vault, covers the top of the King's head while a rosy veil some thirty centimeters long falls from it and covers his face. A long yellow cloak with surplice covers the shoulders of this august figure and, with the crown and signs of solar rays, composes the unmistakable evidence of regal dignity belonging only to the Sun god. The four ritual colors — yellow, blue, red, and white — are represented in the dress of this being which, occupying the chief place in the Chortí pantheon, symbolizes the cosmos. The absence of black in the gamut of cosmic colors should be noted.

The many triangular points that literally radiate from the divine figure stand for the sun's rays. No less symbolic is the yellow cape, the duplication of the resplendent mantle of Gucumatz or Quetzalcoatl in which the elements of feathers, sun rays, breastplates, and hair have the same meaning, are consubstantial, and reduce to a common linguistic denominator according to the native way of thinking. The mantle is yellow to identify the Solar deity or deity of Summer, but is transformed into green — the color of the vegetation — to indicate the Agrarian deity who governs during the winter season.

Since the Dance of the Giants represents a festivity in honor of the Solar god in his aspect as a summer deity, the color of his mantle must be yellow, contrasting with the green mantle that covers the shoulders of the elder of the agrarian worship, just like the cape of the god he repre-

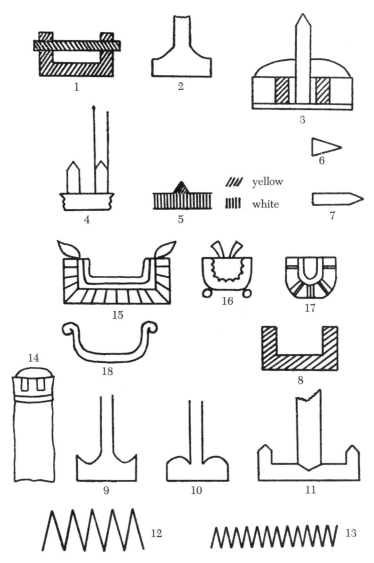

FIGURE 24. 1. Glyph on cap of master of ceremonies. 2. Figure on trouser cuffs of Giants. 3. Shaft of Black Giant's headdress. 4. Insignia of Gavite. 5. Captain's sleeve adornment. 6. Shoulder insignia. 7. Collar spangles. 8. Lunar hieroglyph on Captain's cap. 9–10. Captain's costume, trouser-cuff figures. 11. King's costume, trouser-cuff ornament. 12. Points on King's crown. 13. Points on King's shirt. 14. Cap with veil. 15. Lunar glyph in the Atl sign, Aztec calendar. 16. Atl glyph in the Cospi Codex. 17. Atl glyph in the Nuttall Codex. 18. Atl element in the Laud Codex.

sents when he celebrates the ceremonial corresponding to winter. In similar manner the mythological serpent (*sierpe*) becomes a red snake (*culebra*) and a blue snake (or green since the same word is used for both colors) to symbolize the change of seasons which are clearly differentiated in Chortí liturgy.

All this serves to clarify certain peculiarities in Mesoamerican iconography which until now have not been understood because the researchers had not penetrated into the esotericism that conceals native religious thought, to the point where some pictographic texts have been "corrected" in the belief that the native artist had made a mistake. Such is the case of Lord Kingsborough: when reproducing a plate of the Borgia Codex in which the Solar deity was associated with yellow feathers, he believed there had been a mistake made by the artist because in his view the feathers should have been green. And he, in fact, colored them green, but by doing so he succeeded only in deforming the original meaning of the text.[2]

With respect to the time-reckoning symbolism exhibited in the apparel of the King, we can say that there are represented in it all the basic units of Maya computation. The 10 points of the crown and the 8 of the trousers make the 18 uinals of the tun — a unit of the katún series that we also find in the 18 per year presentations of the famous Chortí drama — while the two series of 10 rays on the crown and a series on one of the sleeves symbolize the basic unit of the native vigesimal system, i.e., the 20 days of the uinal. By extension, the same number represents the katún composed of 20 tuns, as well as the whole ascending series of the katún wheel: baktún of 20 katúns, piktún of 20 baktúns, kalaltún of 20 piktúns, and kinchiltún of 20 kalal-

---

[2] Lord Kingsborough, *Antiquities of Mexico*, London, 1831.

túns. Also the breakdown into the katunic thirteen and the wutz or doubles of 7 katúns is represented by the 13 points of the shirt and the 7 of the other sleeve. This peculiarity is explained in a most picturesque way in the Book of Chilam Balam of Chumayel as follows: "Then, the days went to test each other, and they said, 'Thirteen and seven in a group . . .'" Such is characteristic of Maya computation, and has been preserved traditionally by the Chortí.

The days of the civil year result from multiplication of the numbers 18 and 20 which are figured in the crown, the feet, the umbilicus, and a sleeve of the Solar deity, while the element 13 combined with the 20 gives us the cipher corresponding to the totality of the Tzolkín or ritual calendar of 260 days, whose elevation to a higher power results in the baktún of 260 years just as it is computed in the *u kahlay katunob* of the Mayan Chumayel manuscript. With respect to the series of 9 days of the Tzolkín and its extension to the Long Count, which the epigraphers assign to the glyph G and which corresponds to the 9 forms of the Bolón ti kú in Maya mythology, it is found in the 5 solar rays of the collar and the 4 of the feet; moreover, it is expressed in the 9 days of the year on which "The History" is danced.

Multiplying the 4 points of the foot by the 2 series of 10 elements found on one sleeve and on the crown, we obtain the number 400, a value corresponding to a *bak* in Maya mathematics. Equally can be found the whole ancient arithmetic scale, combining numbers: *hun* = one; 20 *hun* = 1 *kal*; 20 *kal* = 1 *bak*; 20 *bak* = 1 *pik*; and 20 *pik* = 1 *kabal*; that is to say, the same progression noted in the katún wheel. The number 400 also corresponds to the number of days of the loose year employed by the Quichés until the Conquest, while the succeeding unit is arrived at by an operation like that above in which we get the value of 1 *bak*, except that the sum of the elements shown on the *two* trouser legs (8) — rather than a single trouser leg — must be taken into account. In lesser units we find that the 4 points of one ankle in themselves stand for a cycle of 4 years that, multiplied by 13 given us by the belt, turns up the number 52 which has a dual function: as exponent of days it forms a division of the Tzolkín; but representing years it forms a cycle of 52 — that is, the time that must pass before a day can return to the same calendric position. The *xiuhmolpilli* is obtained by multiplying the lower points by those on the belt (8 x 13 = 104). Likewise, the numbers 4, 5, 10, and 13, which appear as multipliers in the formation of subdivisions of the Tzolkín, figure in the elements displayed by this royal personage, as do the mul-tiplicands 26, 20, and 65, this last obtained by the combi-nation of the 5 and the 13.

When the King spreads his legs and lifts his arms over his head, he assumes a posture that can be called a cross and which is nothing more nor less than a representation of the *nahui ollin* or the glyph *kin*. That is, at those moments he assumes the character of a cosmic and solar entity, an affirmation that is confirmed as well by the juxtaposition of the following two numerals in the central point: the 13 of the umbilical cloth and the 5 formed by the cruciform point. Both these correspond to the type-number of the deity of the Cosmic Center, which is also called the navel of the world, so that the Chortí personage embodies it in all of its aspects.

On the other hand, the 4 cosmic entities that according to Chortí religious ideas are positioned in the 4 angles of the cosmos are symbolized by means of 4 red threads sewn into the trousers of the King. Their very color, which in Chortí is called *chak*, eloquently expresses the role of the 4 Mayan Chac. And neither must we forget the cosmic cross formed by the King when standing with arms extended, since this symbolizes the 4 cardinal directions as well as the east and west positions of the sun in its zenith and its nadir, and in this way he is able to represent the cosmic apparatus in toto.

And those triangular cuts which seemingly have no great significance have not been made arbitrarily but with

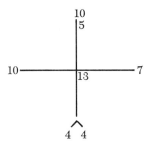

FIGURE 25. Diagram of the numbers represented by "solar ray" glyphs.

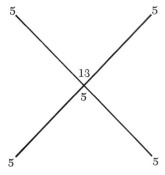

Diagram of the X-shaped cross represented by the King.

premeditation, inasmuch as there are 7 points to one sleeve and 10 to the other. Nor is it coincidence that the 13 points should be placed exactly over the navel. The same is true of the other cuttings of the cloth, needlework, and sewn figures of costume: all have a precise although multiple meaning that is always in accordance with Chortí esoteric knowledge. The adornments of the cuff and the anklets evoke in the Chortí elders the continuous memory of the "strong arms and hands" of their gods, who also possess a tremendous power in their lower extremities since "with only the point of the foot" they keep the terrestrial serpent in its place. We find this very expression of "strong arms" in the narratives of the Dance we are describing, and which brings to mind the Maya name *kab ul*, meaning "powerful arm," which was the specific name of a divinity in their pantheon.

In the same way, the representation of glyphs connoting numbers typical of Maya chronology is an inseparable part of the apparel of the personages sculpted on the Copán stelae, who are richly adorned with collars, armlets, anklets, knee guards, and *maxtlatl*, covered with calendric symbols in the form of discs, balls, quadrangles with signs of *nahui ollin*, conches, etc., that undoubtedly perform the same function as the triangles on the Chortí costume we have been analyzing. Both the glyph of the solar ray and the disc or sphere represent an identical thing, the *kin*, the primary unit of Mayan mathematics and time-reckoning. In confirmation of what was said in the linguistic part of *Los Chortís ante el problema maya* we call attention to the fact that the parts of the body on Copán statuary are treated as units in themselves. For example, on stela A it can be seen that the knee is replaced by a human head surrounded by 18 beads, the unit number in the katún count; but that unit has no value unless it is exactly combined with the whole system expressed in the total aggregate of the personage on which it appears. Thus, we find there is projected in the structure of the calendar the same concept that governs the social organism, where the unit — in this case the individual — has no value by itself but only as a member of a group.

We shall describe next the apparel of the "Captain" who, despite his name and masculine clothing, in reality represents the inseparable feminine companion of the King and on the heavenly plane corresponds to the Lunar-Terrestrial goddess called Ixmucané in the *Popol Vuh*. In Chortí religious terminology, the name of Captain is applied to the moon. And, so that we shall have no doubt

about his identity, he displays on his cap the lunar hieroglyph in the form of a yellow-colored U on a red background (see Figure 24, no. 8). From the actor's headdress
hangs a yellow veil covering his face. Twenty-one rectangular spots, of which 12 are dark and 9 light, respectively violet and yellow in color, appear on the background
of the fabric.

Of great significance is the fact that the King's veil
lacks any markings, while that of his companion exhibits a
ritual series connected with the moon and the earth. As
explained elsewhere, the stellar entities who "work"
during the winter season, which according to the Chortí
Tzolkín is made up of 9 uinals, are 12 in number. During
that whole period the moon has a special role since, as
goddess of Water, it brings down the rains that shall cause
the seeds to fructify. When it is performing this function,
the moon is compared to an immense pitcher full of water,
which pours out its contents upon the world. Moreover,
both numbers represent the night sky full of stars wherein
dwell the 12 companions of the god-Thirteen and the Nine
Lords of the Night who take part in the process of the
maize germination. It is well known that the cabalistic
number 9 corresponds to the Lunar-Terrestrial goddess, a
deity that governs the formative phases of human and
plant life. Its calendric importance is seen in the Tzolkín
and in the series of glyphs G which, as said, figure at the
end of the initial series, playing the same role as in the
Tzolkín and in the so-called Supplementary Series or lunar
computation.

If it is true that the King's veil lacks markings, on the
other hand there emanate from all of his person solar rays
that are projected in the yellow elements of the lunar personage, just as takes place in scientific reality with the
reflection of solar light by the moon. This cosmic principle

was already known to native science, to judge by Clavigero's observation that "the ancient Indians knew that the moon receives its light from the sun." Various popular legends reveal this belief, among other things saying that the sun had covered the face of the moon with pieces of paper. But the use of veils by the personages who embody the sun and the moon has another meaning, one that is found only in the *Popol Vuh* in a passage which tells us that "in the beginning the heaven and the earth existed, but as yet the faces of the sun and the moon were covered. Then there was only very little light on the earth."

To return to the description of the Captain's costume, we find that he wears a frock coat and blue trousers. Upon the vertical seams of the latter runs a wide white band ending at the ankle in a different image for each leg. One presents two figures shaped like a sickle, while on the other this figure is inverted and displays two parts of a disc. The two images together represent the four lunar phases. The triangular shoulder pieces are yellow upon a blue background, and they symbolize luminous bodies in the dark heavens, the reverse of the cap where a blue point shows against a red background. The edge of the frock coat is white, as are the cuffs of the sleeves, and each one exhibits a small yellow triangle in its center. The shirt front and buttons of the frock coat are also white because that is the color of the satellite at night. Two yellow spangles on the collar complete the adornments.

There are 9 elements in toto: 2 on the trouser borders, 2 on the cuffs, 2 on the shoulder pieces, 2 on the collar and 1 — a glyph — on the front of the cap. The latter, representing the lunar hieroglyph, has not varied since the epoch of the Old Empire. If, for example, we compare the Chortí figure with another on the pedestal of stela N at Copán, specifically related to lunar counts and deities, we shall see that the two glyphs are identical in both form and relative proportions. This sign, in the shape of a receptacle and evocative of a feminine function, has been preserved by all peoples of Mesoamerican culture. The essential part of the *atl* glyph in the Aztec calendar is similar to that of Copán and to the one worn by the Chortí actor. That shape is a stylization of a container with water — which is likened to the moon — or a realistic representation of nature, such as found in example 16 in the accompanying illustration taken from the Cospi Codex, showing a vessel full of water.

The Mexicans said that in the beginning the moon shed light with the same brilliance as the sun, the god of Pulque or Frothy Drink, but the latter covered the moon's face with paper as if it were trying to adorn a pot of pulque. The figures of Zapotecan deities which display on their foreheads the same lunar glyph as does our Chortí personage are typical, and we also find it on Xochiquetzal. All of the known codices give us this lunar hieroglyph in one or another form with its variants. We can say that its origin goes back to a far past, inasmuch as we already find it on the forehead of the giant head of La Venta pertaining to the Olmec horizon, and even in our day it is omnipresent on the apparel of the Chortí or Quiché women.

The Gavites, offspring of the White Giant, wear white blouses backstitched with red thread on the one and white thread on the other, tight-fitting at the waist. Both the sleeves of the blouse, as well as the trousers, are rose-colored. Like those of the King, the trousers of the twins have a vertical band, somewhat narrower, that ends at the cuff in two elements having the same form as those adorning the King's trouser cuffs. But here the differences begin. First, we note that the decorative element which one of the Gavites wears on his trouser cuff lacks the triangular symbols of the solar ray, since he embodies the young moon, the Ixbalamqué of the *Popol Vuh*. Also, we should observe that the trouser elements of the Gavites are not placed evenly on each side of the vertical band as they are with the King, but are found on one side. Together with the reduced dimensions of the forms, this distinction manifests a hierarchical rank lower than that of the King and suggests the idea of a sun in gestation.

This concept is found displayed also in the apparel of the Quichés, who through symbolism express differences in age and rank within the family group, as the well-known student of the Quichés, Flavio Rodas, has pointed out. Using the same method employed by the Chortís, the embroidery on the Quiché's trousers announces the three stages of human life — infancy, maturity, and old age. The sign of *akal kij*, infant sun, marks the first stage by means of a drawing representing the incomplete sun, and offers a parallel with the figure on the Gavite's trousers. *Alal kij*, young sun, is the distinctive emblem for those men who have proven their procreating ability; while the sign *ma kij*, grandfather sun, marks the patriarch who has gained a plenitude of wisdom and like the sun sheds his beneficence within the family circle.

The solar Gavite wears a yellow headdress from which hangs a veil sprinkled with 24 rectangular figures, of which 14 are dark and 10 light in color, the first divided into two series of 7 dark elements and the latter into two series of 5 light-colored elements, with the dark and light alternating in each. These latter clearly distinguish the young god who, in numerical terms, equates with god-Five in the divine hierarchical scale, while the septenary series corresponds to his parent, represented in "The History" by the White Giant. Possibly Gavite's wearing of this number is to make clear beyond all question the nature of his ancestral line, a conception very much in accord with the Chortí perspective which asserts that the offspring are like "the face" of their progenitors.

The lunar Gavite wears a white cap having a blue peak, and a white blouse and sleeves, since this is the distinctive color of the lunar entity, as we have seen in the discussion of the dress of the King's female companion. His face is covered by a veil similar to the one his companion wears, the difference being a variation in the number of signs: his veil has only 21 — 9 light and 12 dark in color.

Both the Gavites, as well as the King and the Captain, carry a wooden sword in their right hands, seemingly a Colonial feature. But if we turn to ethnography and archaeology, we quickly find that this element derives from a very old ethnical stage and is found over a very considerable area of the continent. The warriors shown in the pillars of Tula carry in their left hands a wooden sword called *hulche*, a weapon found dispersed over a large part of South America and into the Antilles where "a wooden sword of extremely hard palm is used," according to Columbus's account of his first voyage.[3] Esoterically the sword stands for the solar ray or serpent of fire and, when the Chortí actors raise their swords to the sun, they repeat a classical gesture used by Mexican warriors in their ritual battles. When the master of ceremonies was asked what was his understanding of the origin and object of these wooden swords wielded by the actors, he replied to me that those arms were exceedingly old and no material other than wood must be utilized in their manufacture, certainly not metal, "because it was in that way that Our Lord (*Ka tatá*) gained victory with wooden instruments." This explanation helps confirm for us that in the mythical age

---

[3]Herrera, *Décadas*, II, 1943.

metals were not known, a condition faithfully preserved by tradition despite the fact that the Chortís knew the use of metal, as well as of the bow and arrow, but do not employ in their "History" those arms not consecrated by tradition.

The master of ceremonies wears blue trousers having vertical red bands and a blue jacket with red sleeves, the red being repeated in the trouser cuffs. A green veil covers his face, and over the forehead, on his cap, he displays a yellow lunar glyph crossed by a rose-colored bar that stands out against the reddish color of his headdress. Besides his function as chief of the association of artists and as director of the drama, the master of ceremonies also plays the most difficult roles, i.e., in those moments during which the "account" and the movements must be carried out with complete exactitude and with the precision demanded by the millennial tradition. At those times he is the center of the audience's attention, most so when he plays the role of Gavite, becoming the principal actor. He can do this with propriety since he displays the insignia, reproduced in Figure 24 above (no. 1), that authenticates him as Gavite: the rose-colored band inserted into the lunar glyph is by its color and meaning a distinctive mark of Gavite in his aspect as god-Five, which is symbolized by the Maya sign corresponding to the number five. We find this hieroglyph under a similar form on Zapotec earthen statuary, while in Mayan codices and on their monuments this idea is usually conveyed by the lunar glyph having the figure of a child inside it, in that way substituting for the mathematical sign its anthropomorphic equivalent.[4]

The uniforms of both giants are blue, with wide yellow bands on the trousers that terminate in the figure on the

---

[4]Cf. Girard, *Los Chortís*, section on religion.

cuffs. From their blue cap with yellow stripes rises a high silver-colored cardboard peak terminating in a 30-centimeter-long triangle. This peak or mast has 2 small gold-colored cardboard rectangles on each side. The headdress of the Black Giant displays an 8-pointed star, which is the same as 9 points since the central intersection of the points is considered as itself a point. On the other hand, the cap of the White Giant carries 2 stars each having 4 points. Each actor hides his face under a heavy wooden mask having eyes of glass, the one painted white and the other black to identify their respective persons. In contrast with the other actors, the giants are the only ones to wear wooden masks.

According to the master of ceremonies, the Black Giant formerly used to wear a cardboard gauntlet showing 9 gold stars on a white or silver field. The gauntlet covered his whole forearm and reflected the sunlight when he brandished his sword. The whole of the symbolism displayed in the Black Giant's attire speaks to us of a stellar entity having incomplete solar as well as lunar markings, while his characterizing number, 9, shows him to be a personage from the underworld where the Nine Lords of Night reside. This symbolism is in perfect accord with the description the *Popol Vuh* gives us of "a being, full of self-pride, which boasted of being the sun and the moon," but which is also related with the underworld beings whose chief was Hun Camé, who was then absolute sovereign of the earth. From all this, then, we see that the Black Giant synthesizes at one and the same time — as can be seen in the performance of the drama itself — the mythical giants as well as the Xibalban caste of the Camé: that is, all of the malign forces in the universe before Hunahpú (Gavite), the hero-god of Quiché-Maya tradition, vanquished them and reduced them to impotence and thereby inaugurated a new era. That era is the era of Maya civilization, in contrast with the state of barbarism which characterized the former ethnical cycle and which, because it is barbaric, is personified by the Black Giant.

Now let us describe the armorers who carry out the role of enchanters. They wear red trousers with yellow vertical bands and cuffs, a blue jacket having a yellow-fringed border, and a headdress consisting of a blue cap with rose-colored peak and yellow band across the front, having two small rosy vertical bands across it. One of them hides his face behind a yellow veil sprinkled with 21 rectangular figures, 9 dark and 12 light colored, while his companion's veil lacks any figures. It should be noted that the veil with figures displays the reverse of those marked on the lunar Gavite. Thus the combination of these two series makes visible the contrast between the 2 seasons of the year: winter and summer. Winter is represented by means of the 9 light and 9 dark points which, according to native symbology, show us an exact picture of the distribution of the 18 uinals of the year. As for the 12 elements, we have already explained that they related to the starry heaven formed by 12 pairs of gods. Now with regard to the contrast between the light and dark, the meaning can perhaps be interpreted in the sense that when the moon is shining at its full, that is as the god-Nine, the stars are obscured. In any case, the apparel of the enchanters is related to nocturnal beings.

Each enchanter carries in his right hand a tambourine which he jingles continually during the whole performance, the action being directed to the personage who is acting so as to imbue the latter with courage, according to the master of ceremonies. As Koch-Grünberg has already noted, the enchanter's power is in his tambourine; without it he would lack all force and would, moreover, be deprived of the instrument that is his special attribute.

Two musicians, dressed in blue with vertical red bands on their trousers, complete the group of actors whose dress we have been describing. They respectively play the flute and the upright drum, instruments that, like the tambourine, are used only during representations of a religious nature and are of purely pre-Columbian origin. No other type of musical instrument is admissible as an accompaniment of a theatrical performance of such transcendence as the Chortí "History."

We have already said that the performance begins at midday, exactly at twelve noon, an hour in which the Aztecs also celebrated the fiesta of Xochipilli, their young Solar deity, the equivalent of Hunahpú, in whose honor the Dance of the Giants is presented to commemorate his victory over the malign forces.

Coming from Tisipe, the dancers arrive in the morning in time to get ready in the house of the mayor of Camotán. All of the apparel, articles of equipment, and religious implements, including the musical instruments, are stored in his house. If someone in the mayor's house chances to be sick, the resulting tabu demands that the dancers prepare themselves in the Chapel of Calvary; but when the function is ended all masks, swords, apparel, and instruments are returned to the mayor. The latter also has charge of feeding the actors and master of ceremonies, which he does by contributions from the people of the community. And this is the only stipend the dancers receive, but it is obligatory in nature, being part of their customary law.

From their place of preparation, the actors parade along the street leading to the public plaza, dancing and miming to the tune of native music. And so they enter dancing into the patio of the church in order to "prove the spot" (*convencer al puesto*); in other words, in order to purify the place that will be their theater of operations, driving away bad spirits or, according to the Chortí expression itself, "so that the ugliness will leave" (*para que salga el feo*). (According to Landa, the Mayas practiced the same custom before beginning their ceremonies by performing a rite of purification that cleansed the atmosphere of bad spirits.) This operation is carried out by circular dances in which the dancers separate and then come together while they jingle their tambourines and brandish their swords to the sound of flute and drum, shouting in a great clamor to chase away the invisible malevolent beings. Then the dancers place themselves in a row facing the west, and render honors to the sun by raising on high their swords, tambourines, and magic handkerchiefs in two movements: one directed toward the west and the other toward the east, while they take five steps first in one direction and then in the other as a salute to the daystar. Immediately after this they divide into two groups in measured, rhythmic movements until they form two parallel rows as described above.

Then begins the drama itself, in five parts (a ritual number) named Entrance (*Entrada*), Cross (*Cruzada*), Apparition (*Espanto*), The Sling (*Honda*), and Death (*Muerte*). In each of these scenes, the musicians execute appropriate but different pieces which also have their own special names in the repertory. We can say that the first act, or the Entrance, forms the overture since the purification of the "spot" is accomplished, preparing it for the drama that we have just briefly summarized.

The Cross contains the battle between the White and the Black Giant. Both place themselves face to face and stare in silence at each other for a long moment while the enchanters frantically jingle their tambourines. Then suddenly the White Giant begins the action by moving against his adversary, and they engage their swords in skirmish while the other actors dance from east to west and the reverse.

In the following episode, Apparition, the vicissitudes undergone by the White Giant, who has fallen into the hands of his rival, are mimed. The Black Giant "intimidates" his opponent by beating the ground furiously with his sword while he makes menacing gestures and movements in hopes of touching or wounding the White Giant, who defends himself as best he can by trying to evade and riposte the thrusts. The battle is suspended at intervals while the giants pay homage to the sun, but is then immediately resumed with greater fury. During the whole episode the Black Giant maintains a menacing stance, not only toward his rival but also toward the large audience witnessing the spectacle. Both actors watch each other constantly, trying to take advantage of the smallest error of the other. For whole minutes they are motionless like statues, then cautiously cross swords as they dart glances around in all directions as if fearing some invisible danger. Then they come to grips and each places the point of his sword against his opponent's neck, a tragic pose that lasts but an instant. Finally the Black Giant succeeds in decapitating the White Giant "because his power is greater," an episode that for the Chortí represents the moment "when our Lord was suffering under the dominion of the bad spirit."

This scene in fact reproduces the contest that took place in Xibalbá between Vucup-Hunahpú and Vucup-Camé, in which the former perishes. The head of the vanquished giant is hung in a tree, but is transformed into a *guacal* or calabash. To all appearances the development of the drama contains excessive details; but in reality they are profoundly revealing of the native mentality and the thematic unity of the work, which is as much Quiché as it is

FIGURE 26. Scene of the battle between the Black and the White Giant. Both brandish wooden swords in their right hands and a magic handkerchief in their left.

FIGURE 27. The Gavites bewitch the Giants.

FIGURE 28. The act in which each Gavite (Hunahpú and Ixbalamqué) grip a Giant from behind. One holds the Black Giant while the other rescues the White Giant on orders from the King who, with his Companion, witnesses the action.

FIGURE 29. Scene of the dismemberment. As the *Popol Vuh* says: they cut him into pieces and tore out his heart and, holding it aloft, showed it to the Lords. In the Chortí drama a handkerchief represents the heart that is displayed to the sun. Another actor cuts off the legs, arms, and so on, in succession.

FIGURE 30. Act in which the Black Giant (Hun Camé) kills the White Giant (Seven Ahpú). Note the King at one side, with his crown, sword, mantle and triangular trimming on his trouser and sleeve cuffs.

FIGURE 31. Scene in which Gavite (Hunahpú) uncovers his face after overcoming the Black Giant (Hun Camé), and delivers the latter's sword to the King. From left to right: the Captain (lunar goddess), Gavite, the White Giant (representing the seven Ahpú), and the Black Giant, conquered and disarmed.

Chortí. Worth mentioning as well is the initial pause when the antagonists scrutinize each other's face before they fight, a mute scene which the *Popol Vuh* explains to us as the inherent obligation of the combatants to "make themselves known to each other by their features."

The Gavites come on the scene in the fourth act, The Sling, and, as said, represent the twins Hunahpú and Ixbalamqué who try to avenge the death of their father, the White Giant. The solar Gavite has the principal role and is played by a young boy who, to carry out the action well, must not be more than twelve years old, although in the culminating phases of the drama he is replaced by the master of ceremonies. In this act the enchanters place themselves on each side of the Gavite who, confident of the enormous magical power accumulated about him, challenges the Black Giant, protecting himself with a red handkerchief with which he also provokes his adversary. The Giant assails the handkerchief with the point of his sword and forces Gavite to give ground; but the latter returns to the charge and now it is he who forces the Black Giant to give way in the face of his magic handkerchief. Five times this action, now favoring the one and then the other, is repeated by the two actors, who have placed themselves in an east-west line while the remaining cast hold their original positions. Thus, the scene of combat takes the form of a double T, the same as the model of the ball court in which the opponents occupy the central line and the others are in two perpendicular lines with respect to them.

Exceedingly interesting is the esoteric value of this episode in which, according to the exact explanation of the master of ceremonies, "Gavite always tries to be the target so that he will receive the blows, freeing the rest of his companions, because in this way it is on Gavite that will fall the darts meant for all." In other words, Gavite assumes the role of redeemer of humanity, sacrificing himself only to save the rest, concentrating upon his own person the attention of the evil forces and receiving "the darts" so that they will not fall upon his own kind. In this way Gavite brings out his function as redeemer-god, the equal of what Hunahpú does in the *Popol Vuh*.

Another Chortí characteristic exemplified by Gavite refers to the relations between parents and children. To the latter fall the actual labor to be done, while the former support them through their counseling. This feature of the family code, elevated to the plane of the divine, shows us the personages who represent the sun and the moon in a passive attitude throughout the drama, since they are the grandparents. On the other hand, Gavite assumes the active role, although under the spiritual direction of his divine ancestors, as is seen in the action of the enchanters about whom the *Popol Vuh* tells us also.

Then Gavite performs various magical passes, moving his handkerchief with great dexterity over his adversary's entire body, at the same time appearing to clean the handkerchief by blowing at it so that he can exert his magical influence over the Black Giant. The latter tries to prevent this by cleaning off his clothing with his own handkerchief, especially defending the lower part of his body, since Gavite casts his spell "downward" to conquer the giant by using stratagem instead of force — that is, a method different from the one preferred by his opponent. Following this pantomime, Gavite brusquely turns his back to the west and directs his glance to the east as if imploring supernatural help in a very difficult case. He pays tribute to the sun by the customary salute. And at this point the play is recessed by a short intermission between the fourth and fifth acts.

The fifth and final act begins with *el mento* or the "spoken account," since until now the drama has had the silent character of a ballet. The Black Giant challenges Gavite in the following words:

> O Captain of God, compelled among those loyal to my banner, with due respect I say to you: today we come forth to contend for a kingdom [the dispute is for universal dominion]. Therefore, with those strong arms kill me so that you can begin your reign. Ah! Forces, captains: where are those strong arms with which to fight? And death trembles before me, and showing you other powers, now I want to see your face and I wait. Your hands are going to offend you. Then attack me now with your weapons, which I will turn into ashes and send back to you. And without any more niceties or considerations, let us have at it to prove your mettle and whether you are a brave soldier.[5]

Gavite replies:

> I give you answer to this great cause; they say that you challenge me to come out and fight. I come with my strong arms and hands, which will be your death, and your death awaits you with great patience. I have been well advised, and now all my soldiers come together and are well prepared. From my arms you will not escape to the hell of your power.

The Black Giant continues:

> What does this little unfortunate beardless man dare to

---

[5][This statement of the Black Giant and Gavite's reply immediately following it, as well as later statements made by each in the "spoken account," are rather literal translations of what is an archaic Spanish phrased according to the Indian's elliptical manner of expression. It is useless, therefore, to dwell overmuch on them. The reader should rather focus upon the author's explanations of their meaning for a clear understanding of their significance in the Drama. — TRANS.]

do [referring to Gavite who advances with sword in hand], so small in stature, now he wishes to come and contend with a giant Golillo. If I catch him in my arms, I'll break him into a thousand pieces and eat him. Seven kings have I beaten and seven kings have I vanquished [an allusion to Hun Camé's triumph over the seven Ahpú, or of the Black over the White Giant]. If I am in God, God shall consume me and glorified shall I be. After the world that I have gained [allusion to his universal sovereignty], what dares this beardless little man, born only yesterday, who now wants to have at me without revealing himself. Now play the drum, bugle, and cornet [flute and conch shell] so that we can see that mortal. Well, come here, little beardless unfortunate man; if I were to kick you, the whole world itself would tremble.

Upon the Black Giant's order the musicians play the march titled *del Batallón*, while Gavite and the Black Giant place themselves in the center of the groups so they can dance. The Giant opens combat, saying, "Come here, little beardless unfortunate man, don't be frightened by my name [as said elsewhere, in the native conception the name is the same as the person, and we have here a clear demonstration of this]; there is no one who is not afraid of me." Then a series of skirmishes takes place between the two adversaries, who admirably fit the descriptions given in the *Popol Vuh*. Gavite, flanked by the armorers, takes some steps toward the west and then flees toward the east and hides behind the King, seeking paternal protection. This posture reminds one of the native idea regarding the young sun who "like the child hides behind his father" when the latter ascends through the celestial vault. The two opponents peer at each other for several moments before returning to the center of the square.

It is then that takes place the scene most characteristic

of the drama, which is found exactly described in all its details in the *Popol Vuh*. Just as the Quiché manuscript puts it, Gavite gives a surprising demonstration of his magical power, letting himself be cut up and then becoming his whole person again. He is *"tasajeado"* (cut to pieces), to use the Chortí expression, just as an animal which has been hunted, beginning with the legs and arms as described in the Quiché codex. These pieces taken from the body are triumphantly exhibited first before the sun and then to the audience so that none will doubt that Gavite has really died. A handkerchief is used for the dismembered pieces of the body, as can be seen in the photograph. The Chichicastenango manuscript describes the act as follows:

> Hunahpú and Ixbalamqué did many wonderful things. They cut each other into pieces, killing each other, and the first to let himself be killed was as one who is dead, but immediately revived. The Xibalbans begged them to cut each other up. . . . Immediately they did so. Ixbalamqué cut Hunahpú to pieces, first the legs and arms; cutting off the head, she carried it a distance away, then cut out the heart. . . . "Arise!" she commanded Hunahpú at once, and he returned to life.

This episode of magical dismemberment, narrated in the *Popol Vuh* and dramatized in the Dance of the Giants, is also known in the Huastec culture. Sahagún, telling us of the enchantments effected by these people, says, "they simulated the burning of houses which did not really burn and the killing of each other and cutting the bodies into pieces, and other things which were appearances and not really done." Such an identic tradition among Chortís, Quichés, and Huastecs does much to confirm the great age of the idea which was a patrimony common to all the

Maya peoples before their separation. With respect to the system of enchanting by means of a twisted handkerchief, displayed by Gavite, we find the same custom among the Mayas, for Redfield writes concerning the *badz pach* (hit the shoulder) that the elder gives the patient some taps with twisted handkerchiefs.

On bringing himself back to life, Gavite and his companion and both giants form a cross in the center of the stage, just as depicted in the following diagram, an allegorical sketch marked out twice in succession by means of dances in rectilinear movements north to south and east to west in four turnings: first, from north to south; second, east to west; third, north to south; and fourth, east to west.

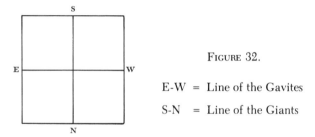

FIGURE 32.

E-W = Line of the Gavites

S-N = Line of the Giants

In relation to these movements, we note a very meaningful detail: the Gavites dance only along the east-west line and the giants along the north-south line, and neither touches the territory of the other. The giants do not participate in the lateral dance marked out by the sun's course, this being reserved for the Gavites, "only themselves coming together," as the textual expression in the *Popol Vuh* has it. Each pair moves about within its own line of dance, both lines together symbolizing the astronomical cross. Later on, when the Gavites have conquered the Black Giant, they also dominate the north-south line and form a homogeneous cross, dancing then along its entire extension.

Following the scene of the cross there is another magical action by Gavite, who runs swiftly toward the giants. These lock arms to block his passage, but Gavite leaps agilely over the obstacle, punching the chest of his rival with his closed fists and tries to separate the giants. This maneuver is repeated four times, Gavite avoiding being knocked down by the kicks given him by the Black Giant. This scene doubtless dramatizes the passage in the *Popol Vuh* in which Hunahpú obliges the Xibalbans to reveal their names by pricking them with a hair taken from his own shinbone, a magical procedure well known to Mayan enchanters who hurl invisible darts at the person they intend to affect. Gavite keeps on surprising the audience with his magical abilities that culminate in the scene called "The Castration," when he grips the Black Giant and makes a gesture as though castrating the latter. This symbolizes the annihilation of the virility, that is, the power, of his opponent. In the same way, the "castration" of others selected from among the spectators is put into effect; these are carried to the center of the patio in reminiscence of the pursuit and destruction of the people of Xibalbá by Hunahpú and Ixbalamqué following the death of Hun Camé. The merriment of the audience now reaches its crescendo: some of them flee to evade being seized and "castrated," others pursue them, and all join in a great hubbub anticipating the scene that will mark the apotheosis of Gavite. In fact, as the master of ceremonies explains: "Gavite already had won the battle because he succeeded in overcoming his adversary."

Then the King intervenes, ordering the Gavites to reunite with their father the White Giant whom they have rescued from the power of his enemy, saying to them: "Go now, take hold of your father, embrace your father." These words fix the grandfather's instructional role in the

family by telling his grandchildren to fulfill their filial
duties, just as is done today within the extended Chortí
family. The King is immediately obeyed and then there
takes place the scene of "The Death," wherein one of the
Gavites takes hold of the White Giant while the other im-
prisons the Black Giant in his arms, immobilizing him.
The pairs, without separating, and preceded by the two
enchanters, place themselves in a single file along the east-
west axis, the King and the Captain standing apart at the
eastern end of the line as follows:

Captain: Ixmucané—	Enchanter	Enchanter	Hun Camé	Hunahpú	Vukup-Ahpú	Ixbalamqué	Distribution of the characters according to the *Popol Vuh*

King: Ixpiyacoc—	Armorer	Armorer	Black Giant	Gavite	White Giant	Gavite	Distribution of the characters according to the Chortí version

The six actors bend their bodies in a simultaneous bowing movement, describing a semicircular figure to the right
and then to the left: that is, toward the south and then the
north. This movement makes perfectly clear the Gavites'
dominion over the whole area of ground covered by the
cross. The King and Captain look on impassively at these
movements, which imitate the ball game, since the ball
describes a semicircle in its flight from one end of the playing field to the other in the same direction marked by the
bowing of the actors, which coincides with the south-north
axis of the ball court at Copán. Once again the figure of

the cross is symbolically traced, but this time vertically rather than horizontally as before, when it was traced out on the surface of the quadrangle. In an erect position, the heads and feet of the actors in accordance with the native conception indicate two astronomical points: the zenith and the nadir. The latter point is beneath the earth, since the Chortís like Ptolemy figure that the terrestrial surface is a fixed quadrangle around which the sun revolves. The actors then pay homage to the sun by bowing to east and west.

Finally, Gavite decapitates the Black Giant and takes away his sword, after the giant humbly says to him: "Rest a moment, child, and I will give you your payment, because I now yield myself, and even my heart trembles." He acknowledges himself vanquished and a tribute-payer to Gavite from thenceforward. But the hero-god replies: "There is no rest now, boastful giant, because we are beginning the end of the labor [*hornada*]." We note here for the reader's better understanding that the word *hornada* means task, act, or ceremony, and is a term frequently employed by Chortí elders in that sense.

There is no discrepancy between the Chortí and the Quiché sources regarding the manner of killing the chief of the infernal forces. Gavite cuts off his head, just as Hunahpú did that of Hun Camé in the *Popol Vuh:* "The first to be cut off was the head of the one called Hun Camé, the great Lord of Xibalbá." Offering the Black Giant's head and sword as trophies to the King and Captain, Gavite says: "Here I bring you the head of this giant, with a blade of steel from my sling, from my battle. It will overcome the whole world, since if you do not subdue it, it will be your subduer." The King answers: "Let us give thanks to the Lord, and let the death of this boastful giant be told [for the gods to speak is the same as to carry the action out, in the Chortí conception]. Today songs of rejoicing will be heard among my people, Gavite. Take my crown, Gavite, we will begin praises to the King. Let this be forever. Amen." Finishing his discourse, the King returns the head and the sword to the Black Giant who will thereafter be his subject. The drama ends as it began: with honors and salutes to the sun, this time beginning from east to west to signify the triumph of the luminous forces over those of the shadows. Without doubt the fifth act, the apotheosis of Gavite, must be related to the fifth day, that of the resurrection of Hunahpú according to the Quiché text.

Reserving for another place the analysis of the teachings to be found in this valuable Chortí theatrical performance, we will here refer to some of the explanations of their "History" that are given by the Indians themselves.

Among other things, they say that the Black Giant could be the chief of the gang of "strong men" because "they gave him the power," but he was overcome and lost it "when they took away his power." In this way the Chortís corroborate and set out the idea found in the Quiché codex, which is that there is always a superior and essentially beneficent force behind universal law even when that force is apparently eclipsed during an epoch of dominion by the giants, that is, by evil. This conception is found in the following aphorism from Chortí philosophy: "Divinity allows evil to exist up to the required point, but no further." Thus there is no dualism in their religious ideas or, in other words, an opposition between a benevolent and an evil god, inasmuch as the omnipotent Supreme Being controls the forces of evil which can act only with its permission, and this can be taken away at any given moment. Carefully analyzed, we see that the divine authorization permitting the forces of evil to come into play to injure humanity serves to punish the latter for offenses against religious ethics and, at the same time, encourages the search for divine protection. It is in this way that the Chortís have resolved the problem of good and evil, so that at bottom the malign forces become instruments of Providence. Man must struggle against the inclinations to evil until he has conquered them, following the example given by Gavite.

Another interesting peculiarity, which clarifies a point in the *Popol Vuh* that until now has been poorly understood, is the incarnation of seven persons in one, as set out in the drama when the Black Giant boasts: "Seven kings have I struck down and seven kings overcome," referring to his triumph over the White Giant. The latter represents seven persons in one single individuality and corresponds exactly to the Vucup-Hunahpú of the *Popol Vuh*; that is, to the seven Ahpú which at one time are presented as a group of seven individuals and at another as one single individual of that name. In terms of Chortí theogony, this concept is explained by the numeral god-Seven who is at once a person but also has the quality of unfolding itself in seven divine hypostases. The god-Seven, or the seven gods, forms the Agrarian deity which, like the Ahpú, fecundates the earth with its own blood.

Moreover, in the personage of the Black Giant the Chortí drama gives us a synthesis of the malevolent beings that peopled the earth in the mythic age, of whom the *Popol Vuh* tells us. Thus we see that by the boastfulness manifested in his words this giant embodies Vukup Cakix and, when he brags that he can make the earth tremble with one stamp of his foot, he plays the role of the giant Zipacná; and finally, his actions as Hun Camé or Vucup Camé, chief of the underworld caste, are clear.

The part, in which Gavite orders that "all my soldiers

come together," is a clear allusion to the native's communal conception by which no action can be undertaken without the participation of the whole collectivity. And with regard to the Black Giant's repeated scoffs at that youth "without beard and luckless," this simply confirms what we have said regarding the ritual value of the beard as an insignia of power, authority, and respect.

Many details, among which we mention only some, closely link the Chortí "History" with the Chichicastenango manuscript. For example, in both messengers are sent by the forces of Xibalbá to deliver their formal challenge to Hunahpú to compete against them in the ball game, a game objectified by the movements of the Chortí actors; and in both sources the one challenged accepts without hesitation the contest that will decide universal authority.

The mythic origin of the drum is also an interesting point brought out by the Chortí drama, since it is an exceedingly ancient musical instrument, already known to an ethnic cycle antedating Mayan culture.

A detailed analysis of the mythologic, astro-cosmic, and ethnologic elements contained within the Dance of the Giants would be out of place here; but these matters are treated in *Los Chortís ante el problema maya* in the chapters on religion and esotericism of the *Popol Vuh*. It is enough here to have pointed out the concordance between the Chortí oral tradition and the written account in the Quiché codex, in both of which is found the theme that dramatizes the story of the young Solar deity. This circumstance permits us to make comparisons between the two traditions not only for their mutual corroboration but also for their better comprehension.

The form in which the text and other aspects of the Chortí drama have been handed down from generation to generation gives us an idea of how the contents of the *Popol Vuh* have been transmitted within the Quichés from very remote times. In the case of the Chortís, the master of ceremonies, whose function is hereditary, acts as a real historian who has the obligation to take scrupulous pains to see that no detail of "The History" shall be lost. Thanks to that fact, in the middle of the 20th century the Chortís can still sing the episodes of their remote past history and recite passages from their mythology.

Nevertheless, important differences exist between the Quiché and Chortí traditions; these are found in the Chortís' time-reckoning methods which are based upon the patterns of classical Maya culture, and which we do not find in the *Popol Vuh*. This fact would seem to show that the common mythographic theme, which goes back to a period before that of the classical Maya, was extended in a unilateral manner to incorporate into the original drama the most outstanding and characteristic feature of Maya culture which the Chortís, their direct descendants, have passed down to us right to this day. This innovation, absent from the Quiché tradition, goes to show that before the Quiché and Maya separation both peoples had a common mythographic patrimony faithfully expressed in the mythic portion of the *Popol Vuh*.

Appendix A

A comparative list of words for food plants in Central and South American language groups which proceed from equivalent roots in one or another of them.

iximah	(maize grain produced by sorcery)	Maya
ixim	maize	Xinca
aima	maize	Matagalpa
ima, ama, eima	maize	Lenca
eima	ear of maize	Xinca
im	tortilla	Matagalpa
am	maize	Paya
nama	maize	Chiapanec-Chorotega-Mazatec
ma	maize	Miskito
man	maize	Tapachultec
cama	*milpa*	Mixe
ajam	young maize	Huastec
ama, am	maize	Sumo-Ulua

ma-ya	*milpa*	Xinca
tsak	bean	Popolaca
isak	bean	Tzotzil
isaka	bean	Paya
aska	*milpa*	Paya
ik	red pepper	Quekchi
ichi	maize	Tlapanec
is	tuber	Mame, Maya
ucho	red pepper	Quechua
pik	ear of green maize	Quiché
ij	ear of green maize	Mame
böcö	ear of green maize	Chontal
pa	tortilla	Chortí
ba	maize leaf	Mame
pak ká	tortilla	Paya
pakah	tortilla	Maya
bacam	tortilla	Huastec
opa	maize	Cuna
aba	maize	Chibcha
nar	food	Chortí
or	tortilla	Lenca
ma ix	(ma is) maize (meta-thesis of iximah)	Taino
xi, chi	maize	Guaimi
aima ka	bean	Yurumangui
chiscam	black maize	Chibcha
kimi	maize	Kulina-Araua
kinak	bean	Quiché
ti kin	to farm	Poconchi
mi koy	food	Quechua
man	manioc, cassava	Motilon
man	manioc, cassava	Amuesha
mama	manioc, cassava	Jívaro
ma	manioc chicha	(Changuena)

alma si	ear of green maize	Carib
ma-yaca	manioc, cassava	Yuruna (Tupi-Guaraní)
ma-tsoaka	manioc flour	(Pano)
ma-niac	manioc, cassava	Yuruma
ma-tsuka	manioc flour	(Piapoco, Arawak)
auma	hardwood palm tree	Yurumangui
auas	maize	Carib
au	threshed maize	Xinca
inchi k	peanut	Quechua
skik	bean	Mixe
iche	bean	Bintuka
ik	manioc, cassava	Rama
ik ué	maize	Guatuso
xik	bean	Lenca
pöpö	maize	Cofan
arepa	maize	Chayma (Carib)
arepa	manioc, cassava	(Cariniaco)
pak	bean	Matagalpa
eyrapa	food	Carib
alepa	food	Galibi
tapa	maize	Arawak
papa	potato	Quechua
ara	*milpa*	Carib
porosh	maize cob	Lenca
sara	maize	Quechua
poroto	bean	Quechua

pete ma = tobacco in languages of the Orinoco (note the root *et* which in other languages is applied to the bean, and *ma*, to maize or manioc).

tit'am	bottle gourd	Chortí
tin'am	cotton	Chortí

atz am	salt	Chortí
ama	corn beer	Quiché
qhy	bean	Otomí (Buelna)

(the phonetic mutation $ki < ik$ is regular in languages derived from the proto-Maya, as has been shown with the word for sun: $ik < ki.$)

Appendix B

Comparative list showing the parallelism between words for maize or food plant and mother, father, and grandfather or ancestor in generically related Central and South American languages.

nan, mam	grandfather	Chortí, Maya, Poconchi, Pocomam, Chol
mam	father	Mame, Jacalteca
mamá	grandfather	Cakchiquel
mi	mother	Jacalteca
min	grandmother	Chol
mai	mother	Xinca
mim	grandmother	Maya
chi ima	mother	Chorotega
mim	mother	Huastec
ibama	woman	Guarauno
nan	mother	Cuna
mama	mother	Rama, Atanque, Guarauno, Sumo, Quechua

mina	mother	Lenca
imini	mother	Lenca
ami, w-ambi,		
mia	mother	Arawak
imi	mother	Bribri
ima	girl	Rama
dama	grandfather	Rama
maa	father	Yurumangui
mayi, maa	mother	Uru
gáma	son	Guamaca
ama	aunt	Cuna
akama	son	Arawak
ab'áma	grandfather	Koggaba

Etymologically related, with the root pa, ba, opa, aba (tortilla, maize leaf, and maize in Chortí, Mame, Cuna, and Chibcha), we have the following words:

pap	father	Huastec, Chontal, Maya, Mame
paba, pabe, pabi	father	Lenca
apé	father	Tapachultec
apú	grandfather	Tapachultec
ayú	mother	Tapachultec
apé	father	Xinca
ap	grandmother	Mixe
abin	daughter	Uspantec, Quekchi
apin	male cousin	Xinca
paba, pabi	father	Chibcha
baba	father	Carib
aba, abo	father	Achagua
abua	grandmother	Xinca
epe	mother	Chicomuceltec
rahpa	father	Subtiaba
bal	father	Ixil

bal	son-in-law	Tzental
pabi	uncle	Lenca
pale	father	Chuj-Jacalteca
bapay, papay, baa	father	Hicaque
apo	chief	Quiché (Imbelloni)
abo	chief	(Cuba)
apo	sun	Carib
pap	father	Cuna
abi	father	Araua
apé	uncle	Trumai
abú	mother	Guamaca
abé	grandfather	Paressi
abi	person	Boruca
apa	aunt	Rama
q'apa	family name	Chortí
apin	uncle	Rama
apin e	brother	Trumai
aba	mother	Koggaba
abú	mother	Guamaca
aba	man	Tupi-Guaraní
apai, apa, apak	father	Uru
epe	grandmother	Uru
aparo	father	Jívaro
api tsi	grandfather	Nahuacúa
wabú	friend, brother-in-law	Carib, Araua
inábo	woman, female	Kaduveo
papané	father	Sumo
abi	father	Arawak
apo	chief	Quechua
apo, apu	chief	Araucan
avo	maternal uncle	Carib
avo	maternal uncle	Tamanac

mapo	chief (or head)	Pano
pol	head	Chol
poo	white hair	Mixe
powa	grandfather	Jívaro
apoto	chief	Tamanac
mapo	chief (or head)	Pacaguara
poo	moon	Mixe
poo	moon	Quekchi
kapo-i	grandfather	Chiapanec

Glossary

Ahau "Lord." The reigning Regent of a Maya calendric cycle; the final day of the month. The Fourth Regent is equated with Hunahpú.

Ajbit Singular of Bitol, a class of "builder" gods; in Quiché-Maya theogony, Ajbit is associated with Ajtzak.

Ajtzak Singular of Tzakol, a class of "builder" gods in Quiché-Maya theogony; associated with Ajbit.

Alom One of six hypostases of Cabahuil or god-Seven. Especially associated with the three other hypostases: Tzakol, Bitol, and Cajolom; these four are regent gods of the 4 cosmic angles. Their mediation produces light.

Bacabs The four cosmic bearers of the Mayas. The four "world pillars" whose foundations are in the underworld. During the Third Age, the four primeval giants (Vukup Cakix, his wife, and their two sons) are transformed into these "world pillars."

Bitol One of six hypostases of Cabahuil or god-Seven. More especially associated with the three other hypostases: Tzakol, Alom, and Cajolom; these four are regent gods of the 4 cosmic angles; their mediation produces light. A class of "builder" gods.

Bolón ti kú   The god-Nine: the Nine Lords of the Night, who cooperate with god-Thirteen (Oxlahun-oc) in cosmic work. The Nine Lords of the Night are headed by the old Fire god, the oldest in the Maya pantheon, who is the divine nahual of Vucup Hunahpú, or the Seven Ahpú.

Brujo   Spanish, the "black magician," doomed to hell in Xibalbá, the underworld. His nahual is the *culebra*. The elder of an earlier cycle of Maya prehistory.

Cabahuil   "Heart of Heaven (and of Earth)"; god-Seven or the Creator deity, having six hypostases; integrated by the three suns of the line of parallel (rising, at zenith, setting). Equated with god B of the Mayan codices. Corresponds to the sun at zenith. (See Gucumatz.)

Caban   Earth. As a goddess, a hypostasis of Hunrakán; as a cosmic plane, an unfoldment or reflection of the celestial or heavenly plane. The fertility of, likened to human fecundation. The four giants of the *Popol Vuh* personify the forces of Earth.

Cajolom   One of six hypostases of Cabahuil, or god-Seven. Especially associated with the three other hypostases: Tzakol, Bitol, and Alom; these four are regent gods of the 4 cosmic angles; their mediation produces light.

Camé, Vukup   "Seven Death." A sevenfold entity (Hun Camé) of false gods, Lords of Xibalbá, the underworld. Antagonists of Vucup Hunahpú, the true gods, whom the Camé challenge to a ball game in Xibalbá where they defeat the Seven Ahpú and behead them. The Camé are later vanquished by Hunahpú and Ixbalamqué, the divine twins who are the offspring of the Seven Ahpú, for the deliverance of mankind from thralldom.

Camé, Hun   "One Death." Lord of Xibalbá, the equivalent of Cimi, the Second Regent in the Maya primary calendric series of regents or Ahau; assumes the regency from Ixmucané. God of Death.

Caprakán   "He of two feet." The theogonic antithesis of Hunrakán, son of Vukup Cakix and his wife, Chimalmat, and brother of Zipacná. With these three, one of the four primeval giants of the *Popol Vuh* who are vanquished by Hunahpú and Ixbalamqué in the Third Age and become transformed into the four "world pillars." God of earthquakes, associated with his brother, Zipacná.

Cerbatana   "Blowgun." The divine weapon of Hunahpú; emblem of the solar ray. It operates magically for Hunahpú.

Chac   Of Maya mythology; the four Chac are the equivalent of Tzakol, Bitol, Alom, and Cajolom of the *Popol Vuh*; the gods of the four sectors of heaven. The Chac are the owners of the wild plant and animal life of the earth.

Chan   "Serpent." The name the Chortí Maya apply to themselves: "people of the serpent," whose chief is called Hor chan (head of the serpent). The generic name of the Maya as a whole, whose cultural totem is the serpent, as a divine nahual. The equivalent of the Quiché word *cumatz*.

Chilam Balam, Books of   Manuscripts written in the Mayan language but in Roman letters by native Mayans during the late 17th and early 18th centuries, after Spanish conquest of the Yucatán Peninsula and suppression of the native religion. The principal ones among these manuscripts, the Chumayel, Tizimin, and Maní, are named after the towns in Yucatán where they were found. About nine other manuscripts are known at the present time; it is likely that more are preserved in secrecy. The so-called Books of Chilam Balam are the sacred books of the Yucatán Mayas, and probably very many of them existed in towns and villages during the Colonial period.

Chimalmat Wife of Vukup Cakix, and mother of Zipacná and Caprakán. Together, these are the four giants of Quiché-Maya theogony.

Chortí A Maya people, direct descendants of the builders of classical Copán, the apogee of Maya culture. The Chortí now live in a number of villages and hamlets on the border territory of Honduras and Guatemala, not far from the ruins of Copán.

Chuen Third in the Maya primary calendric series of regents or Ahau, equated with Hun Chouén of the *Popol Vuh*; god C of the Maya codices, who symbolizes the Third Regent, and has the face of a monkey. Associated with the sign Chuen and the Third Age of the *Popol Vuh*.

Cib "Light, torch." Fourth in the Maya primary calendric series of regents or Ahau, equated with Hunahpú of the *Popol Vuh* as Regent of the Fourth Age or Age of Quiché-Maya culture.

Cimi Second in the Maya primary calendric series of regents or Ahau, equated with the Camé of the *Popol Vuh*.

Copal   The sap from various Central American trees which is used by Mayan natives for incense for purificative and other purposes. Equated with blood and rain as a divine substance or exudation in nature.

Culebra   Spanish, "snake," a pejorative term for the Seven Camé, their hellish nahuals, and the *brujos* or black magicians who represent them on earth (see *Sierpe*).

Guacamayo   Spanish, "macaw." Six macaws, with the game ball, compose the symbol of the god-Seven (Cabahuil), the disguise or nahual of the Solar deity.

Guaman Poma de Ayala, Felipe   "Falcon Puma." An Andean Indian nobleman of the Inca caste, the author of the *Nueva Corónica y Buen Gobierno*, an illustrated codex or manuscript describing the origins of the Incas, the four ages of mankind, and related matters from indigenous Andean pre-Conquest belief. The manuscript severely indicts Spanish treatment of the native Andean peoples. Prepared sometime between 1567 and 1615, it was directed to King Philip III of Spain, but somehow found its way to the Royal Library in Copenhagen, where it lay untouched for 300 years, until 1908, when European scholars interested in the early New World brought it to light.

Gucumatz   "Serpent-bird" or "Feathered Serpent." One of six hypostases of Cabahuil, it is especially associated with Cabahuil itself and another hypostasis, Tepeü, as the three suns of the line of parallel (rising, at zenith, setting). Corresponds to the sun at setting. Identical with the Quetzalcoatl of Toltec tradition. Stands also for the class of creative gods as a whole.

Hor chan "Head of the serpent." The Chortí Maya caste of elder-chiefs, equated with Gucumatz, the Agrarian deity of which they are the earthly representatives. This elder caste is of divine origin, but the individual born into it must win the right to exercise of the post through his or her personal merit and exemplary conduct.

Hunab ku The Supreme Being of the Maya; also called Hun Itzamná. Equated with the Quiché's Cabahuil, the god-Seven of the *Popol Vuh*.

Hunahpú "One Blowgunner." The Quiché name of the Maya savior deity that incarnates to enlighten mankind and show the way to divinity; born immaculately at dawn on the winter solstice. With Ixbalamqué, the civilizing hero of Quiché-Maya culture; god-Five, the young Solar and Maize god, in Chortí imagery symbolized by a cross (four points plus the central point); son of the Supreme Being, and alter ego of Hunrakán. A hypostasis of the Agrarian deity (god-Seven); as the young Maize god, is born from the foot of Cabahuil in the bowels of the earth. A twin of Ixbalamqué, grandchild of Ixpiyacoc and Ixmucané. God B of the Maya codices; god of Dawn; compared with Osiris; symbol of chronological unity; apotheosized with Ixbalamqué at the end of the Third Age in the *Popol Vuh*; the Fourth Regent or Ahau; god of the Woods; one of his zoological nahuals is the fish.

Hun Bátz "One Big Monkey." A son of one of the Seven Ahpú, he is a hero and great sage, singer, orator, engraver, sculptor, etc., of the Third Age of the *Popol Vuh*. A cousin or older brother of Hunahpú and Ixbalamqué and Regent of the Third Age. Together with his brother, Hun Chouén, transformed into a monkey at the end of the Third Age. The monkeys of the forests are the only record of his existence.

Hun Chouén   "One Monkey." Like his brother Hun Bátz,
          a son of one of the Seven Ahpú and sage
and hero of the Third Age, sharing its regency. Transformed into a monkey with Hun Bátz at the end of their
regency, or the Third Age.

Hunrakán   "He of the single foot." A variant of Caba-
          huil, having a precise functional meaning. A
nahual of Hunahpú and Ixbalamqué. Identified with the
constellation Ursa Major.

Imix   First in the Maya primary series of regents or Ahau.
          Associated with Ixmucané, and the First Age of
the *Popol Vuh.*

Ixbalamqué   With Hunahpú, her inseparable "twin," the
          hero god of the Quiché-Maya. The feminine
aspect of god-Five; new-moon goddess. Grandchild of Ixpiyacoc and Ixmucané. Her nahual is the jaguar. With
Hunahpú, apotheosized at the end of the Third Age of
the *Popol Vuh.*

Ixcanleos   The Maya equivalent of the Quiché Ixmucané,
          "the mother of the gods."

Ixmucané   With Ixpiyacoc, the Supreme Pair of Quiché-
          Maya theogony, grandparents of the Mayas
and of humanity as a whole. A feminine deity, the old
lunar-earth goddess. Identical with the Maya Ixcanleos.

Ixpiyacoc   The equivalent of Hunab ku, the Supreme
          Being of Maya tradition. With Ixmucané, the
Supreme Pair of Quiché-Maya theogony, and grand-
parents of humanity. A masculine deity, the father of the
Seven Ahpú.

Ixquic   The mother of Hunahpú and Ixbalamqué in the
          Popol Vuh; a lunar goddess and earth goddess,

associated with the four cosmic bearers. Immaculately fertilized by the Seven Ahpú, she bears their offspring, the twin savior deity. Her nahual is the jaguar.

Milpa   Spanish, "seed field." The native maize planting field. The symbolic equivalent of the altar table, the sacred ball court, the plane of the Earth.

Nahual   An alter ego of a person, of vegetable, animal, human or godlike nature. An inner relationship, fully defined, exists between the person and his or her nahual(s) from birth to death: e.g., a nahual of Hunahpú is the fish; of Ixbalamqué, the jaguar; of both as the divine twins, Hunrakán itself. Nahualism as a belief continues among today's Indians.

Oxlahun-oc   "Having thirteen feet." The god-Thirteen; the Solar deity in its zenith position, with its twelve stellar companions.

Popol Vuh   A document written down in the Quiché-Maya language but in Latin letters by a Quiché Indian shortly after the Spanish Conquest. It contains the Quiché rendition of Maya cosmogony, theogony, and sacred history, as well as a history of the Quiché-Maya peoples themselves down to the year 1550. Hidden from Europeans for 150 years, it somehow was discovered at the end of the 17th century by Father Francisco Ximénez, a learned priest of the Dominican Order, in his parish at Santo Tomás Chichicastenango, located north of Lake Atitlán in Guatemala's highlands. Ximénez transcribed the original Quiché text and translated it into Spanish. His manuscript was found in 1854, in the library of the University of San Carlos, the city of Guatemala, by the European, Carl Scherzer. The original Quiché document has never been found, and was perhaps returned to the Indian donor by Ximénez after he had copied it.

Pucbal-chaj   The place where the Camé buried the Seven
                  Ahpú after beheading them in Xibalbá.

Quiché-Maya   At the time of the Conquest, the principal
                  Maya people living in the highlands of
what is now Guatemala, north of Lake Atitlán. Its chiefs
claimed descent from ruling families in Tula, Mexico. Like
all Maya tribes, the Quiché-Maya regarded themselves as
the direct descendants of the Supreme Being and the
creator and builder gods.

Sacerdote   Spanish, "elder" or "white magician." The el-
                der defends the community against the *brujo*,
and represents the true gods. His nahual is the *sierpe*.

Sierpe   Spanish, "serpent." A sacred term for the Seven
             Ahpú, the serpent being their divine nahual. It is
also the totem of the Mayas (*chan*). The *sierpes* are in
eternal opposition to the *culebras*.

Tamoanchan   "Place of the Hawk and the Serpent." The
                 ancestral homeland of the Mayas, which
was the Pacific coast of Guatemala. The mythological
place of origin of the Mayas, where the hawk brought the
blood of the serpent from the sea, to knead with the maize
which entered into the formation of man of the Fourth
Age.

Tepeü   One of six hypostases of Cabahuil. Especially
            associated with Cabahuil itself and with another
hypostasis, Gucumatz, as the three suns of the line of
parallel (rising, at zenith, setting). Corresponds to the sun
at rising.

Tepexpan   The site in Mexico where in 1947 a human
               skull and a considerable part of the skeleton
were unearthed in association with bones of extinct mam-

moths and bone and stone artifacts. Tepexpan man is given a geological horizon of 11-12,000 years before the present.

Tzakol One of six hypostases of Cabahuil. Especially associated with three other hypostases: Bitol, Alom, and Cajolom; these four are regent gods of the 4 cosmic angles. Their mediation produces light.

Tzolkín A sacred 260-day period, the Maya ritual calendar, called *cholquih* in Quiché. This 260-day count, calculated as 13 times the 20-day month, was intricately connected with other time-reckoning cycles, and applied to all important acts in life.

Uuc-cheknal The god-Seven of Maya mythology, identical with the Seven Ahpú or god-Seven of Quiché myth.

Vukup Cakix "Seven Macaw," or "Seven Feathers of Fire." A false creator deity of the First Age in the *Popol Vuh* who, while the world was still enveloped in semi-obscurity, pretended to be the true solar or illuminating deity. After being vanquished by Hunahpú and Ixbalamqué, he and his wife Chimalmat and two sons, Zipacná and Caprakán, four giants, were transformed into four cosmic bearers.

Vucup Hunahpú The god-Seven of Quiché myth, identical with Uuc-cheknal of the Mayas. The Seven Ahpú, produced by the Supreme Pair, Ixpiyacoc and Ixmucané. Hypostases of the Supreme Being (Ixpiyacoc). Their nahual is the old Fire god, oldest in the Maya pantheon, who is the father of the Maize god (Hunahpú). Their celestial ideogram is the constellations Orion and Ursa Major. Identical with Heart of Heaven

(Cabahuil) and the Agrarian or Creative deity (Hunra-kán). "The Descendant of Seven Generations."

Xibalbá The underworld, as a locale and an inferior cos-mic plane, but having additional meanings. The abode of the Lords of Death (Camé). In Maya cosmogony, it appears later than the time of creation of the universe, at an interval of eight stages or epochs removed from that of formation of heaven and earth.

Zipacná Son of Vukup Cakix, brother of Caprakán. His mother is Chimalmat. These four are the primeval giants of the *Popol Vuh*, transformed into the four cosmic bearers after being vanquished by Hunahpú and Ixbalamqué. Zipacná causes the death of the Four Hundred Boys (associated with the Pleiades), who are resuscitated by the divine twins.

Index

356

Rite(s), Ritual(s)
  four colors 29, 289
  Ixquic inaugurates, of confession
    132
  of agrarian religion 10, 263
Rodas Corzo, Ovidio 19, 175
Rodas, Flavio 18–19, 22, 26, 153, 224,
    265, 299
Román, Gerónimo 31
Ross, Patricia Fent 74
Rubber 101–2, 171, 252–3

Sacrifice(s)
  animal 46
  flint knife and cup used in human
    118
  human, regarded as barbaric;
    repudiated and prohibited 46,
    121, 183–4
  reinstated among Quichés by Mexi-
    can tribes 280
Sahagún 176, 208, 229, 250, 259, 315
Salvador, Republic of 275
San Agustín 257
San Buenaventura, Fray Gabriel de
    238
Sanchuniathon 41
Sapper 98
Scheler, Max 228
Schulte-Jena 18, 108
Sea of Cortez 44
Seler, Eduard 18, 174
Seri 43
Serpent(s), Snake 212, 269, 272–3,
    300
  -bird 33, 270
  blood of 255–6
  divine 197
  divine nahuals 225, 268–9
  Earth god and 270
  great White (Zakicaz) 170–1
  mythological (sierpe) 291
  terrestrial 294

Seven Ahpú. See Ahpú, Seven
Seven Macaw. See Vucup Cakix
Sex(ual)
  act 194
  conceptions of 192, 199
  contact prohibited before maize
    sowing and ceremonies 150
  instinct 264
Sherzer 18, 68, 108
Shuller, R. 79, 106, 110, 221, 257
Solar. See also Sun
  bird 89
  calendar 55
  god(s) 88, 102, 171, 224, 285, 288
  ray 33, 71, 83, 177, 186, 300
  young, deity 144, 168, 322
Sol Invictus 226
Solstice(s) 287
  four points of 28
  Hunahpú born at winter 134–5,
    149
  summer 103, 285
  winter 235–6, 285
Sorcerer 71
Soul 245
  Quiché-Maya doctrine of immor-
    tality of 77, 195–6
Sparrow Hawk. See Hawk
Spencer 18
Spirit(ual) 64
  descent of, into carnal a mystery
    115
  enters man in Fourth Age 244–5
  material and, relations resolved
    196
Starr, Betty 11
Steam Bath 204
Steinen, Karl von den 112
Stoll 18
Stone(s)
  Great, of Grace 31, 65
  grinding 96, 167, 252
  tool kit 45
Sumos 23, 106, 109, 129, 274, 276